Please
return
materials
on time

HIGHLINE COMMUNITY COLLEGE
LIBRARY
P.O. BOX 98000
DES MOINES, WA 98198-9800

CONSTANTINE AND ROME

Constantine &Rome

R. ROSS HOLLOWAY

Yale University Press   *New Haven and London*

Designed by Rebecca Gibb. Set in Adobe Minion by Duke & Company, Devon, Pennsylvania. Printed in the United States of America by Sheridan Books, Ann Arbor, Michigan.

Library of Congress Cataloging-in-Publication Data
Holloway, R. Ross, 1934–
Constantine and Rome / R. Ross Holloway.
p.   cm.
Includes bibliographical references and index.
ISBN 0-300-10043-4 (alk. paper)
1. Architecture, Early Christian—Italy—Rome. 2. Architecture—Italy—Rome. 3. Constantine I, Emperor of Rome, d. 337—Art patronage. 4. Christianity and art—Italy—Rome. 5. Rome (Italy)—Buildings, structures, etc. I. Title.
NA5620.A1H65 2004
722′.7—dc22
2003018712

A catalogue record for this book is available from the British Library.

The paper in this book meets the guidelines for permanence and durability of the Committee on Production Guidelines for Book Longevity of the Council on Library Resources.

10 9 8 7 6 5 4 3 2 1

GVGLIELMO LOVELACE

SERVIENTI AD LEGEM

OCTOVIRO VERAE RELIGIONI RESTITVENDAE A D MDLIX

AEVO AVCTOR

Contents

Preface

THIS BOOK had its beginnings many years ago in the excavations below St. Peter's. Standing beside one of the Roman tomb buildings that had been filled in and then covered over by the floor of Constantine's basilica, I could look up through a modern ventilator into the nave of the vast Renaissance St. Peter's that replaced Constantine's shrine for the apostle. Pagan antiquity and medieval Christianity were around me just as much as was their Renaissance successor. Constantine the Great set these changes in motion, but the Constantinian moment in Rome was brief, hardly more than thirteen years between 312 and 326. In fact it was even shorter because in 326 Constantine returned to a capital that he had not seen for a decade. And his sights were already set on Constantinople, the new Rome on the straits between Europe and Asia where he was about to establish his new capital. Yet the cityscape of Rome of 326 was not that of Rome of 312. It was significantly Christian, but it was also overwhelmingly pagan. And in this way it mirrored, I have come to believe, the personality of its ruler. Constantine was a Roman emperor and continued to carry out the civic and religious duties of the pagan emperor. He was the patron of the Christians but exercised his patronship from an exalted position in respect to the ministers of the church, a position which, as a divinized ruler, he maintained even in respect to the Christian God. Yet Constantine had prepared for death in a tomb of imperial dignity on the Via Labicana in the company of two Christian martyrs and with provision for a following of the faithful beneath the roof of the apse-ended hall attached to the imperial mausoleum. This complex and the group of other apse-ended basilicas which were built in the cemeteries along the roads leading south and east from the city are the most notable architectural innovations of Constantine's Rome, even more than that first great cathedral of Christendom and church of the bishop of Rome, San Giovanni in Laterano.

The planning and writing of this book took place during a sabbatical leave from teaching duties in 2001–02. Part of that time was spent as a Visiting Scholar at the American Academy in Rome, where I enjoyed the advantages not only of that great institution but also of the numerous resources of the city, while during my time in Providence I relied on the unsurpassed resources of the Brown University Library. I am particularly indebted to the Photographische Abteilung of the German Archaeological Institute and to Dr. Sylvia Duebner, its director, and to Dr. Katrin Stump for access to resources on which I have drawn heavily for illustrations. A similar debt is owed to the Fototeca Unione presso l'Accademia Americana and to Dr. Lavinia Ciuffa. The Ernest Nash archive at the Seminar für Griechische und Römische Geschichte and Dr. Margarita C. Lahusen have made it possible for me to illustrate Dr. Nash's portrait of Pope Pius XII. Dr. Olof Brandt has favored me with permission to reproduce his reconstruction drawing of the Lateran Baptistry, and Dr. Archer Martin arranged for reproduction of the plan of the newly discovered Christian basilica at Ostia. The map and figures 4.7, 4.17, 4.23 illustrating the Tomb of St. Peter have been drawn with care and skill by Ms. Alice Walsh. The Brown University Library made a special reproduction of the engraving of Etienne du Perac, fig. 1.3. Mr. Harry Haskell took an early interest in my work on Constantine and encouraged the presentation of the resulting manuscript to Yale University Press. It has been a pleasure to have Mr. Lawrence Kenney as my editor. Names of buildings and places are given in what I consider to be the most familiar form of each, Italian, English, or Latin. All dates not otherwise specified are A.D.

The most powerful tool for dating Roman construction is the brick stamps which at various periods, including that of the tetrarchy, were applied before firing and frequently dated by the consuls of the year. The second tool, of more importance in studying buildings of the Constantinian period, is the height of the courses of brick facing on concrete walls. In giving dates based on the latter criterion I have not exercised my own judgment but have accepted the opinions of scholars dealing directly with the monuments in question.

Debts to friends are many. But it is a particular joy to record the help of some of my oldest Roman friends. Prof. Silvio Panciera and Prof. Mara Panciera Bonfioli encouraged my uncertain steps on the borders of the late antique and undertook to read the first draft of the manuscript. Dr. Giuseppe Sicari and Prof. Mariella Sicari Montana kept me abreast of the ever-surprising world of archaeological exhibitions in Italy, which for Christian Rome culminated in the frenetic activity of the Jubilee Year 2000. Prof. Stefania Quilici Gigli invited me to illustrate my views on Constantine's Rome in two lectures at the Seconda Università di Napoli, Santa Maria di Capua Vetere. At the Fabbrica di S. Pietro in Vaticano I was received with great courtesy by Dr. Alfredo Maria Pergolizzi. I made one new friend during the course of writing whom I wish I had known in life but whose spirit I have grown to treasure. This is

Richard Krautheimer. It is not only the monumental achievement of the *Corpus basilicarum christianarum romae,* the flesh and blood of the third chapter of this book, that has made Krautheimer my guide and friend. It is his good sense and his humor, which on more than one occasion during the course of this work made me feel that I was listening to his voice more than reading his prose. And finally, a word must be said in memory of the departed vice prefect of the Apostolic Vatican Library, who introduced me to the complexities of Christian archaeology. Mgn. José Ruysschaert would not have agreed with the conclusions I have reached concerning the explorations below the confessional of St. Peter's, but he would have listened and smiled as he replied. My wife has played her now oft-repeated role of muse.

Abbreviations

AC	*Archeologia Classica*
AJA	*American Journal of Archaeology*
BC	*Bullettino della Commissione archeologica comunale di Roma*
BEFAR	*Bibliothèque des écoles françaises d'Athènes et de Rome*
CBCR	*Corpus basilicarum christianarum Romae*
CEFR	*Collection de l'Ecole française de Rome*
CIL	*Corpus Inscriptionum Latinarum*
DAI	Deutsches Archäologisches Institut
EAA	*Enciclopedia dell' Arte Antica*
JAC	*Jahrbuch für Antike und Christentum*
JdI	*Jahrbuch des Deutschen Archäologischen Instituts*
JRA	*Journal of Roman Archaeology*
LP	*Liber Pontificalis*, ed. L. Duchesne
LTUR	*Lexicon topographicum urbis Romae*
MEFRA	*Mélanges de l'Ecole française de Rome. Antiquité*
NAC	*Numismatica e Antichità Classiche*
PG	*Patrologia Graeca*
RAC	*Rivista di Archeologia Cristiana*
RendPont	*Pontifica Accademia di Archeologia Romana, Rendiconti*
RIN	*Rivista dell'Istituto nazionale d'archeologia e storia dell'arte*

RM   *Römische Mitteilungen*
RQ   *Römische Quartalschrift für christliche Altertumskunde und Kirchengeschichte*

CONSTANTINE AND ROME

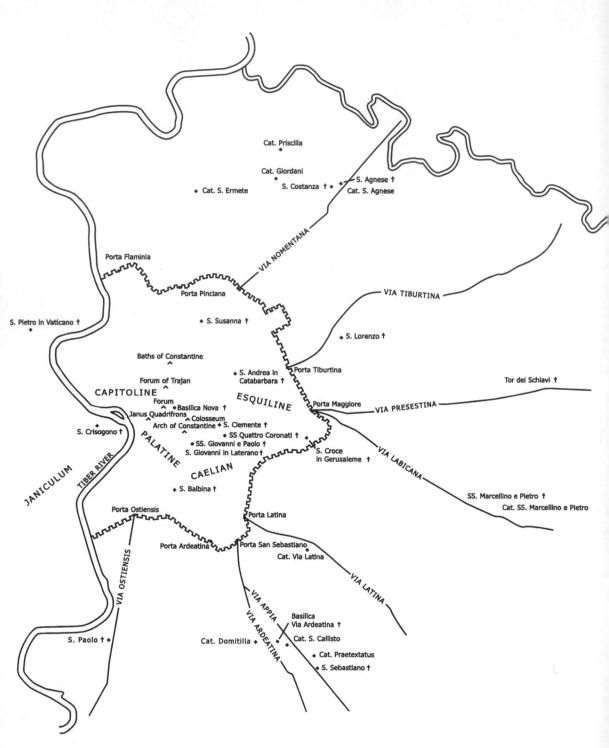

Map of Rome

I Constantine and the Christians

AT THE END OF OCTOBER 312 a Roman warlord was leading his army south from its latest victory toward the capital (fig. 1.1).[1] The struggle for the succession to Diocletian's regime of shared imperial authority was entering a crucial phase. Diocletian's tetrarchy of two emperors and their two lieutenants had given Rome four rulers ready to defend the long frontier against barbarians and the threat of Persian invasion. The division of command had served the empire well. But since Diocletian, with a self-control known to few rulers, had laid down his office in 304, an inevitable power struggle had taken place. In 312 Licinius and Maximinus Daia still figured as members of a reconstructed tetrarchy in the east, although Licinius was soon to eliminate his partner. In the west the struggle was between Constantine and Maxentius, both sons of members of the original tetrarchy.[2] Constantine had almost reached the gates of Rome before his opponent came out to face him at the Mulvian Bridge on the twenty-eighth of October. The victory was Constantine's. Maxentius drowned in the Tiber with many of his army.

Constantine's success is commemorated in a monumental inscription on the Red Cliffs (Saxa Rubra) that overlook the scene of the battle:

Emperor Constantine the Great
On the Fifth Day before the Kalends of November in the year 312 here at the
Red Cliffs
With divine inspiration, Maxentius defeated,

Fig. 1.1 Portrait of Constantine the Great. Capitoline
Museum. Photo Koppermann, DAI Rome, Inst. Neg.
59.1721. Copyright Deutsches Archäologisches Institut.

> Carried the standard bearing the name of Christ into the city
> Inaugurating a happier era for the human race.

This majestic statement, only the first half of the text but all that can be read today because
of the growth of trees on the slope of the cliffs, is not an ancient but a modern inscription,
put in place in 1912 on the seventeen hundredth anniversary of the battle by Pope Pius X.[3] The
message is a simple interpretation of events. Constantine by divine grace carried Christianity
to victory.

But Constantine was fighting to win the empire for himself, not for the Christians. His
patronship of the church and, more important, the thoughts, schemes, and anxieties that
lurked behind his imperious countenance have been examined by modern historians of every
generation. But just as each generation, and sometimes each country, has given us a different
Alexander the Great and a different Augustus, so along the bookshelves Constantine wears a
score of faces. His biographer, Eusebius bishop of Caesarea in Palestine, who became an inti-
mate of the emperor's late in his reign, made his subject the willing instrument of divine grace.
Jacob Burckhardt dismissed Eusebius's portrait as a pious fraud and gave us Constantine the

Renaissance prince.[4] Between these extremes there are a host of historians who have attempted to chart Constantine's conversion, progressing steadily on the road to salvation or haltingly unsure, from the time of his vision or dream before the battle at the Mulvian Bridge until he took the momentous step of founding a New Rome, Constantinople, which he inaugurated in 330 and where he accepted baptism on his deathbed in 337.[5]

On that fateful day in 312 Constantine's standard carried his own portrait, as we learn from Eusebius.[6] The name of Christ, in the form of a ligature of its first two letters, Chi-Rho (less familiar in 312, about the time it began to be used, than it is today), was displayed in a wreath made of precious stones and gold which topped the staff. It was, however, significantly less prominent than Constantine's portrait. It is from Eusebius that we have the account of Constantine's vision of the cross-shaped trophy in the sky with the legend "By this conquer"; then of Christ appearing to Constantine in a dream and urging him to adopt the celestial apparition as a charm to protect himself from his enemies. Eusebius assures us that he heard this recollection from the lips of the emperor. And one detail in his account inspires confidence. Constantine, he says, wore the Chi-Rho on his helmet, and a silver medallion struck at Ticinum probably in 315 and coins issued at Siscia in 317–18 show that this was the case.[7] Such an appearance of a Christian symbol was a rare occurrence in the Constantinian coinage.[8]

Our other source of information concerning the Chi-Rho at the battle of the Mulvian Bridge is Lactantius, another Christian and a member of the emperor's circle. Instead of the Chi-Rho crowning the standard, Lactantius reports that the soldiers of Constantine's army bore the Chi-Rho emblem on their shields. For Eusebius both the celestial apparition and the dream occurred some time before the march on Rome. In Lactantius's account, the dream seems to come to Constantine immediately before the battle.[9] He does not mention the portent in the sky. The vision of an army advancing with a wall of shields adorned with the talismanic Chi-Rho is a dramatic one, but if Constantine's dream did occur just before the day of battle while the army was on the march, how, one may ask, was the paint procured to carry out the transformation? All told, Eusebius's version of the event seems more credible, not only because Eusebius heard Constantine's recollections directly from the emperor but also because his account suggests a personal, even hesitant, use of the Christian charm by Constantine at the Mulvian Bridge.[10]

It is certain, nonetheless, that Constantine carried a Christian talisman into battle and that he attributed his success to its power. Constantine's move toward Christianity, however, was far different from the vision that overtook St. Paul on the road to Damascus.[11] Paul's conversion was the result of an overpowering apparition. Constantine's approach to the Christian God was no more a conversion than Sulla's dream in which the Anatolian goddess Ma-Bellona offered him a lightning bolt with which to strike his enemies.[12] It was not conversion, it was accommodation.

At the outset it is important to place Christianity in the context of Rome of 312. What was the community with which Constantine was now allied? In the centuries following the creation of the Augustan regime the energies of the Roman Empire had been drawn in two directions. The first was toward the European frontier, reaching from England and the Rhine to the shores of the Black Sea and fronting on the ever-present threat of barbarian incursion. The second pole that attracted Roman energy was the eastern frontier bordering on Persia but also containing within it Palestine, where revolts by the Jewish population troubled the reigns of Vespasian and Hadrian, and the lands that formed the domain of Queen Zenobia of Palmyra in the third century. From the Balkan provinces fronting on the Danube toward the east there came the new rulers of the empire, beginning with Maximinus Thrax (emperor 235–38) and triumphing in the persons of Diocletian and his associates after 284. From the east there came religion.

In the view of the Romans in the first two centuries of the empire Christianity was an unauthorized and repugnant branch of Judaism. As a consequence of the Jewish revolts the Romans destroyed the temple of Jerusalem and canceled the name of the city from the map. But the religion of the Jews was tolerated because it was a religion established of old and because it identified a nation, albeit a nation whose members were dispersed throughout the Greek- and Latin-speaking lands of the empire. The Christians seemed more like a conspiracy. They adored a Leader who had been executed as a subversive and likely revolutionary. They preached his imminent return in glory to establish a thousand-year reign on earth. Their rites were secret, but in public they affected a snobbish purity and when pressed often defied common sense by enthusiastically embracing martyrdom. They shunned the theater and the arena as much as they did the pagan temples. Such refusal to accommodate their worship into the family of pagan cults was as offensive to their neighbors as the exclusivity of the Jews, but in comparison to the Jews the Christians were far more fervent in their proselytizing. Worse, they seemed to be full of a hatred for the society around them.

The Romans had had experience with such cults before. In 186 B.C., they had suppressed a Bacchic cult that seemed conspiratorial in nature.[13] More recently the cult of Isis had been banned by Tiberius.[14] The Jews too were not immune from repression under Tiberius and Claudius, and Domitian punished "Jewish superstitions" in his immediate family.[15] Thus, in dealing with the Christians Roman officials could count on a general atmosphere of suspicion and dislike among the populace.[16] Nero capitalized on the Christians' unpopularity to place the blame for the great fire in Rome of 64 squarely on their shoulders. Tacitus has left an account of their grisly executions, which excited pity from the usually pitiless Roman throng.[17] From the time of Nero's persecution until the third century the Christians were subjected to accusations which brought them before the Roman authorities in the provinces. Such instances could be called to the attention of the Roman governor, as they were when Pliny the Younger as governor of Bithynia turned to the emperor Trajan for clarification of procedure in such cases.[18] Trajan's reply was that there was to be no hunting down of Christians and that anonymous accusations were not to be countenanced. The government thus kept a hands-off policy, unless faced with a specific charge. Like most Romans Pliny despised the Christians for what the Romans considered atheism (that is, an unwillingness to see their God as part of the pagan pantheon) and punished them if they persisted when charged. But he also clearly felt that they were not a menace to public order and that the accusations of orgies involving men and women who called each other brother and sister and the charges of infant sacrifice leveled against them were unfounded. This was the message he transmitted to Trajan.

The mob, however, believed the Christians to be capable of the worst, and the mob more than once forced actions against them. This was the case in both Lyons and in Smyrna in the late second century. The Martyrs of Lyons came to occupy a prominent place among the Christian martyrs, and at Smyrna bishop Polycarp suffered for the faith.[19] The martyrologies display the unflagging courage of the Christians in its most edifying form, secure that Paradise beckons them in imitating the Passion of the Lord. Cyprian of Carthage, who was to die before the persecution ended, exhorted his fellow Christians when Valerian's repression began in the tone of the martyr's defiance and expectation of a spectacle of divine vengeance on the oppressors:

Let us take these arms, let us fortify ourselves with these spiritual and heavenly safeguards, that in the most evil day we may be able to withstand, and to resist the threats of the devil: let us put on the breastplate of righteousness, that our breast may be fortified and safe against the darts of the enemy: let our feet be shod with evangelical teaching, and armed, so that when the serpent shall begin to be trodden and crushed by us, he may not be able to bite and trip us up: let us bravely bear the shield of faith, by the protection of which, whatever the enemy darts at us may be extinguished: let us take also for protection of our head the helmet of salvation, that our ears may be guarded from hearing the deadly edicts; that our eyes may be fortified, that they may not see the odious images; that our brow may be fortified, so as to keep safe the sign of God; that our mouth may be fortified, that the conquering tongue may confess Christ its Lord: let us also arm the right hand with the sword of the Spirit, that it may bravely reject the deadly sacrifices; that, mindful of the Eucharist, the hand which has received the Lord's body may embrace the Lord Himself, hereafter to receive from the Lord the reward of heavenly crowns. Oh, what and how great will that day be at its coming, beloved brethren, when the Lord shall begin to count up His people, and to recognize the deservings of each one by the inspection of His divine knowledge, to send the guilty to Gehenna, and to set on fire our persecutors with the perpetual burning of a penal fire, but to pay to us the reward of our faith and devotion! What will be the glory and how great the joy to be admitted to see God, to be honored to receive with Christ, thy Lord God, the joy of eternal salvation and light—to greet Abraham, and Isaac, and Jacob, and all the patriarchs, and prophets, and apostles, and martyrs, to rejoice with the righteous and the friends of God in the kingdom of heaven, with the pleasure of immortality given to us—to receive there, "What neither eye hath seen, nor ear heard, neither hath entered into the heart of man"[20] for the apostle announces that we shall receive greater things than anything that we here either do or suffer, saying, "The sufferings of this present time are not worthy to be compared with the glory to come hereafter which shall be revealed in us."[21] When that revelation shall come, when that glory of God shall shine upon us, we shall be as happy and joyful, honored with the condescension of God, as they will remain guilty and wretched, who, either as deserters from God or rebels against Him, have done the will of the devil, so that it is necessary for them to be tormented with the devil himself in unquenchable fire.[22]

The satirist Lucian saw the suffering of the persecuted Christians in a different light. His view is that of the average citizen of the empire, who saw the Christians as a herd of simpletons, preyed on by swindlers turned prophets and cult leaders.[23]

It was in this context of official restraint but occasional sporadic repression and universal suspicion that the debates between pagan critics and Christian apologists began. The record of the pagan voices was largely erased by the triumphant Christians but the attacks of two of them, Celsus, who wrote in the time of Marcus Aurelius, and Porphyry, who lived on into the opening years of the next century, can be reconstructed from the refutations offered by their Christian opponents.[24] Beside the prejudices of the ordinary pagan citizen, we find in these writers a searching refutation of Christian theology. The Jewish God is a self-contradictory being because He is both omnipotent and at the same time plagued by counter forces. The Christian's idea of God wavered between celestial detachment and all too human passion. Christ is a poor, weak figure hardly measuring up to divinity, whose pronouncements were far from clear and unequivocal. In reality, He was a magician playing on the credulity of the people He encountered in His wanderings. The prophecies of the Old Testament, in which the Christians found foretelling of the coming Christ, are dismissed as vague traditions which only sophistry could turn into the message sought by the Christians. The miracles surrounding Jesus are no more than claimed for various other magicians. Belief in the resurrection must rely on the testimony of a hysterical woman (or two or three such) deluded by sorcery or else suffering hallucinations. The Christian appeal is not by logic but by emotion. The defenselessness of the Christians is proof that their God is powerless to save them.

This anti-Christian literature, however, makes another point by its very existence. Christianity had become sufficiently important that rebuttal was necessary. And so before the third century was much advanced Tertullian could claim, perhaps with less exaggeration than has been thought, that the Christians were experiencing phenomenal growth: "Day after day, indeed, you groan over the increasing number of the Christians. Your constant cry is, that the state is beset; that Christians are in your fields, in your camps, in your islands. You grieve over it as a calamity, that each sex, every age—in short, every rank—is passing over from you to us; yet you do not even after this set your minds upon reflecting whether there be not here some latent good."[25]

At the same time the Christian apologists rose to the challenge with eloquence and the impelling certainty of faith. Furthermore, these Christian luminaries were masters of the Jewish scriptures (in Greek translation, the Septuagint, which had been in common use among the Jews of the diaspora since Hellenistic times) and masters of Greek and Roman classical literature.

In comparison to the works of their opponents, their writings are abundantly preserved. With Justin Martyr in the second century, Tertullian, who lived on into the first two decades of the third century, and later in that same century Origen there must be counted Minucius Felix, Novatian, Tatian, and other voices.[26] They pointed out, to no small advantage, that pagan religion had no logical foundation. Its gods were morally repulsive. In fact, they were demons in masquerade. Its rituals were centered on disgusting exhibitions of the slaughterhouse. The Greek philosophers, moreover, refuted their own cults because they had groped their way toward the knowledge of Supreme Divinity, lacking only the revelation of the Gospels to fulfill their quest. The Old Testament was clear in its prophecies of the coming of Christ. And Christ on earth had given ample proof of His divinity and powers, not the least by His resurrection. By assuming the sins of the world, He opened the road of salvation to all. The second coming, the reign of the saints, and the final judgment were at hand.

Reading the tracts of the defenders of the faith, one realizes a further strength of Christianity. It had attracted first-class intellects into its fold. Christianity was young, vigorous, and utterly confident of its coming triumph. The pagan apologists could only defend inherited cults which no longer spoke with spiritual meaning to the ancient world. This division, of course, takes into account only the traditional pagan cults. To be reckoned with also were the exotic cults and mystery religions, Isis and Serapis, Mithras, the Syrian gods, Sabazius, Anahita and Men, and the rest, which together with Christianity may be set over against the old Greco-Roman cults.

The search for a new and better religion was a consequence of the growth of ancient cities. The old cults belonged to families, tribes, and small cities in which one was born, lived, and died. They rested on a sense of kinship with family and kinship with location. These divinities, even those few who developed mystery cults, were in origin the spirits of the family and the spirits of the landscape. To appreciate them and feel protected by them, as even Socrates did, a sense of belonging to a family, to a clan, and to a place was absolutely necessary.

The metropolises of the Roman Empire offered no such emotional or religious security to their residents. The populations were mixed in a confusion of languages and foreign origins. At Rome, the security of the grain ration was only for the Roman citizen. The security offered by the formal client-patron relationship, which had buffered the urban ills of an earlier day, could not stretch over the vast population. So too the associations of tradesmen were not there for all. Religion, in its traditional form, also reflected the closed nature of the early state. What ties did the soldier from the provinces or the barbarian slave confined to an urban workshop feel with Vesta, Jupiter, or Janus? Where were his ancient gods in the Roman pantheon? No message of hope and liberation such as flowed into the ear of the American slave from the Bible's story of the tribulations of Israel came to the slave or pauper of ancient Rome. Rome, like the other metropolises of antiquity, was a city in which the security of place, of patron, and of settled family was denied to a large number of its inhabitants. In an hour of need or in troubles of the spirit, many, many were lost souls, despairing even of a decent burial for their remains.[27]

The cities of the empire, and Rome first among them, must have offered a lively scene of the hawkers of new cults and their promises. The Christians were the greatest proselytizers, and Christianity presented a spectrum of cults, both what became the organized and dominant church and other shades of opinion, from those closest to Judaism to those most influenced by Greco-Roman philosophy and the various mysticisms of the day, all competing for converts. It is true that a long preparation (measured in years) was required for a postulant before baptism and admission to the eucharistic service. In this respect Christianity was as much a mystery religion as any of its competitors. But the Christians were not bashful in spreading the good news of salvation. And Christian teachers of all stripes held forth in lecture halls resembling the "storefront" churches of modern America.[28] It is in one of these settings that one can hear the words of the North African apologist Tertullian reaching for the sympathy of the pagans:

> I do not call upon thee who art formed in the schools, practiced in the libraries, nourished in the Attic academies and porticoes—thou who dost belch forth wisdom. I address thee who art simple, unskilled, unpolished and uneducated, that is, of such a nature as they have thee who have thee alone, that very soul in its entirety coming from the crossroad, public square and workshop. It is thy inexperience that I need, since no one has any faith in thy little bit of experience. I shall demand from thee an answer concerning those things which thou bringest with thee into man, which thou hast learned to perceive, either from thyself or through thy author—whoever he may be. Thou art not a Christian, as far as I know, for, as a rule, the soul is not born Christian; it becomes Christian.[29]

A different scene, but one that gives a vivid picture of the growth of Christianity, comes from the pagan Celsus, who emphasizes the way in which the message of hope and salvation was spread through the streets and alleys, to shops and kitchens by word of mouth, from the Christian missionary to the slave, from the slave to his fellow slave to the mistress of the house and to the household:

> Further, we see that these Christians display their trickery in the marketplace and go around begging. They would not dare to enter into conversation with intelligent men, or to voice their sophisticated beliefs in the presence of the wise. On the other hand, wherever one finds a crowd of adolescent boys, or a bunch of slaves, or a company of fools, there will the Christian teachers be also—showing off their fine new philosophy. In private houses one can see wool workers, cobblers, laundry

workers, and the most illiterate country bumpkins, who would not venture to voice their opinions in front of their intellectual betters. But let them get hold of children in private houses—let them find some gullible wives—and you will hear some preposterous statements: You will hear them say, for instance, that they should not pay any attention to their fathers or teachers, but must obey them.[30]

This is the ground in which the seeds of Christianity and the other eastern cults took firm root. The converts to these other beliefs, among them the narrator of Apuleius's *Golden Ass* to Isis, were as sincere as the Christians.[31] But the Christians had three great advantages over their rivals in addition to openness to all converts, their eager search for them, and the good news of hope and salvation that they preached. The first was the organization of the church led by its bishops. The second was the social services provided for its members by the Christian community, not the least of which was the provision for a decent burial. The third was the growing wealth in the hands of the church. By the middle of the third century the church in Rome had a large staff: forty-six presbyters, seven deacons, seven subdeacons, forty-two acolytes, fifty-two exorcists, readers, and doorkeepers. Its funds were supporting fifteen hundred widows and other needy cases.[32] In the time of the Severans Tertullian testifies to the organized program of charity of the church at Carthage, which, we may suppose, was no different from that of the church of Rome. The church feeds the poor and buries them. It cares for orphans and aged house slaves. It assists the prisoners, those confined on remote islands and those condemned to labor in the mines.[33] What the pagan temples could not do for the masses in distribution of food because the offering of animals for sacrifice was falling off, the church does.[34] The church, albeit a confederation of bishoprics and frequently beset by schism and doctrinal feuds, was becoming a state within a state.[35] It was to be Constantine's achievement to incorporate this Christian state into the Roman state.

The worldly figure of the church meant that its leaders became worldly too. In the wake of the first general persecution of the church, which took place under the emperor Decius (249–51), Cyprian gives an unflattering picture of a number of his colleagues: "Not a few bishops who ought to furnish both exhortation and example to others, despising their divine charge, became agents in secular business, forsook their throne, deserted their people, wandered about over foreign provinces, hunted the markets for gainful merchandise, while brethren were starving in the Church. They sought to possess money in hoards, they seized estates by crafty deceits, they increased their gains by multiplying usuries."[36]

Things were no better at Rome. Cyprian and Pope Cornelius exchanged letters about the activities of the deacon Nicostratus. This man, one of the seven deacons of the Roman church, lost his post of financial administrator after stealing the ecclesiastical revenues and refusing to give up the deposits of widows and orphans.[37]

Pope Zephyrinus (199–217) and his successor Callixtus I (217–22) were both subject to a vehement attack which passed under the name of Origen.[38] Some of the tone of early Christian debate comes through the charge against the two occupants of the Chair of St. Peter: "Callixtus attempted to confirm this heresy, a man cunning in wickedness, and subtle where deceit was concerned, [and] who was impelled by restless ambition to mount the episcopal throne. Now this man moulded to his purpose Zephyrinus, an ignorant and illiterate individual, and one unskilled in ecclesiastical definitions. And inasmuch as Zephyrinus was accessible to bribes, and covetous, Callixtus, by luring him through presents, and by illicit demands, was enabled to seduce him into whatever course of action he pleased."[39]

The indictment continued by dredging up Callixtus's past, portraying the pope as a former slave, owned by a Christian, who bilked the depositors in his master's bank, fled, was recovered and relegated to the *pistrinum*, where wayward slaves took the place of donkeys turning grain mill and mixing basins for flour. The brethren implored the master for the slave's release, but, having obtained it, Callixtus repaid their attention by causing a disturbance in a synagogue and was condemned to the living death of the mines in Sardinia. Enter Marcia, the Christian mistress of the emperor Commodus. She obtained an amnesty for the Christians at hard labor in the mines, and Callixtus implored his way into liberation. Returning to Rome, he set to work on poor Zephyrinus and became administrator of the Christian cemeteries and from this post, using the money it brought in for bribes, succeeded Zephyrinus as pope.[40]

It is remarkable how little is known of the growth of the Christian movement, even though we possess a lengthy history of the church by Constantine's biographer Eusebius written in the second quarter of the fourth century. Its leaders and its martyrs and the bitter disputes over doctrine and over policy toward the lapsed in the aftermath of persecutions crowd Eusebius's pages, but about numbers and organization, church property, and the scale of church activities he says almost nothing. He gives us the first description of a church building.[41] But beyond this description and the remarkably frescoed house church from Dura-Europos on the Syrian frontier of the empire, there is almost no evidence for pre-Constantinian structures.[42] Still, from the evidence just reviewed it would appear that the church had become much more than a small and struggling creed by the first decades of the third century. It was not the economic and military crises of the half century before Diocletian came to power in 284 that gave Christianity its initial success, but the efforts of the Christian preachers and converts in the generally peaceful years of Christianity's existence in the empire before the post-Severan crisis that built the fabric of the Christian state within the state. With the crisis, however, with barbarian invasion, with dangers on the eastern frontier with Persia, and with economic stress, there came a series of general persecutions throughout the empire.

The fifty years that followed the end of the Severan dynasty in 235 are practically bereft of pagan records.[43] The collection of imperial biographies forming the so-called Historia Augusta has been exposed as a thoroughgoing invention concocted at the very end of the fourth century.[44] Otherwise, the historian of the period can draw only on epitomes and Byzantine chronicles. For the tetrarchy the situation is much the same, assisted only by the contemporary, but colored, account of the last persecutions given by Lactantius and in Eusebius's writings composed a generation later. In dealing with the persecutions, therefore, one is left groping for the answers to basic questions.

The widespread persecution of the Christians began under Trajan Decius (249–51). The trials of the empire, especially the barbarian incursions deep within its borders, would naturally encourage a search for scapegoats, and the old prejudices against Christian atheism and hatred of mankind would not be slow to surface.[45] Indeed it was apparently a desire to revive the old ways and through them the former successes of the empire that triggered the assault on the Christians. At least such an explanation is in agreement with the little we know of Decius's admiration for the ancient Roman character.[46] The emperor's death cut short the persecution, but it was shortly resumed under Valerian (253–60). Valerian did not begin his reign as a persecutor. But in 257 he issued his first edict against the Christians, a mild ordinance which required that the principal officers of the church perform some act of recognition of the traditional Roman observances.[47] The next year a decree of far wider implications was issued.[48] Now the death penalty was ordered for bishops, presbyters, and deacons. The Christian members of the Roman ruling class were to be punished. Senators and Roman knights forfeited their property, and if they failed to renounce Christianity, they too were to be put to death. Lesser members of the civil service were to be enslaved. High-ranking married women were to lose their property and suffer banishment to one of the inhospitable islands the Romans reserved for the purpose. Valerian's edict has two important implications. First, Christian senators and high officials now make their first concrete appearance as a group. The message of the gospel had reached into the ruling class. Second, the persecution would net an immediate profit for the treasury. In fact, one source cited by Eusebius accuses Macrinus, the imperial treasurer, of fomenting the persecution with an eye to plundering the Christians to meet the state's expenses.[49] Cyprian says the same thing: "Moreover, the prefects in the city are daily urging on this persecution; so that, if any are presented to them, they are martyred, and their property claimed by the treasury."[50] The persecution of Valerian thus had much of the shakedown about it. And one may suspect that Decius's was motivated, at least in part, by similar aims. Just in the mid–third century the financial situation of the empire was becoming serious. Kenneth Harl summarizes the situation:

> Problems begin in 235 and after when Emperors debase the coinage, expecting
> in every instance that the profits of victory will restore the situation. But that did
> not happen. At the same time taxes were raised. The civil war of 238 makes matters
> worse. The Antoninianus was revived by the senatorial candidates—the Gordians
> in Africa and Pupienus and Balbinus—but quickly debased. By 253 the Antonini-
> anus was a billon coin. By this time denarii and earlier Antoniniani have disap-
> peared—into hoards or the melting pot. Trajan Decius reduced the Antoninianus
> to 4 grs. at 40 percent fine. He restruck surviving denarii and earlier Antoniniani.
> But conditions continued to worsen under Trebonianus Gallus. [251–53]

The bronze coinage fared no better: up to 235 it had been dependable and its widespread use stood behind the unprecedented monetization of the Roman economy, but within fifteen years debasement and inflation ruined the token bronze coins so vital in daily transactions and taxation.[51]

Confidence failed: "Egyptians panicked by the mid 250's, hoarding earlier coins, hallowed by such nicknames as 'ancient' or 'Ptolemaic-looking silvered money,' over 'newfangled money.' The mint of Alexandria, just like imperial mints, was swept up into wasteful recycling of tremendous numbers of recent billon coins into more debased ones." Finally, the crisis continued under Valerian: "Valerian (253–260) degraded the Antoninianus to a billon piece approximating the weight and size, but not the fineness, of a Severan denarius."

At the same time exactions in kind capriciously collected by the army made taxation a nightmare. It was part of a system that has been described as "permanent terrorism which from time to time assumed acute forms."[52]

The persecutions of Decius and Valerian both passed rapidly. Within two years of the beginning of the persecution Decius was assassinated. Valerian, after a similar time of repressing the Christians, was captured in battle by the Persian monarch Sapor. The new emperor, Valerian's son Gallienus, restored the Christians' property to them.

The Christians quickly regained lost ground, gathering the victims of fright and misery into their fold while penetrating further the upper ranks of society, who felt no less than their inferiors the insecurity of the times. By the end of the century Christians were prominent in the palace and in the army.[53] And when Diocletian, after almost twenty years' work restoring the stability of the empire, took aim at the Christians in 303, his palace in Nicomedia faced a Christian church across the street.[54] Why did he do so when he was on the verge of retiring to his native Dalmatia to hoe his turnips in the garden of the palace at Split? Perhaps it was the influence of his lieutenant Galerius, who proved to be an intractable foe of the Cross until he admitted defeat as he lay dying in pain.[55] Perhaps it was momentary pique such as he felt on the occasion of sacrifice gone wrong when the haruspices claimed that the presence of Christians had disturbed the reading of the entrails of the victims. Perhaps it was the voice of the oracle of Apollo at Didyma that accused the Christians of interfering with his prophecies. Perhaps it was a desire to complete restoration of the empire as a totalitarian state of perfect order and uniformity.[56] Whatever the immediate cause, he determined to deprive the Christians of their sacred books, destroy their meeting places, and enforce nominal reverence by a simple sacrifice of incense before the magistrate. This policy met some success, but when two fires broke out within days at the palace at Nicomedia, Diocletian saw it as the work of the Christians and gave full vent to his imperial rage. The persecution was intensified. The state within the state was to be destroyed.

The persecution was unequally pursued in the eastern and western halves of the empire.[57]

In the east, after Diocletian bade farewell to his duties, Galerius pursued the persecution un-remittingly until he lay on his deathbed, when he issued an edict calling a halt (311). But Maxi-minus Daia (Caesar in the reconstituted tetrarchy) pressed on, and Licinius, the eastern Augus-tus, despite joining Constantine in the letter commanding toleration that was issued at Milan (313) later returned to the persecution of the Christians. In the west, the persecution was far less serious. In particular, Constantius Chlorus, Constantine's father, formerly Caesar in the original tetrarchy and then the western Augustus of the reconstituted tetrarchy, contented himself with pulling down a few churches. Considered as a whole, the persecution was a failure. The Roman state had not been able to stamp out Christianity or the Christian organization.

On the eve of Constantine's victory the religious landscape of the Roman Empire was thus composed of three parts.[58] One part was the Christians, unbroken by persecution and a force to be reckoned with by the ruler who would emerge victorious in the end. The second element was composed of the cults, largely of eastern origin, that had become the focus of pa-gan devotion, Isis, Mithras, Ma-Bellona, and the rest. No matter how large the numbers of their adherents or how widespread their penetration of the empire, as a force they were weak-ened by their lack of cohesion, by their lack of organization to match the episcopal adminis-tration of the Christian churches, and by their often exclusive practices (the cult of Mithras excluded women). The third factor was composed of the traditional cults of the Roman state. The Roman state religion was a venerable relic of the Republican city restructured by Augustus. Its divinities were the familiar Olympians, ancient Italian gods, and two notable additions, Aesculapius and the Magna Mater. At its head were the ancient patrician priesthoods, the *sacerdotes publici.* The Arval Brethren, the Salii, the Fetiales, and Luperci were among the older of these priesthoods, their origins lost in the distant past. Some, such as the Albani and the Lanuvini, were reminiscent of a particular locality. Some were attached to Greek cults or the Magna Mater. The Quindecemviri Sacris Faciundis had charge of the Sibylline Books, that mysterious collection of oracles that the Romans consulted only in dire emergencies. At the apex of the imperial organization were the pontifices, who regulated the *sacra publica* as a whole. And at the head of the pontifices was the *pontifex maximus.* Since the time of Augustus the emperor had been pontifex maximus, while the members of the great priesthoods owed their dignity to imperial favor. On the pontifex maximus and his colleagues fell the responsibil-ity of regulating that delicate balance between the Roman state and its attendant divinities that the Romans called the *pax deorum.* Should any untoward event disturb that balance, the pontifices took the corrective action prescribed by long tradition.

One has only to glance at the reliefs of the Arch of Constantine (see chap. 2) to realize how the duties of the emperor were punctuated by religious ceremony. Whether in prepara-tion for war, celebration of victory, or in the midst of the hunt, the emperor carried out sacrifice as a priest. His goings and comings were escorted by the goddess Roma and Victory. And in attendance he had augurs and haruspices, whose skill in reading omens confirmed the decisions

Fig. 1.2 Gold medallion. Obv. INVICTUS CONSTANTINUS MAX AUG, jugate busts of
Constantine laureate bearing a spear and shield decorated with the Sun God in his
chariot seen frontally and the Sun God radiate, Rev. FELIX ADVENTUS AUGG NN in
the exergue SMT (mint mark), Constantine mounted, bearing scepter and raising
right arm in salutation preceded by Victory and followed by a standard-bearer.
Paris, Cabinet des Medailles. After Maurice, *Numismatique Constantinienne.*

of the imperial will. The emperor in the reliefs of the arch, as dedicated to Constantine, is not
Trajan or Hadrian or Marcus Aurelius, even though the various sculptures had been originally
prepared for monuments of those emperors. In each relief the head of the emperor is Constantine's, and the act has become his. As Zosimus put it, "He still practiced the traditional cults,
not because of reverence but because he needed them. He believed the soothsayers since by
experience he knew that they had predicted his victories accurately."[59]

It is against this background that Constantine had himself portrayed on the arch that celebrated his victorious entry into Rome.[60] Whatever his private inclinations, whatever the influence of his mother and sister, who appear to have been practicing Christians, Constantine was
tied to paganism by his office. At the same time he moved among mortals as a god himself.

Beginning with Aurelian, more than a quarter century before Constantine, the emperor
claimed divine status as an attribute of his office rather than as an honor bestowed by the Senate after death. He became Dominus et Deus. The mindset of a late Roman emperor has been
approached in modern times—and then only distantly—by the self-image of a captain of the
Royal Navy in the age of sail, "Striving by secluding himself in his cabin behind a marine with
a drawn sword to acquire an air of divinity."[61] And the Royal Navy captain was spared the per-
fumed haze spread over the emperor by that most loathsome form of ancient rhetoric, the
panegyric. Alone, separated from the rest of mankind by his assumed divinity and court ritual
of an oriental cast, endowed with despotic power but ever watchful lest foreign peril or domestic
conspiracy hurl him into the pit of failure, the emperor had no one beside him save the gods.[62]
In the generation before Constantine one god stood particularly close to the ruler, the sun
god, "As it were that companion and ally of Your Majesty."[63] And it is in just such an attitude
of easy friendship with the sun god that we find Constantine on a gold medallion in Paris,
which must date after 312 because on it there appears the title Maximus Augustus voted Constan-

Fig. 1.3 Baths of Constantine. After Etienne du Perac, *I Vestigi dell' Antichità di Roma*, edition of 1652.

tine in that year (fig. 1.2).[64] Even in the new capital at Constantinople Constantine placed his own image radiate, like the sun god, on a column which stood prominently in the city.[65]

Constantine was never represented in familiar company with Christ. His view of his relationship with the New Divinity, however, was made clear by the plans for his burial in the new capital of the empire. There in the Church of the Holy Apostles a chamber was made to receive the remains of the twelve to be brought from their scattered tombs to Constantinople. And in the center of the company there was the tomb of the new companion of Christ, "Emperor Equal of the Apostles," as he remained ever after for the Byzantines.[66] Constantine presided at the Council of Nicaea. He not only presided but exercised final authority. To this day millions of Christians repeat the words of the Nicene Creed dictated at one crucial point— the relation of the essence of the Father and the Son—not by episcopal wisdom but by an unbaptized layman.[67] That same emperor, at the same time, was issuing from the mint of Antioch, newly seized from Licinius, gold coins showing Constantine together with the sun god and carrying the legend "To the Sun, Companion of our Augustus."[68] Constantine moved on a plane that defies any analysis by the historian seated in the armchair of modern conventions. As the nearest being to the Christian God in the universe, he took charge not only of Christ's church but of the pagans as well. He was, as he said, "the bishop of those without."[69] And while he incorporated the Christian state into the imperial administration, granting the privileges of high office and remission from taxes to its officials and encouraging the imitation of imperial ceremony that still dignifies Christian worship in churches governed by episcopal hierarchy, he did not disturb the pagan foundation of the empire.[70] Bishop Eusebius's best efforts were

Fig. 1.4 Basilica Nova. Photo Sichtermann, DAI Rome, Inst. Neg. 58.1006. Copyright Deutsches Archäologisches Institut.

necessary to parade the closing of a few temples in the east, where the promiscuity of their rites offended public morals, as a concerted attack on paganism.[71] Constantine even permitted the erection of a pagan shrine to the genius of his family.[72] On his arrival in Rome he took over the grandiose building projects of Maxentius and finished them in his own name.[73] The Baths of Constantine on the Quirinal Hill were the last of these grand thermal establishments that gave every citizen the opportunity to relax in palatial surroundings (fig. 1.3).[74] Of the Basilica Nova situated between the Forum and the Colosseum only one side aisle is standing today. But this is more than sufficient to suggest the grandeur of the enormous vaulted structure (fig. 1.4). In the western apse of the basilica a gargantuan seated statue of Constantine oversaw the proceedings in the hall (fig. 1.5).[75] The head and parts of the body are preserved today in the Capitoline Museum. The center of Constantine's Rome thus remained a pagan city, and it was to remain a stronghold of paganism after the founding of New Rome and the emergence of Christian intolerance as the century progressed.

At the same time Christian buildings arose around the periphery of the city. The church of S. Giovanni was built in the Lateran. St. Peter's martyrium was created in the Vatican, and in the Christian cemeteries a series of great covered coemeteria began to be built. One of these,

Fig. 1.5 Portrait of Constantine the Great. Rome, Capitoline Museum. Photo Koppermann, DAI Rome, Inst. Neg. 59.1720. Copyright Deutsches Archäologisches Institut.

on the Via Labicana, was connected with a mausoleum where Constantine may have planned to be buried before he founded Constantinople and decided to build his tomb in the company of the apostles. (His mother, the empress Helena, took his place in the Roman tomb.) The complex of mausoleum and basilica that constituted the Roman tomb is a monument that takes us very close to Constantine in his role as Christian ruler, as will be explained in chapter 3.

Constantine ruled until 337. Following his death there was a bloodbath in a family already troubled by Constantine's elimination of his wife, Fausta, and Crispus, his son by a previous marriage. Two other sons, Constantius II and Constans, emerged victorious and ruled jointly until 350, when Constans died. Constantius II overcame a powerful usurper, Magnentius, and continued as emperor until 361. At this juncture Constantine's nephew Julian, whose troops had proclaimed him emperor in Gaul in 360, became ruler of the empire. His attempt to revive the official pagan cults was cut short by his death in 363. Christianity would never be challenged again in the Roman west or in the empire of the east until the rise of Islam.

Constantine was in Rome from October of 312 until January of 313. He returned for two months in 315 and again briefly to celebrate twenty years of rule in 326.[76] It was in the space of these thirteen years that he set in motion the initiatives which the old capital would see realized in the next quarter century and more. These are the work of an emperor who was equally Emperor of the Christians and Emperor of Those Outside the Christian Fold.

II   The Arches

The Arch of Constantine

I have always had a soft spot in my heart for the Arch of Constantine (figs. 2.1 and 2.2). The evening before I left Rome in 1962 after two years as a postdoctoral fellow, I walked down to look one last time on this monument, which was completed within three years of Constantine's triumphal entry into the city. Standing between the arch and the Colosseum, with the vista of the valley between the Palatine and Caelian Hills in the background and the warm light of a Roman evening in August around me, I could easily read the arch's inscription, on which Pius X had drawn for his inscription on the cliff face of the Saxa Rubra.[1] The dedicatory inscription of the Arch of Constantine, repeated on both façades and standing out as the largest element of the design, is as follows:

> To the Emperor Flavius Constantinus Maximus
> Father of the Fatherland the Senate and the Roman People,
> Because with inspiration from the divine and the might of his intelligence
> Together with his army he took revenge by just arms on the tyrant
> and his following at one and the same time,
> have dedicated this arch made proud by triumphs.[2]

Two phrases of the text have provoked discussion but give clear sense. The inspiration from on high ("instinctu divinitatis") acknowledges Constantine's dream/vision before the battle at the Mulvian Bridge, but it does so in a way that does not compromise the pagan character

Fig. 2.1 The Arch of Constantine. South face. Photo Rossa, DAI Rome, Inst. Neg. 77.1641. Copyright Deutsches Archäologisches Institut.

of the monument (Pius X made the reference overtly Christian in the version at the Saxa Rubra). In the last line it is not a single triumph but triumphs that have glorified the arch. This is, of course, an exaggeration. But late antique rhetoric fed on exaggeration, and no emperor or warlord of the day would have been satisfied with anything less than total victory.

Of all the Roman arches with three passageways this is the most harmonious. The relief decoration of the exterior is extensive, but unlike some other heavily decorated arches—the Arch of Septimius Severus in the Roman Forum or the arch at Orange in southern France, for example—the relief work does not overpower the architecture. The four tall, detached columns of the façades, each topped with a solemn barbarian captive, emphasize the structure of the whole and give depth to the façade. And in what seems to be a masterstroke of design, each façade carries four large reliefs in circular or almost circular frames. These are comfortably placed two over each of the side openings, with sufficient space around them for a background of porphyry revetment. The purple color of this background must have stood out royally against the white marble of the arch, and it contrasted with the *giallo antico* marble of the freestanding columns.[3] The subjects of these reliefs are unusual. They are a series of imperial hunting scenes punctuated by sacrifices to sylvan divinities. The attic is brought alive by the

Fig. 2.2 The Arch of Constantine. North face. Photo Koppermann, DAI. Inst. Neg. 61.2297. Copyright Deutsches Archäologisches Institut.

rectangular reliefs of imperial duty in war and peace that flank the dedicatory inscriptions. There is other sculpture on the façades of the arch. But the round tondos and the attic panels dominate the visual impression made by the monument.

The sculpture that achieves this stately and even quiet atmosphere was not created for Constantine's arch but was borrowed from other monuments. It was spolia. The practice of reusing marble from earlier monuments had begun on a large scale in tetrarchic times. Another arch in Rome, built by Diocletian, was no less shamelessly decorated with sculpture of earlier date.[4] And the practice was to become standard in the building of Christian churches. The reuse of sculpture, however, should not deceive one into thinking that the reused panels were meant as a tribute to the emperors originally represented. The figures fitted with portrait heads of Constantine became Constantine and showed the new ruler in his various roles as emperor.

The series of eight tondo reliefs are Hadrianic (max. diam. ca. 5.4 m). Hadrian's portrait (117–38) in the scene of sacrificing to Apollo on the north side of the arch and in the sacrifice to Hercules on the south side has been transformed into a likeness from the tetrarchic period,

Fig. 2.3 The Arch of Constantine. South face. Departure for the hunt. Photo Faraglia, DAI Rome, Inst. Neg. 32.56. Copyright Deutsches Archäologisches Institut.

Fig. 2.4 The Arch of Constantine. South face. Sacrifice to Silvanus. Photo Faraglia, DAI Rome, Inst. Neg. 32.67. Copyright Deutsches Archäologisches Institut.

possibly Constantius Chlorus, Constantine's father.[5] Otherwise the head of Hadrian was recut to represent Constantine. These reliefs are exceptional examples of the graceful sculpture of the Hadrianic times. The divine figures, Apollo especially, are examples of Roman classicism at its best. The secondary figures, especially the bearded individuals and youths, such as the almost nude boy of the departure scene, are also typically Hadrianic. The trees and foliage are typical of the so-called Neo-Attic reliefs.[6]

On the south side of the arch to the left (west) of the central opening we find the departure for the hunt (fig. 2.3) and a sacrifice to Silvanus. The hunters assemble before the arch of a gateway. A tree suggests that they are already outside the city. A frontal figure in the center is the leader. His head, both original and replacement, is missing. Two companions, one with a spear, stand to his left. A mastiff and a horse are ready for the hunt.

Beside the departure scene there is the sacrifice to Silvanus (fig. 2.4). The emperor, in the center, stands in the same pose as in the departure scene. The figure has been obliterated down to the waist. Two companions flank him, one in profile against the background of the relief who raises his hand in salutation toward the god. The shrine is in the open air as shown by the tree limb which spreads out in the background of the scene. There is an altar and the statue of the god standing on a high pedestal. Silvanus is nude save for a cloak on his shoulder in the fold of which he holds a selection of fruit. Another companion in the hunt stands behind the statue.

On the right side of the central passageway of the arch there is first the tondo of the bear hunt (fig. 2.5). Three horsemen close in on the fleeing animal. The horseman of the foreground again must be the emperor; he raises his right arm to strike home with his lance.

Fig. 2.5 The Arch of Constantine. South face. Bear hunt. Photo DAI Faraglia, Rome, Inst. Neg. 32.57. Copyright Deutsches Archäologisches Institut.

Fig. 2.6 The Arch of Constantine. South face. Sacrifice to Diana. Photo Faraglia, DAI Rome, Inst. Neg. 32.85. Copyright Deutsches Archäologisches Institut.

Next comes the sacrifice to Diana (fig. 2.6). The sanctuary again is in the open air. A garland and a pine cone are piled on the altar center foreground. Behind there is the statue of the goddess on a high base. She stands frontally wearing the dress of the huntress, tunic and boots. There is a torch beside her. Two gnarled trees mark the background. The four hunters are grouped around the altar, two on each side. The offerant of the sacrifice is the first figure to the right. His head is covered, in the Roman mode. He extends his right hand over the altar. His head is half destroyed and worn otherwise. Of his companions only the young man beside the altar on the left has his features largely intact.

These four tondos were originally intended for display in such a way that their lower edge below the ground line of the sculptured scene was hidden. This is the original condition of the reliefs. It is not due to reworking at the time they were installed on the Arch of Constantine.

Moving to the north side of the arch, first on the left we find the boar hunt (fig. 2.7). The scene is set on the banks of a stream. A tree grows from the bank covered with rushes while the surface of the water is indicated behind the boar. The boar is a fearsome animal, not shown in flight like the bear but with feet planted, ready to stand his ground. Above and behind him three horsemen ride to the attack. On the foremost a tetrarchic head has been substituted for the original. His hunting gesture with the lance is the same as in the bear hunt. The figures of his two companions, and the horse of one, are well preserved. The horseman directly behind the emperor has been identified as Hadrian's favorite, the young Antinoos.[7]

The next relief, a sacrifice to Apollo, is the best preserved of the set (fig. 2.8). The composition is much the same as in the scene of sacrifice to Diana. On center is the altar, behind it

Fig. 2.7 The Arch of Constantine. North face. Boar hunt. Photo Fototeca Unione Neg. 4222F. Copyright.

Fig. 2.8 The Arch of Constantine. North face. Sacrifice to Apollo. Photo Faraglia, DAI Rome, Inst. Neg. 32.54. Copyright Deutsches Archäologisches Institut.

the statue of the god on a high pedestal, and finally in the background two trees, now laurel trees. The longhaired god wears a robe which has slipped to expose his torso to the groin. He has beside him his tripod, snake, and lyre. To the right there stands a youth holding the bridle of a horse. To the left there is the emperor, whose portrait is intact, and a companion.

To the right of the central opening of the arch first comes the lion hunt (fig. 2.9). The hunt has ended, and the carcass of the beast is sprawled below the ground line of the scene. Above, the hunters and two horses stand before two trees in the background. The emperor's head (he is second from the left) has been recut and a halo added behind it.

A sacrifice to Hercules terminates the series (fig. 2.10). The emperor, head veiled but features recognizable, stands in the center, his hands stretched toward the altar, on which a fire has been kindled. A companion faces him and two stand behind. The god, in the pose of the Heracles Epitrapezios of Lysippus, appears in miniature in the upper field of the relief. He holds a Victory in his outstretched left hand. He is flanked by a cuirass to each side. His right hand holds the end of a swag of foliage which is fixed to the border of the image and also hangs down toward the sacrificial party. Finally, the lion's skin is displayed along the right border of the relief.

Unlike the tondo reliefs of the south side of the arch, the full circumference of the tondos of the north side was intended to be seen. The boar hunt and scene of sacrifice to Apollo are finished along the lower edge. The Hercules sacrifice relief is less so.

Despite these anomalies of display in their original setting, the tondos, measuring 2⅓ m

Fig. 2.9 The Arch of Constantine. North face. Lion hunt. Photo Faraglia, DAI Rome, Inst. Neg. 32.55. Copyright Deutsches Archäologisches Institut.

Fig. 2.10 The Arch of Constantine. North face. Sacrifice to Hercules. Photo Faraglia, DAI Rome, Inst. Neg. 32.66. Copyright Deutsches Archäologisches Institut.

and all of Luna marble, appear to be a set. They have no close parallels among surviving Roman imperial relief sculpture. Their origin is unknown, although hypotheses about their original situation have been advanced.[8]

The attic reliefs belong to a series made for a monument of Antonine date. Their style is comparable with that of the reliefs of the Column of Marcus Aurelius in the Campus Martius. It is probable that the reliefs were executed during the reign of Marcus's son, the emperor Commodus (180–92). The heads of the principal figure in each scene (certainly the emperor) were replaced in antiquity. One assumes that the new portrait was of Constantine, but the heads one sees today were put on the sculptures in 1732 as part of the restoration of the arch by Pope Clement XII. The reliefs are made of Luna marble and are somewhat over 3 m high.

These reliefs take us away from the hunt to the business of government and war. The melancholic seriousness of the reliefs is the same that marks other official reliefs of the Antonine Period. Even on the best occasions, the arrival of the emperor or the payment of support to the Roman citizenry, there is hardly a happy face to be seen. The reliefs replay standard themes of imperial iconography.

They begin, on the south face of the arch, at the west with the presentation of an allied chieftain to the army (fig. 2.11). The scene is a military base. The general's headquarters, the praetorium, is in the background. On the left the emperor, in campaign dress, tunic and cloak, addresses the army from a podium. With him on the podium is a figure which recurs beside the emperor in each of the military scenes of the series.[9] Standing below the emperor and fac-

Fig. 2.11 The Arch of Constantine. South face. Presentation of barbarian chieftain. Photo Fototeca Unione Neg. 28747. Copyright.

Fig. 2.12 The Arch of Constantine. South face. Imperial address. Photo Fototeca Unione Neg. 28743. Copyright.

ing the crowd of soldiers is the subject of the presentation. Being a friend of Rome, he is a noble barbarian, but as a mark of his identity he wears a fringed cloak. Behind the soldiers of the foreground the standard-bearers of the army appear in their characteristic animal-pelt headgear. They hold standards which carry figures among which one can distinguish Victory, Mars, and Hercules.

Directly beyond the great inscription over the central openings, one sees next a relief showing another address of the emperor to the troops (fig. 2.12). The emperor and his general stand on a podium to the right side of the panel. The time of battle is approaching, and the soldiers appear with armor, helmets, and spears. In the background there are again two standard-bearers holding legionary standards (the "eagles").[10]

Beside the relief just described, we find first a scene of sacrifice before combat. Among the crowd of soldiers and victims the emperor offers a pinch of incense over a flaming tripod (fig. 2.13). He holds a scroll in one hand. A youthful assistant, long hair reaching his shoulders and secured around his head by a chaplet, holds the incense box. A slightly older assistant, bearing the sacrificial ax, stands on the far left. Two attendants kneel holding the pig and sheep. The bull is behind. On the right a trumpeter, facing inward toward the host, sounds his instrument while another musician, his head wreathed, adds the shrill note of the double flute.

Fig. 2.13 The Arch of Constantine. South face. Sacrifice. Photo Fototeca Unione Neg. 287414. Copyright.

Fig. 2.14 The Arch of Constantine. South face. Barbarian prisoners. Photo Fototeca Unione Neg. 4234F. Copyright.

The general, bareheaded, mingles with the crowd. Spears and ensigns, both the legionary eagles and the vexilla carrying a cloth standard from a crosspiece, fill the background together with large wreaths which we should imagine suspended in some way behind the gathering. A standard-bearer, grim in his lion skin headdress, looks out from the throng.

Returning to the left side of the arch, we find that the battle is over, and two captured barbarians are being brought before the emperor (fig. 2.14). The emperor stands in the podium to the left with his constant companion. Soldiers in battle dress with spears crowd below, two of their number dragging the captives forward. The faces of the defeated warriors are marked with the signs of downcast resignation or wild-eyed despair. The Romans maintain a serious dignity. In the background there are two vexilla and a gnarled tree.

On the north side of the arch the attic reliefs bring the emperor to Rome. At the east end he arrives. Following the standard iconography of this scene, the emperor is accompanied by Mars and Dea Roma (fig. 2.15). A Victory flies overhead. Two women, one veiled, the second bearing an offering tray with fruits, stand behind. In the background are a garlanded arch and a temple. The arch is a quadrifrons; that is, it has two major openings that cross in its center. The pediment of the temple has a figure of Fortuna, identified by the globe and a wheel between which she sits. There is a cornucopia in each angle. The temple is thus identified as the Temple

Fig. 2.15 The Arch of Constantine. North face. Arrival of the emperor. Photo Fototeca Unione Neg. 28741. Copyright.

Fig. 2.16 The Arch of Constantine. North face. Departure of the emperor. Photo Fototeca Unione Neg. 28740. Copyright.

of Fortuna Redux, a most appropriate divinity for an imperial return to the city. This temple in Rome was rebuilt by Domitian in 93.[11]

There follows a departure scene (fig. 2.16). The emperor, again with his scroll, faces toward the personification of the highways of the empire (a seminude female figure seated on the ground and resting her arm on a wheel). A bearded figure behind the emperor represents the Roman Senate. His companion would be the Roman People. Soldiers in armor and two warhorses crowd to the right. Two military standards are unfurled overhead. In the background is the same garlanded arch as on the preceding relief. Now we see something of the sculpture which it carried, four elephants (that would have been yoked to a chariot), a Victory, and a barbarian.

To the right of the central opening of the arch (east side) there are the final pair of Antonine reliefs. First comes a scene of *liberalitas,* the emperor distributing support payments to Roman citizens (fig. 2.17). Here in action is the famous dole, which was a concrete advantage of the citizenry of the capital. The emperor, the scale of whose figure dwarfs the other participants in the scene, is seated on a high podium. Three dignitaries are grouped around him. A slave passes him purses of money from a sack beneath his feet. In the foreground at the foot of the podium there are gathered the recipients of the emperor's generosity. Turning away after receiving their allotment are a father carrying his child on his shoulders, a woman, and

Fig. 2.17 The Arch of Constantine. North face. Imperial generosity. Photo Fototeca Unione Neg. 28746. Copyright.

Fig. 2.18 The Arch of Constantine. North face. Submission of the defeated. Photo Fototeca Unione Neg. 28748. Copyright.

an elderly man with his slave boy. Another man looks up toward the emperor in anticipation of receiving his share. The scene is set before a colonnade in which garlands are displayed.

Finally, we return to the camp for the submission of the defeated (fig. 2.18). The emperor sits on a podium, his attending commander standing behind him. Before him a defeated barbarian, embracing his downcast son, begs for the mercy of the emperor. Soldiers, including three standard-bearers, look on. In the background there are three eagles and a military standard.

Many students of the subject believe that these eight reliefs, together with three others now preserved in the Capitoline Museum (Galleria dei Conservatori), originally belonged to an arch erected in honor of Marcus Aurelius. This arch, furthermore, is identified with the "Arcus Aureus" located on or near the road ascending the Capitoline, the Clivus Capitolinus, at the northwest corner of the Forum. The theory of an arch in this location is supported by the inscription from the Capitoline (or the area of the Capitoline and possibly belonging to the arch) which appears in the medieval pilgrim's guidebook known as the "Anonymous Einsiedelensis" and by the fact that the three additional reliefs now in the Conservatory Palace were brought there from the Church of S. Martina, which stands beside the Curia near the Clivus Capitolinus in the northwest corner of the Forum.[12]

The Arcus Aureus, however, is quite possibly a figment of the imagination. In the various manuscripts of the Einsiedeln itinerary, we find not only Arcus Aureus but also Arcus Panis

Fig. 2.19 The Arch of Constantine. South face. Statues of barbarians and Antonine Relief Panels. Photo Fototeca Unione Neg. 28742. Copyright.

Aurei, the later title referring, as Paolino Mingazzini pointed out, to a well-known bakery on the south side of the Capitoline Hill toward the Tiber. Consequently, there is no guarantee that an arch dedicated to Marcus Aurelius ever graced the slopes of the Capitoline on the opposite side of the hill.[13] The source of the reliefs is uncertain.

Topping the freestanding columns of both façades of the arch there are figures of defeated barbarians standing with hands clasped in a sign of resignation and defeat (fig. 2.19). The figures are 2.75 m high and are made of Pavonazzetto marble. The barbarians of the Arch of Constantine have usually been assumed to have been removed from the Forum of Trajan, where fragments of similar statues of similar size have been found.[14] But this is far from certain. A cache of these figures, in fragments, has been found in the Campus Martius, where other stores of unused sculpture are known, most notably the so-called Cancelleria Reliefs, originally intended for a monument of Domitian.[15] It was at such a way station that the plinth of one of the barbarians was marked with a cursory "ad arcum," when it was about to be sent to the arch.[16] The very fact of this annotation makes it unlikely that the statue was taken directly from the Forum of Trajan to the arch; rather, with other spolia it had been stored in a marble yard in the Campus Martius, where it was selected to be used where we now find it.

Without doubt the most impressive sculptures that were incorporated into the arch come from a monumental frieze in Pentelic marble, closely comparable to the reliefs of the Column of Trajan and commonly known as the Great Trajanic Frieze. Sections of the frieze were used on either side of the central passage of the arch and in the attic on its two short sides. When

Fig. 2.20   The Arch of Constantine. Central passage. The Great Trajanic Frieze. Photo Faraglia, DAI Rome Inst. Neg. 37.328. Copyright Deutsches Archäologisches Institut.

reassembled, as was done by M. Pallottino, the Great Trajanic Frieze becomes a monumental band of sculpture 18.28 m long and almost 3 m high.[17] This grand opera relief is a paean to the victorious might of Roman arms and of the emperor, now given the features of Constantine. On one side of the central passage, the emperor mounted on his fine steed, cloak flying behind him, only one trooper at his side and the legionary standard-bearer a pace behind, dashes forward, and the barbarians melt away before him (fig. 2.20). Behind, the legionaries mop up. Ahead, captives await their fate. Great though it is, the frieze is still incomplete. On the opposite side of the central passage there is another section of the frieze showing the emperor's arrival (fig. 2.21). Victory crowns him, assuring success, and Dea Roma accompanies him. Other sections of the frieze on the east and west sides of the attic fill out the action (figs. 2.22, 2.23, 2.24), and further fragments of the reliefs are preserved in Paris and Rome (Villa Medici and Villa Borghese). The original length of the frieze has been calculated to have been some 36 m.[18]

The Great Trajanic Frieze is spolia, but from where? The obvious answer would seem to be the Forum of Trajan, that grandiose complex comprising the Column of Trajan, the Basilica Ulpia, and libraries, which is located not more than 600 m (about one-third of a mile) west

Fig. 2.21 The Arch of Constantine. Central passage. The Great Trajanic Frieze. Photo Faraglia, DAI Rome, Inst. Neg. 37.329. Copyright Deutsches Archäologisches Institut.

of the arch. But as James Packer has pointed out in his full-scale study of the forum, it is difficult to find a location on the building for a frieze 3 m high.[19] Other ideas have included the perimeter wall of the Forum of Peace (Vespasian's monument to the Jewish War located between the Forum of Trajan and the arch) and the perimeter wall of the Forum Iulium (situated between the Forum of Trajan and the Capitoline Hill).[20] If, however, one is searching for a true parallel for this magnificent band of sculpture, it is to be found in the Aegean. The monument in question is the Antonine Altar at Ephesus.[21] This monument is in the tradition of the Great Altar of Zeus at Pergamon, and the height of the frieze encircling its base is 3 m, exactly comparable to that of the Great Trajanic Frieze. In an earlier article I have argued that the Great Trajanic Frieze originally adorned a monumental altar located far from Rome in some city that had suffered during the barbarian invasions of the later third century, when much of region bordering the Aegean Sea, including Athens, was devastated.[22] Following the sack, the altar was dismantled, just as many Athenian monuments were dismantled after the Herulian Sack of 267.[23] The frieze was shipped to Rome to supply the ever-growing demand for spolia in the tetrarchic period, and from the storage yard came to the arch.

Fig. 2.22 The Arch of Constantine. West face. Photo
Faraglia, DAI Rome, Inst. Neg. 38.701. Copyright Deutsches
Archäologisches Institut.

Finally we come to the sculpture contemporary with the arch. In the two side passageways,
there are found a group of busts. They measure ca. 90–100 cm high by 110–25 cm wide. In the
east side passage on the east wall there was a bust of a figure in armor flanked by a Victory.
The face has been disfigured. The second panel on this side of the passageway has been removed
from the wall. On the west side, east wall there is a bust of Sol, identified by the radiate crown,
and a second panel now missing. In the west side passage we find a second bust of a man in
armor. His head and chest are disfigured. There is a second similar figure. He was surrounded
by two Victories. His head, which was made separately and inserted into the body, is missing.
On the west side there is a figure in civilian attire. The head, now disfigured, was crowned and
was attended by a Victory. The three cuirassed busts are surely those of emperors, as was the
last. Hans Peter L'Orange and Armin von Gerkan, who published a detailed monograph on
the late antique decoration of the arch, considered two of them to have been portraits of Constantine and Licinius, his coemperor until 324.[24]

The series of tondo reliefs of the two façades of the arch was filled out by two additional
reliefs, one of Sol, the other of Diana, on the east and west short sides (figs. 2.25, 2.26). The

Fig. 2.23 The Arch of Constantine. West face. The Great Trajanic Frieze. Photo Fototeca Unione Neg. 28750. Copyright.

Fig. 2.24 The Arch of Constantine. East face. The Great Trajanic Frieze. Photo DAI Rome, Inst. Neg. 1271. Copyright Deutsches Archäologisches Institut.

Fig. 2.25 The Arch of Constantine. East face. Tondo with the Sun God and frieze of Constantine's entry into Rome. Photo DAI Rome, Inst. Neg. 3134. Copyright Deutsches Archäologisches Institut.

Fig. 2.26 The Arch of Constantine. West face. Tondo with the Moon Goddess and frieze of Constantine's army on the march. Photo DAI Rome, Inst. Neg. 3135. Copyright Deutsches Archäologisches Institut.

style of these reliefs is dramatically different from the Hadrianic tondos and typical of the Tetrarchic Period.

There are Victories in the spandrels of the central opening of the arch on both façades, each bearing a trophy and accompanied by a cherub figure, each representing one of the four seasons. The spandrels of the side arches were decorated with figures of eight river gods.

On the fronts of the plinths of the freestanding columns on both façades there are carved Victories. On the sides of the plinths there are representations of Romans and barbarians.

Specific recording of Constantine's recent achievements and activities was restricted to a small band of continuous relief that encircles the arch just below the Hadrianic tondos midway up the shafts of the detached façade columns. These reliefs are a picture of Constantine's victorious campaign of 312 and views of the victor fulfilling the duties of the Roman emperor. They are executed on a band of stone no more than 1.2 m in height.[25]

The series of scenes begins on the west side of the arch (the short side toward the Roman Forum, fig. 2.27). The army is on the march. The first two figures, however, are around the corner on the north frieze of the arch, squeezed in between the northernmost column of the façade and the edge of the monument.[26] They are a cavalryman and a foot soldier about to pass through an arch. This is taken to suggest the city gate of Milan from where the army set out toward Verona, its last stop on the way to Rome. On the west face proper a wagon emerges from under the arch. The soldiers wear leggings as well as tunics. The rank and file, including musicians and standard-bearers, have helmets. The quartermasters following in the line of march wear the pillbox hats that were the hallmark of the tetrarchs and their retinue. There is a packhorse and, not surprisingly for an army used to war in the east and service in North Africa, a camel.

The south side of the arch brings us to the continuation of the campaign and the siege of Verona (fig. 2.28). Constantine, dismounted while his charger waits behind, is immediately visible one-third of the way along the frieze. He towers over his men. Victory flies up to crown him. The attack is led by a line of legionaries brandishing their spears. Above them in the relief one sees the first of the light-armed North African auxiliary troops, distinguished by their feathered headdress.[27] Among the regular troops some wear crested helmets, some a helmet decorated with a horn. The latter are the Gallic corps d'elite. One of their number rushes ahead to the foot of the wall. At the same time a defender plummets to his death. The resistance is fierce, however, and the defenders crowd the walls.

Beyond the main opening of the arch on its south side, the victory of the Mulvian Bridge was celebrated (fig. 2.29).[28] At the left Victory and Dea Roma stand beside the emperor, whose figure is largely destroyed. They are standing on the remains of a bridge through which the Tiber flows. A great mound of bodies occupying most of the scene are the troops of Maxentius floundering in the Tiber under the weight of their chain armor. Above them, like fishermen around a school of netted fish, Constantine's soldiers, mostly cavalry moving along the banks of the river, dispatch whoever raises his head. Two musicians sound horns. Beyond the corner column of the façade there are two soldiers who belong to the victory procession entering Rome (found on the east, short side of the arch).

In the procession Constantine rides in a chariot drawn by four horses (fig. 2.30). Victory walks by his side leading the team.[29] A formation of infantry precedes the emperor. Then comes the cavalry, serpent standards above them. Finally, there is another regiment of foot approaching an arch. Around the corner on the north side of the arch two horsemen complete the scene. The elephants on the arch above them identify it as the Arch of Domitian in the Campus Martius.

We now come to the friezes of the north front of the arch. On the left of the central opening the emperor addresses the people in the Forum (fig. 2.31). In the center Constantine appears in military dress on the Rostra. Behind the Rostra the arch with triple openings is the Arch of Septimius Severus. The single opening arch is the no-longer-existing Arch of Tiberius. To the left one sees the Basilica Julia and on the right the Basilica Aemilia. At the ends of the Rostra there are two seated figures, seemingly statues of Hadrian to the right and Marcus Aurelius to the left. In the background are five honorary columns. The central column carries a statue of Jupiter flanked by standards and the others statues of the four members of the original tetrarchy, Diocletian, Maximian, Constantius Chlorus, and Galerius. The party on the Rostra are senators dressed in the old-fashioned toga. The people and their sons below are content with less elaborate dress.

Finally, balancing the oratory to the left there is the *congiarium,* the imperial bounty distributed to the citizens (fig. 2.32). Constantine occupies the dais. The upper register gives us a series of four windows through which we can see officials (in toga) and their assistants at work. In the two windows at the left they are sorting coins from a strongbox into trays. The trays are specially made with cavities to accept—and clearly display—the number of coins in each citizen's allotment. A tally is kept by a secretary with a scroll. The tray is then passed to an official in the central group with the emperor. The official then empties the tray into the cloak or mantle of the waiting recipient below.[30] On the right the same operations are repeated (but without trays). The crowd behaves exactly as one would expect—in confusion with gesticulation and pushing to the front.

The sculptors never quite finished work on the *congiarium* relief. The feet of the waiting recipients were supposed to be cut from the course immediately below the frieze, as in the oratory scene on the other side of the central opening of arch. But this was never done.

The small historical frieze of the Arch of Constantine is commonly looked on as a marker of a turning point in ancient art. The late antique, already visible in the arts of the tetrarchs, is here apparent in all its directness and roughness on a major commemorative monument of Rome itself.

Sadness at the decline and fall of ancient art has marked more than one critic's response to the frieze. Bernard Berenson found the military scenes depressing enough, but the civil scenes of the north façade brought him to despair: "Indeed the individual figures suggest

Fig. 2.27 The Arch of Constantine. West face. Constantine's army on the march. Photos Faraglia, DAI Rome, Inst. Neg. 32.76, 77, 78, 79. Copyright Deutsches Archäologisches Institut.

Fig. 2.28 The Arch of Constantine. South face. Siege of Verona. Photos Faraglia, DAI Rome, Inst. Neg. 32.75, 81, 82.
Copyright Deutsches Archäologisches Institut.

Fig. 2.29 The Arch of Constantine. South face. Battle of the Mulvian Bridge. Photos Faraglia, DAI Rome, Inst. Neg. 32.72, 73, 74, 80. Copyright Deutsches Archäologisches Institut.

Fig. 2.30 The Arch of Constantine. East face. Constantine's entry into Rome. Photos Faraglia, DAI Rome, Inst.
Neg. 32.62a, 63–65. Copyright Deutsches Archäologisches Institut.

Fig. 2.31 The Arch of Constantine. North face. Constantine's address in the Forum. Photos Faraglia, DAI Rome, Inst. Neg. 32.7–10. Copyright Deutsches Archäologisches Institut.

Fig. 2.32 The Arch of Constantine. North face. Distribution of the *congiarium*. Photos Felbermeyer, DAI Rome, Inst. Neg. 31.2068, 2070, 2071. Copyright Deutsches Archäologisches Institut.

nothing so much as an assemblage of rudely carved chessmen . . . we find huge heads out of all proportion to their bodies. These stunted bodies are swathed in heavy blankets or covered with scanty shifts, both with the folds of the draperies as unfunctional, as helplessly chiseled as ever European art sank to in the darkest ages."[31]

Verdict: the Roman sculptors of Constantine's day were simply inept. Their art was not on the way to barbarism. It was already barbaric.

Others have a more hopeful view of the style of the reliefs. In the first part of the twentieth century claims were made that the Persian influence on imperial ritual and the presentation of the imperial office had carried over into the art of late antiquity.[32] But at the same time a new stream of expression in Roman art itself was being explored. This is the art of action, without the pretensions of the Greek past, a new art for new themes, whether the tradesman's signpost or the sarcophagus with the newly introduced images such as hunting scenes of game driven into nets that came into the artistic repertoire with no Hellenistic prototypes behind them.[33] This stream then melds with that of the art of the provinces, where Hellenized Roman art had never been really at home, becoming the vehicle of expression for the late antique world. Still another group of scholars, with Marxist affinities, sees an affirmation of popular as opposed to patrician art.[34] And the "symmetrical crystallization of the composition" has been seen as the reflection of the rigidified social structure of the tetrarchic and Constantinian age.[35]

But there is another perspective on the way that the presentation of Constantine's achievements was handled on the arch. First, one must emphasize that the band on which the reliefs

were to be carved was only about 1 m high. Second, one must realize the fact, which I shall attempt to establish in what follows, that when Constantine's sculptors came to do their work on the arch, they had very little choice in the placement of their reliefs or their dimensions. They had to cut the frieze on a band of stone that was already in place.

Their battle scenes, which bothered Berenson so much, are reminiscent of the work of another group of sculptors, from the finest period of Greek art in Greece and Asia Minor, who undertook to carve battle scenes, including a siege, on the basement of the tomb known as the Nereid Monument at Xanthos (fig. 2.33). These sculptures were done about 400 B.C., yet they show the same tendencies toward distortion of the human figure (venturing toward dwarfism) and the same rendering of fortifications in a Lilliputian fashion that we see on the Arch of Constantine. This is the result of the problems of achieving wide perspective on a narrow frieze without making the buildings look gigantic and without allowing the figures to all but disappear if they are kept in correct proportion to the buildings. What we find on the Arch of Constantine are the devices of the comic strip artist, the dwarfish figure with head too large for his body and the stunted building, all part of an effort to keep the action from being lost and to keep the setting subordinate to the figures involved. At the same time the sculptors of the frieze in common with other artists already working under Diocletian abandoned the formulas of traditional imperial art and its Hellenic sources in order to render these scenes with the utmost clarity. The historical frieze of the Arch of Constantine is thus a study in the tricks of the artist's trade. In late antiquity the high classical style was not forgotten, and the late antique craftsman was technically just as accomplished as his forebears. But even though remaining dominant

Fig. 2.33 Detail from the upper podium frieze of the Nereid Monument from Xanthos. London, British Museum. Crown Copyright Reserved.

in the best work in the minor arts, silver plate, for example, the high classical style was no longer the only vehicle, or indeed the favored vehicle, for official or ecclesiastical monuments.

Why were Constantine's sculptors in such a predicament? Let me anticipate the discussion to come.[36] The Romans (Senate and People as the inscription has it) took a partly finished arch and converted it to honor the new emperor. The arch was being erected to honor Maxentius. The body of the arch was ready, but the attic had not been built. The Hadrianic tondos were already installed, as were the Luna and Sol tondos of the sides that had been prepared to extend the series of tondos around the arch. The secondary sculpture around the archways had been carved.[37] But the panels of Marcus Aurelius were probably on the site waiting to be lifted into place when the attic was ready for them. The Trajanic frieze was possibly on the site too, but more likely it was still in a marble depot, where it had been brought from a great altar somewhere in the Aegean which had been despoiled during the barbarian invasions of the third century.

In short order Constantine saw to finishing the attic with its two grand inscriptions and the Marcus panels. All of the attic is a marble veneer over brick, unlike the lower parts of the structure, which are solid marble.[38] Far less care was taken with the appearance of the work than was the case in the lower part of the arch, and in fact not until the investigations of the 1990s was it realized that all the marble blocks composing the walls of those parts of the arch already prepared for Maxentius, as well as decorative elements of the arch, were spolia. In Constantine's honor the small course below the tondos was transformed into a historical relief of his victories and attention to imperial duties. But the arch still lacked the battle scenes on a big scale that the victory of the Mulvian Bridge required. Therefore in completing the attic Constantine's architects added two slabs of the Trajanic frieze on the short sides of the arch and two other sections in the main passage. The latter two sections have clearly been let into the wall that was cut out for the purpose. The "vota" inscriptions of the façade and the inscriptions over the sections of the Trajanic frieze in the main passageway were added at this time.[39] Finally, the façade was completed with other sculpture, barbarians above and Victories, Romans, and barbarians on the column bases. Constantine did not, however, have the usual statuary of a triumphal arch placed on the roof, once again acknowledging that this was a monument to victory in a civil war.[40]

The evidence for this history of the arch comes from the excavations carried out around it during the 1990s. The results of modern archaeological work applied to a monument which was by no means unknown resulted in enormous progress in our knowledge of the arch. The marbles of the arch were identified. Numerous details of construction were clarified. And the phases of construction were documented by evidence excavated around the foundations. There were, however, two teams of excavators involved, and the conclusions of each were therefore drawn from incomplete evidence.

Of particular interest for the following discussion are the results of the excavation of the foundations of the arch. On the south side the team led by Alessandra Melucco Vaccaro discovered two deposits, in direct contact with the concrete foundations, which were composed purely of material of the second century. These had survived despite the continual building and pitting that had gone on in the area.[41] The testimony of these deposits is unequivocal. They must have been laid down when the foundation was already in place. This means that the Arch of Constantine stands on a much earlier foundation. The Melucco Vaccaro team, however, drew an erroneous conclusion from this evidence. They hold that the arch itself was erected during the second century, in fact under Hadrian. The Hadrian tondos were, therefore, in place on a Hadrianic arch.

The arch sits askew on and considerably overlaps the early foundation. This leaves open the possibility that the foundation was intended for a monument that was erected and subsequently torn down or that was never in fact built.[42]

Patrizio Pensabene, Clementina Panella, and their associates dug (on a limited scale) against the foundations of the arch on the north side. At the northwest corner they excavated a feature which they believed was part of the construction trench for the foundations of the arch.[43] Yet inspection of their plans and sections does not inspire confidence in this identification. The feature is a pit, 6 m broad at its top and irregular in outline. Foundation trenches, in my experience, are never wider than necessary and always tidy. The feature, therefore, may be considered one of those intrusions that Melucco Vaccaro and her collaborators also found on the

Fig. 2.34 The Arch of Malborghetto before restoration. Photo courtesy L. Quilici.

south face of the foundations. The fill of the feature dated its closing to the early fourth century. But this is not a date for the foundations, only for the pit that was dug down beside them.

The observations of Pensabene and Panella on the structure of the arch itself are of outstanding value. It is they who identified the marbles involved. And it is they who established that the structure of the arch throughout, wall blocks as well as sculpture, is spolia, betrayed by traces of moldings, molding decoration, setting, and working. This cannot be a Hadrianic arch or an arch of any emperor before the late third century.

One may suggest, however, that the foundations partly underlying the Arch of Constantine were built in late Flavian or Hadrianic times but that *the arch was never built above them.* They were, however, finally employed for an arch at the beginning of the fourth century. This arch was only partially completed when Constantine entered Rome.[44] It is certain that the fourth-century arch was not a single project because of the way the walls were cut out to receive the sections of the Trajanic frieze placed in the main passageway and the busts of emperors and divinities in the side passages.

On the basis of this reconstruction, we can better understand the character of the historical reliefs that were added in Constantine's honor and the practical necessities that determined their style. In this case physical limitations far more than decay of style, proletarianism, or an eastern influence played a decisive role in their creation.

The resulting arch was a patchwork. There are no subtleties of program to discover.[45] But the arch and its sculpture still conveyed a message of absolute clarity. Constantine, the com-

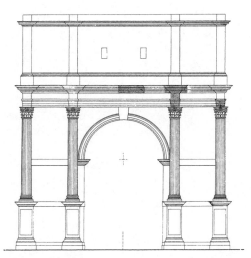

Fig. 2.35 The Arch of Malborghetto. Reconstructed north elevation. Courtesy G. Messineo.

Fig. 2.36 The Arch of Malborghetto. Reconstructed west elevation. Courtesy G. Messineo.

panion of the pagan gods, is triumphant in war and fulfills the religious and civic duties of the emperor.

Malborghetto

The Via Flaminia runs north from the Saxa Rubra along the last ridge flanking the Tiber plain. At some distance (five kilometers) along this road, where the small railroad to Viterbo and the modern Flaminia run side by side with the ancient highway, there is a squarish brick tower, once a farmstead, once an inn, before that a fortified church and originally a Roman commemorative arch (fig. 2.34). Due to the careful surveillance of the authorities of the branch of the Archaeological Superintendency of Rome in charge of this area the landscape along the Flaminia has been preserved in all its simplicity, edged by umbrella pines and subtly hinting at the centuries of cultivation of this very human landscape.

The Arch of Malborghetto may well have been the real monument to the victory at the Saxa Rubra. It figures in no history of Roman art and is often ignored even by archaeological visitors to Rome because what remains is brick work denuded of its marble revetments, inscriptions, and sculpture. Yet the structure of the arch is preserved almost complete, and it requires little imagination to see it as it was originally. The arch is a *janus quadrifrons* (that is, a four-way arch). Until 1982 it was, as it had been for centuries before, the core of a farmstead. Now property of the Italian state, it was restored between 1984 and 1988.[46]

The wider axis of the arch, which spans the Via Flaminia, the major highway north from Rome up the Tiber valley, is 14.86 m (fig. 2.35). Its narrow side, which accommodated a side road crossing the Via Flaminia, measures 11.87 m (fig. 2.36). Actually, the traffic on the two roads did not pass through the arch but was diverted around it on a widened paving—thus

Fig. 2.37 The Janus Quadrifrons in the Forum Boarium. At right the church of S. Giorgio in Velabro. Photo Fototeca Union Neg. 1746. Copyright.

creating what may be the world's first traffic circle! In the absence of writing or images, there is nothing to connect it with Constantine. Töbelmann, however, argued that this could well have been the site of Constantine's camp and that this would, therefore, have been the spot where Constantine (in Lactantius's version of events) dreamt the dream that changed history.[47] In addition, the character of the brickwork and the practice of erecting a brick core to be sheathed in marble are characteristic of the time.[48] The date is further supported by brick stamps of 292–305.[49]

Not all the decorative marble covering of the arch has been lost. There are fragments of the façade and flank columns and their capitals. On the north side there is a bit of the cornice including the frieze, which because it projects forward shows that the columns of the façade were detached as in the Arch of Constantine. Recent widening of the excavated area around the arch has brought to light further documentation of the cornice and a large part of one column. On the basis of this evidence it has been possible to make a graphic reconstruction of the monument.[50]

Fig. 2.38 The Janus Quadrifrons in the Forum Boarium. At right the church of S. Giorgio in Velabro. After Rossini, *Archi Trionfali e Funebri*, 1836.

The Janus Quadrifrons *in the Forum Boarium*

The purpose, date, and original appearance of the four-way arch that stands in part over the great drain of Rome, the Cloaca Maxima, near its outlet into the Tiber are all in doubt. It is a massive monument measuring 12 by 12 m on the ground and standing 16 m high (figs. 2.37,

2.38). The arch has never been much admired because in its present state it is squat and ugly. It has lost its upper part, which was marble veneered brickwork and was removed in 1830 on the mistaken assumption that it represented a medieval addition.[51] The columns which originally flanked the forty-eight niches of the exterior are gone, and any sculpture that once filled the niches is lost.[52] Only the restoration of Rossini gives some idea of what the arch was like when it was new, although the delicate channeling around the niches and the scalloping crowning their interiors show something of the elegance that was intended. Heads of Minerva and Dea Roma still decorate the keystones of the openings north and south. Christian Hülsen wished to restore the arch supporting a cone above it.[53]

There is, however, no certainty that the entry in the fourth-century Regionary Catalogue for Regio IX referring to an arch of Constantine refers to this arch, and even if it does, that the reference is not to one of his sons rather than to Constantine himself. There are fragments of a monumental inscription, possibly from the arch, preserved in the nearby church of S. Giorgio in Velabro, but they are too small to permit the restoration of any text.

The purpose of the monument is cloudy. Giuseppe Lugli saw it as a shelter for merchants in this commercial center of Rome.[54] Filippo Coarelli raised the possibility that it served as a boundary marker in the Forum Boarium.[55] But the solution of this problem as well as a full publication of the arch is a matter for the future.

III   Basilicas, Baptistry, and Burial

The First Christian Churches of Rome and the Birth of the Christian Basilica

The basilica of S. Giovanni in Laterano stands on the highest point of the Caelian hill just inside the Aurelian walls (fig. 3.1). There are no steep approaches, only a gradual ascent from the area of the Colosseum to the point where the Caelian ridge meets the Esquiline plateau. The eighteenth-century façade of S. Giovanni magnifies the height of the church through five grand arches carried from the ground level to the cornice far above. Along the top of the façade there is a glorious epiphany in which a company of saints gesticulates fervently around the figure of Christ Himself beckoning from a raised podium. Because of the open space fronting on the church the building retains something of its appearance before the modern expansion of Rome after 1870 when it was an isolated urban monument amid the cloisters, villas, and gardens surrounding it. The same held true for the early Christian basilica at a time when the area was also one of gardens and great properties.

The interior of the church has no traces of its early Christian appearance. The nave, flanked by gigantic figures of saints to left and right, was designed by Francesco Borromini in the seventeenth century. The crossing is dominated by the tabernacle over the papal altar, a Gothic structure of the fourteenth century. The frescoes of the transept are important works of the Mannerist period in the sixteenth century.

This is the seat of the bishop of Rome and has been ever since the church was built by the emperor Constantine beginning possibly within a month of his victory at the battle of the Mulvian Bridge and dedicated several years later.[1] The work required first clearing the ground,

Fig. 3.1 S. Giovanni in Laterano, façade. Photo Fototeca Unione Neg. 1627. Copyright.

which had been occupied by the barracks of the Equites Singulares, a corps faithful to Maxentius that was suppressed by the new emperor.

The corner of Rome where the basilica arose adjoined the Sessorian Palace, where Constantine made his Roman residence, which he ceded to the dowager Empress Helena after he decided to transfer the capital of the empire to Constantinople in 326.[2] The bishop of Rome and his church were very much guests and the emperor the host. Constantine intended to keep this newly favored cult and its leader firmly under the imperial thumb.[3]

The church that was erected, the Basilica Constantiniana, is vivid evidence of the size of the Christian community at Rome at the end of the Great Persecution (fig. 3.2). No small band of faithful could have prompted the building of a giant cathedral. The church was 333⅓ Roman feet (a Roman foot equals 29.6 cm, shorter than the English foot by less than one cm) in length and 180 Roman feet wide (including the thickness of the outer walls). The Constantinian building is known principally from its foundations, exposed in 1934–38, and Borromini's plan of 1646.[4] It was a large rectangle divided into a wide nave and four side aisles, two on each side. Each side aisle was 30 Roman feet in width, and the nave was equal to two side aisles. However, a small apse projected at the west end (radius 30 Roman feet). The church also had a transept, although a modest one created by two small projections at the western

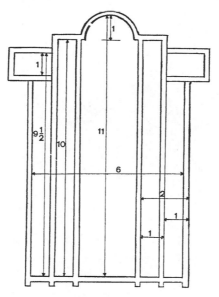

Fig. 3.2 S. Giovanni in Laterano,
plan. After *CBCR*.

end of the nave arranged so that they cut across the outer aisles of the church but did not in-
terfere with the inner ones. There were twenty or possibly twenty-one columns on each side
of the nave. The twenty-four columns of *verde antico* marble employed to flank the niches of
the huge saints of the present nave originally belonged to the colonnades between the side
aisles north and south. The capitals of the nave colonnade, obviously taken from various earlier
buildings, are documented in seventeenth-century painting as well as by Borromini's survey
drawings, which show that the columns supported arches.[5] The brickwork of these continued
into the walls above.[6]

What we can thus recapture of this large hall, with double side aisles and a small apse, is
a ghost of the first great church of Christendom (fig. 3.3). But some idea of the sumptuous-
ness of its original state is given by the list of furnishings that were provided by the founder.[7]

A silver paten weighing twenty pounds.
Two silver scyphi each weighing ten pounds.
A gold chalice weighing two pounds.
Five service chalices each weighing two pounds.
Two silver amae each weighing eight pounds.[8]
A silver chrism-paten, inlaid with gold, weighing five pounds.
Ten crown lights each weighing eight pounds.
Twenty bronze lights each weighing ten pounds.
Twelve bronze candlestick chandeliers each weighing thirty pounds.

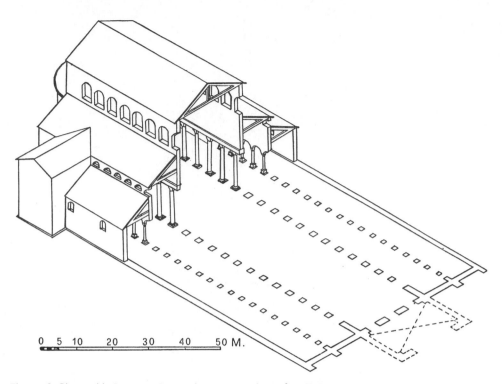

0 5 10   20   30   40   50 M.

Fig. 3.3 S. Giovanni in Laterano. Isometric reconstruction. After *CBCR*.

The total revenue of the estates assigned to the church gave it an annual income of 413 gold
solidi. Fragments of yellow marble found in 1934 and hooks for the attachment of revetments
hint at the decoration of the interior. And, if we can judge from the decoration of the original San Pietro, the bishop's seat in the apse was emphasized by the gilding of its half dome.
Irrevocably lost are the hangings, paintings, and mosaic work that we can imagine beautified
the church in its original state. And missing are the crowds that were expected to fill the vast
hall. For this building, as for so many early Christian churches, there is no evidence for decoration of the exterior. The simple brick of the Christian churches, although perfectly in keeping
with Roman utilitarian architecture, was a jarring contrast to the exteriors of pagan temples.

    The church existed for the celebration of the Eucharist. Baptism was given by the bishop
in the adjoining baptistry (see below). But the ceremonies that marked these and other occasions are most imperfectly known.[9] During the excavations of the 1930s two parallel rows of
sockets came to light in the nave.[10] These seem to have been intended to support the posts for
barriers at either side of the processional corridor by which the bishop and clergy entered the
church in state.

    By day the church would have been awash with light. The windows in the clearstory of
the nave were blocked up in the seventeenth century, but originally the church would have
been lit from this source. The aisles, too, seem to have been provided with smaller, semicircular

or arched windows both in the outer wall and in a clearstory above the colonnade where the two aisles meet. The apse apparently had windows, and there would have been others, no doubt sizable ones, in the façade.[11]

To recapture the atmosphere of this and other early Christian churches in Rome one must go to the church of Santa Sabina on the Aventine (figs. 3.4, 3.5). The church is fifth century, and it has been restored to much of its original state. There are a nave, side aisles, and an apse. The building was entered directly from the west. The central doors still have the famous set of carved cypress wood panels contemporary with the building of the church. The interior is full of light. It enters through the three high arched windows of the apse, through the clearstory windows, and through five large arched windows over the doorways. This is the atmosphere that must have prevailed in the large basilicas by day. No Romanesque darkness, no claustro-phobic, underground setting like the chapels of Mithras, but the light of the world shining on the gathering of the faithful. Those who have attended divine service in a Christopher Wren church, or any of the grand progeny of the master across the sea in North America, will appre-ciate the psychological effect of light radiating through the congregation at prayer.

And so one must imagine San Giovanni, but with a sea of Roman Christians joyful and triumphant. Three thousand could be accommodated within its walls. The communicants would fill the nave, the catechumens, as yet unbaptized and thus inferior in status, would gather in the aisles (this point will be argued further below). The clergy, in no small numbers, surrounded the bishop on his throne. Constantine and his architects did not overestimate the size of the gatherings, as is shown by the need that was felt to create an artificial corridor through the throng by means of the sockets and posts mentioned above, just as barriers create a passageway for the pope today when he enters San Giovanni or San Pietro on the great feast days. No one who has not experienced the mystery of the consecration as part of such a vast congregation can appreciate the power of the eucharistic service in San Giovanni of Constan-tine's day. In the evening and at night the effect of Constantine's lamps and candles, gold and polished bronze, must also be imagined in the setting of rich furnishings and intense piety they illuminated.

It is clear that a large hall such as the new church of the bishop of Rome was a building in the tradition of Roman indoor assembly halls, whether the public basilicas of the fora or the auditoria of the mansion and palace. The question surrounding the appearance of the basilical church is thus not one of building experience and scale, but whether conscious tradi-tion from such earlier secular buildings was felt by Constantine's generation when they con-fronted the new Christian basilicas. To pursue this question I want to consider how Christians not blessed by imperial patronage and the requirements of an episcopal seat, or even the im-perial family when adapting part of a palace to Christian worship, met their needs.

We cannot achieve this end by turning to Christian churches of the third century. Aside from the famous house church at Dura Europos, a Mesopotamian outpost of the empire in the east, there is scant evidence of where the Christians met and prayed.[12] We do, however,

Fig. 3.4 S. Sabina. Photo Bartl, DAI Rome, Inst. Neg. 61.2507. Copyright Deutsches Archäologisches Institut.

have good documentation in Rome for the adaptation of Christian worship to the city in various churches of Constantinian and later date. And these buildings repeat, I believe, the expedients of earlier generations of Christians.

The best-known house church *(domus ecclesia)* of Rome is to be found underneath the church of SS. Giovanni e Paolo (fig. 3.6). SS. Giovanni e Paolo, built in the early fifth century, is also on the Caelian hill, but it is to be found at its western end, toward the center of the city, rather than at the eastern extremity, where S. Giovanni in Laterano was built. The church is oriented east–west. Its southern flank (and so the flank of one of the long sides) borders the ancient Clivus Scauri, a street running steeply downhill in the direction of the Palatine and the Circus Maximus. From this little piece of the distant past one gains a vivid idea of the appearance of many other streets in the populous quarters of Rome. The street was narrow. The brick apartment houses were multistoried. Behind a portico running partway down the street shops opened directly on the exterior. Brick arches thrown across the street supported the houses on either side. Those familiar with the old quarters of Naples will have no difficulty imagining the bustle and noise of the street in the fourth century. The artisans of the shops must have daily practiced their trades under the porticoes, mending pots, making shoes, and beating out brass. The housewives, then as now, would have been at the windows of the upper

Fig. 3.5   S. Sabina, interior. Photo Bartl, DAI Rome, Inst. Neg. 61.2514. Copyright Deutsches Archäologisches Institut.

stories to lower a basket to passing peddlers with all kinds of wares and all kinds of food. They gossiped across the alley, and in the midst of conversation hailed their children with the shrill voices that Italian women still have at their command. Only the smell is beyond our ability to imagine.

In the second century, there were at least four houses under and around the area now occupied by the church (fig. 3.7). The façades along the Clivus Scauri belong to two Roman apartment blocks. The eastern one (uphill) is essentially unexcavated. Its brickwork places it in the third century. The ground floor of its neighbor downhill was a building with a series of shops on the ground floor (each with the characteristic Roman plan of the shop proper and another room behind). The brickwork is of the mid to later second century. The eastern part of the building was rebuilt in the third century. From the façade along the Clivus Scauri and the windows opening on it one can form an idea of the interior of the second-floor apartments. It has been suggested that the uphill section of the building was renovated at some time to create a single large room divided by a set of arches in place of the apartments on its second floor.[13]

Behind the two apartment houses facing on the Clivus Scauri there was an alley and on

Fig. 3.6 The Clivus Scaurus and SS. Giovanni e Paolo. Photo
Fototeca Unione Neg. 645. Copyright.

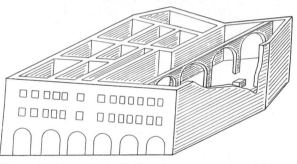

Fig. 3.7 SS. Giovanni e Paolo. Tentative reconstruction of the
early Christian phase. After *CBCR*.

its opposite side another building, which Richard Krautheimer interprets as follows: "It appears to have been either a private residence with a thermal establishment on the lower floor, or a thermal establishment with apartments on the upper stories."[14] The marine fresco in a small nymphaeum with a fountain found in this building shows that its occupants had some pretensions, as do the other pagan frescoes of the building (fig. 3.8). At some time the courtyard in the eastern part of the house was vaulted over, creating a large room above.

The first evidence of Christians on the spot comes from the ground floor of the down-hill building on the Clivus Scaurus. In the back room of the third shop (counting from the west) there are frescoes and among them a figure with arms uplifted in prayer (an *orans*). With the orans figure there is a philosopher figure (but in this context possibly an apostle), then a

Fig. 3.8 SS. Giovanni e Paolo. Fresco. Photo Hutzel, DAI Rome, Inst. Neg. 65.2035. Copyright Deutsches Archäologisches Institut.

pair of seahorses (hippocamps) and goats.[15] The identification of these isolated figures as Christian, however, is far from certain. The decoration of this and the adjoining room, in which there is an elegant series of male figures alternating with birds, peacocks and ducks among them, the whole surmounted in the ceiling vault with a vine motif with cupids gathering the grapes, is of high quality (fig. 3.9). It may be dated to the opening of the fourth century and, together with the decorations of the nymphaeum in the courtyard, suggests that this was a period in which the entire complex on both sides of the alley was a residence of some style and the shops under the arches were suppressed.[16]

The alley behind the structures with their façades on the Clivus Scaurus had at some time been vaulted over, creating a cryptoporticus. A stairway was subsequently built against the rear wall of the same structures. The stairs are judged to have been built in the first half of the fourth century.[17] This stair led to a landing on the level of a window (or *fenestrella*) which opened onto a shaft rising from the ground level below (figs. 3.10, 3.11). This arrangement, constituting a confessional for the adoration of the relics housed at the bottom of the shaft, is described by Krautheimer as follows:

Fig. 3.9 SS. Giovanni e Paolo. Fresco. Photo Hultze, DAI Rome, Inst. Neg. 65.2048. Copyright Deutsches Archäologisches Institut.

The upper part of the confessional, as it rises now at the level of the landing, that is at the mezzanine level of the apartment house, presents itself as a small square box-like construction. Its front wall, facing the landing, is pierced by a small window, a "fenestrella," and so are its side walls. The "fenestrella" in its front wall is surrounded by a fresco which, below the "fenestrella," shows a male figure, possibly Christ, adored by a man and a woman in proskynesis (prostrate), and at the sides, Saint Peter and Saint Paul. On the left projecting wall of the landing appears the martyrdom of two Saints, possibly Saints John and Paul, on the right wall the martyrdom of three others, two men and one woman. The top of the confessional was later cut off by the pavement of the basilica. Yet, certainly its ceiling originally projected beyond the level of the mezzanine floor into the second floor of the house. On this level, near the first right-hand pier in the present church, the site of the confessional is marked by a marble slab indicating the place where an altar stood up to 1573. It is likely that there was always an altar at this place; remnants of one dating possibly from the V or VI century were found in the excavations. Nothing precludes the existence of an altar on this spot from the time the confessional was built.[18]

The space at the bottom of the shaft has a monochrome mosaic floor. Below it, two cavities were excavated in 1912. They could have been tombs, and they have been interpreted as those of Saints John and Paul, who, according to tradition, were put to death and then buried "in their palace" on the Caelian hill in 365.[19]

This reading of the evidence has been disputed by Beat Brenk. This author holds that the fenestrella itself held a repository for whatever relics were the subject of Christian veneration in the house.[20] In his view this was a private chapel of a Christianized family in the fourth century and remained so until the creation of the Titulus Pammachii, the first phase of the present church of SS. Giovanni e Paolo, during the fifth century.

Returning to the large room on the second floor of the uphill section of the building fronting on the Clivus Scauri, we find what Krautheimer suggested was the Christian meeting room. It was reached by the staircase from the cryptoporticus and was adjacent to the confessional. Although the identification of this room as a Christian hall is hypothetical, there was surely a Christian presence in the building.[21]

SS. Giovanni e Paolo illustrates how the Christians could find room for their services and made a space for their relics in the ordinary houses of the city. Any important house or palace, however, had halls that were easily adapted to a new purpose. This is the case at S. Croce in Gerusalemme, also located behind the Aurelian walls a short walk from S. Giovanni. This church adapted a hall in the Sessorian Palace, which was the residence of the empress Helena. And it was to this church that the empress brought a relic of the cross of the crucifixion that is still preserved there today.

The piety of Constantine's mother and her devotion to the shrines of the Holy Land were famous. It is more difficult to know whether her recovery of the true cross and her bringing a relic of the cross to Rome is fact or fiction, but the burden of the evidence is against accepting it.[22] Whether the cross was even known during her lifetime (she died before 328, the date is variously fixed) is a matter of dispute. Eusebius, who would certainly not have let such a wonderful discovery go unnoticed, says nothing about it, although St. Cyril, bishop of Jerusalem from 348 on, is loud in its praises.[23] This problem bears on the date of S. Croce. Although the church is attributed to Constantine by the *Liber Pontificalis,* initially a simple list of the bishops of Rome expanded in the sixth century and later into biographies of each, this information could be a conflation of the great emperor's name with a building sponsored by one of his sons.[24]

The original hall, the masonry of which dates to the third century, measured 133 Roman feet in length and 84 Roman feet in width (fig. 3.12).[25] The height of the room is 75 Roman feet, almost the same as the interior width of 74 Roman feet. In the long walls there are five arched openings and five rectangular windows above them. On the north side there is a cornice between these apertures. On the south side there is no cornice but there is a setback below the upper windows. The shorter walls also seem to have had five windows each (this arrangement must be assumed for the east end, where the present apse is located). There were secondary

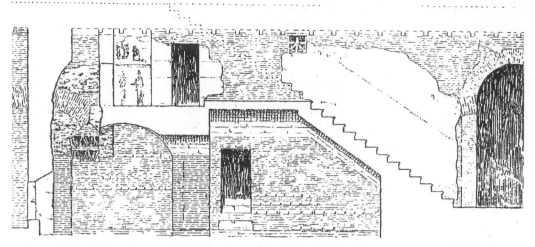

Fig. 3.10 SS. Giovanni e Paolo. Section through the courtyard and staircase adjoining it. After Colini, *Storia e Topografia del Celio nell' Antichità.*

Fig. 3.11 SS. Giovanni e Paolo. *Fenestrella* of the confessional and frescoes. Photo Hutzle, DAI Rome, Inst. Neg. 65.2038. Copyright Deutsches Archäologisches Institut.

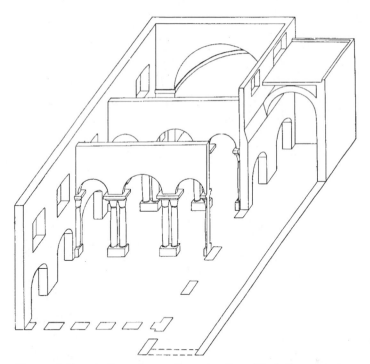

Fig. 3.12 S. Croce in Gerusalemme. Reconstruction of the hall converted
into a church. After *CBCR*.

structures attached to the east side and the south side. Also part of this structure was a small
room beyond the southeast corner which is the present Chapel of St. Helena.

The transformation of the hall into a Christian church was easily accomplished. An apse
was installed at the east end (and most of the earlier wall across the east end was removed in
the process). The entrance was now shifted to the west. The secondary structure on the south
side was maintained. It became an aisle and communicated with the nave through the original arches in the south wall. On the north the arches and windows remained open, giving onto
the outside. At some point two transverse walls were built across the nave to carry triple-arched
openings. It is noteworthy that the south aisle of the church was matched not by another aisle
but by an arcade leading to the outside. This arrangement occurs in other churches and, as
we shall see below, is related to the treatment of catechumens in the early Church.

An almost identical transformation occurred in the case of Santa Susanna, a church justly
famous for its early baroque façade by Carlo Maderno (fig. 3.13). Santa Susanna is situated
along the ancient road, now the Via XX Settembre, that runs along the top of the Quirinal
ridge to the Porta Nomentana. It preserves the two side walls of a hall that was evidently part
of a magnificent domus located at the edge of the ring of gardens and villas that surrounded
the populous quarters of Rome. Glimpses of the eastern side wall can be obtained from the
outside of the building. This long wall of the hall was originally pierced by three tiers of arched

Fig. 3.13 S. Susanna. Exterior elevation. After *CBCR*.

windows. The hall was built in the fourth century, and when it was transformed into a church an apse was added at one end and side aisles with galleries above were installed along the long walls. The church was 120 Roman feet in length, and the nave 45 Roman feet wide. The height of the clearstory walls was 55 Roman feet.

In some cases existing halls were taken over with practically no modification. Such may be the case of Santa Balbina, which is located in a modern Roman green zone within a stone's throw of the Baths of Caracalla. Santa Balbina is a large hall, 82 Roman feet long and 50 Roman feet broad. It has an apse but no side aisles. Instead there is a series of niches in the side walls. The masonry of the building dates it to the fourth century, but its conversion to ecclesiastical use is surely much later. The theory of a secular origin of this church and a late date for its transformation is supported by the case of S. Andrea in Catabarbara, the fourth-century Basilica of Junius Bassus. This building, which stood in the populous part of the Esquiline, did not become a church until the end of the fifth century under Pope Simplicius.[26] It has seemed natural to attribute it to the Junius Bassus who died in 359 at the age of forty-two and whose sarcophagus in the Vatican is one of the major monuments of early Christian art.[27] An inscription copied before the building was torn down, partly in the eighteenth century and finally in 1932, gives the name of the builder Junius Bassus *consul ordinarius*.[28] Two consuls of that name are known, one in 317, the other, apparently the father of the Junius Bassus of the sarcophagus, in 331. This basilica, known from Renaissance drawings, was a simple hall fronted by a porch. There was an apse, and the interior was lighted by three large windows on the sides and three more over the porch. The interior was covered with elaborate decoration in colored marble (*opus sectile*), of which some pieces are preserved.

In another of the densely built-up quarters of ancient Rome, the valley between the Esquiline and the Caelian, which runs from the Colosseum in the general direction of S. Croce in

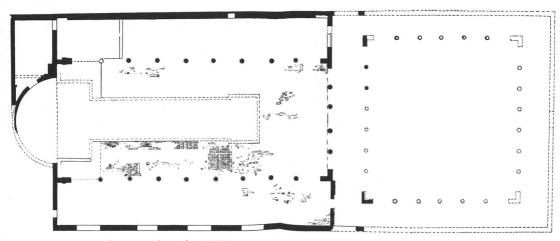

Fig. 3.14 S. Clemente. Plan. After *CBCR*.

Gerusalemme, we find the church of the SS. Quattro Coronati. The church is of Carolingian date (ninth century), but it too incorporates a large hall of the fourth century, originally terminating in an apse.[29]

Located nearby there is a church well known to all enthusiasts of subterranean Rome, S. Clemente, memorable not least because the lowest level below the church contains the remains of a mithraeum. The church belongs to the end of the fourth century (fig. 3.14).[30] However, it is certain that there was a house church *(titulus)* on the spot before.[31] The early basilica (known in detail from the excavations) was created from a Roman house which had a hall with wide openings on its sides. The openings were left in the south wall of the basilica. The church was a simple wide hall with two aisles and ending in a shallow apse. It was entered directly from an atrium through a wide opening with four columns. The date of the basilica is the later fourth century.

S. Crisogono, built as a church and as early or earlier than S. Giovanni in Laterano, is to be found across the Tiber from the center of ancient Rome in Trastevere, the district that has kept its name unchanged since antiquity. This was the riverfront, and the character of its life and people reflected the fact. Like Santa Susanna, the church was situated on a major street which led up the Janiculum hill to the beginning of the Via Aurelia. The early Christian church lies below its twelfth-century successor. Apparently there was a courtyard between the street and the church, set with its long axis parallel to the roadway. Originally the church consisted of a simple room 100 Roman feet by 58 Roman feet. The room had a series of arches opening into it from the east (that is, its short side). In the south wall there were two doorways. At this time the building resembled nothing so much as one of the warehouses of this riverbank quarter of the city. In a second phase the hall was lengthened (fig. 3.15). It was divided by a screen wall into two sections, the eastern one 78 Roman feet in length and a shorter one, 21 Roman feet, to the west. At this time a row of doorways, for which there is evidence of at least three, was

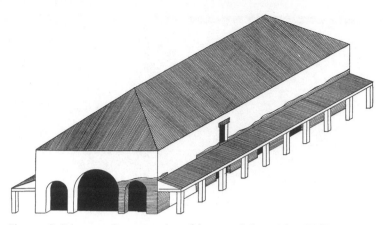

Fig. 3.15 S. Crisogono. Reconstruction of the second phase. After *CBCR*.

opened through the north wall giving onto the courtyard. There was a window above one of these. Finally in phase three the building was lengthened again so that the nave became 115 Roman feet long. Behind the entrance in the east a narthex was added. The apse was added and two side rooms. The southern member of this pair of rooms contained a font and was thus surely a baptistry.

It is possible, but not sure, that the original building was a church. If so, S. Crisogono would be the simplest kind of ecclesiastical building.[32] S. Andrea in Catabarbara (ex–Basilica of Junius Bassus) would be the nearest comparable church in Rome, but its transformation into a church did not occur until the fifth century. By its second phase, however, S. Crisogono was certainly a place of Christian worship. The masonry of the building favors a date in the first third of the fourth century; it can be compared, for example, to the masonry of the Basilica Nova and of S. Giovanni in Laterano. The third phase of its history belongs still to the fourth century.

A distinctive feature of S. Crisogono is the presence of porticoes on its two long sides. That of the south side could be original. The portico to the north, giving onto the courtyard entered from the street, belongs to the second phase of construction, when the doorways that connect it with the church were cut into the north wall of the building. This modification occurred still within the fourth century.

It is likely that the porticoes of S. Crisogono are connected to the conduct of Christian worship at the time. The early Christian community was not a unitary body. There were the baptized. And there were those waiting for baptism, the catechumens. The period of probation for the catechumen was far from short, lasting up to three years before baptism. The catechumens were not admitted to the mysteries of the Eucharist. They attended but before the consecration they were excluded from the service. Did they depart or were they in some other way separated from the baptized congregation? The openings to the exterior on the long sides of S. Crisogono may be interpreted as arrangements to permit the catechumens to withdraw before the beginning of the culmination of the service. Such an interpretation gains weight by comparison with similar provisions found in other Roman churches. In the house church below S. Clemente, if the remains are interpreted properly, the openings in the side walls inherited from the Roman buildings on the spot were not closed up by the Christians. At Santa Croce in Gerusalemme the openings to the courtyard on one side of the nave remained open throughout the Middle Ages. In none of these cases did the doorways give directly on the street. They led rather to a courtyard or other protected area.

When the catechumens were present in churches without such arrangements, these buildings were provided with side aisles such as we find installed in Santa Susanna.[33] And a great new church like S. Giovanni in Laterano was also built with aisles.[34] In late antique buildings hangings were commonly draped in the openings of a colonnade.[35] When the drapes were open, the catechumens in the aisles could see as well as hear. When they were closed, they could hear but were prevented from seeing the mystery of the consecration.

The question of the origin of the Christian basilica can now be viewed from a viewpoint of strict functionality. A large room, otherwise unaltered, was fully acceptable as a place for Christian services. So much we learn from SS. Giovanni e Paolo and S. Crisogono.[36] The dignity of the altar and the clergy, however, was emphasized by a domed apse in every Roman church built or renovated from a preexisting building after the Peace of 312.[37] In the Christian church additional space for the clergy could be required around the altar. This need was clearly accommodated at San Giovanni without a true transept. The full transept, which gave the Christian church its cruciform ground plan, arose from the piecemeal development of S. Pietro in Vaticano, as we shall see below.

The distinction between the baptized and the catechumens, which necessitated their separation and the exclusion of the latter from the culmination of the service, was achieved either by provision of connection with areas outside the church proper or by the introduction of aisles within the church.

No architectural feature of the early Christian Church was there because it was inherited from an established pagan building type. The Christians could be satisfied with the simplest surroundings for their services. And even when success and recognition made their churches grander, the same churches remained simple and functional.[38]

The Lateran Baptistry

Baptism at Rome in the fourth century was a solemn occasion. The years of preparation for the catechumen culminated at Easter, when the bishop repeated the rite first practiced by St. John the Baptist when he baptized Jesus in the river Jordan.[39] The baptistry of S. Giovanni in Laterano, octagonal on its exterior and centered on the baptismal font, is thus a building of particular importance (fig. 3.16). Today the interior of the baptistry is punctuated by an octagonal colonnade which divides the aisle from the center (fig. 3.17). This structure is the result of modifications made by Sixtus III (432–40), as are the elliptical antechamber and the portal of

Fig. 3.16 The Lateran Baptistry and post-Constantinian porch. Photo courtesy of Virginia Chieffo Raguin.

Fig. 3.17 The Lateran Baptistry, interior. Photo Rossa, DAI Rome, Inst. Neg. 75.1729. Copyright Deutsches Archäologisches Institut.

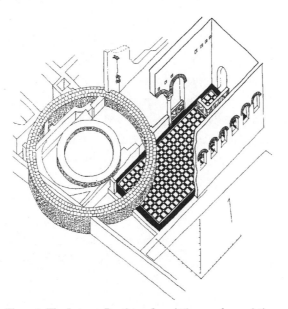

Fig. 3.18 The Lateran Baptistry, foundations and preexisting buildings. Reconstruction by O. Brandt. Courtesy Olof Brandt.

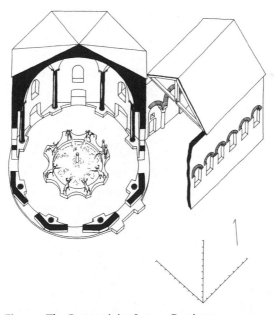

Fig. 3.19 The Constantinian Lateran Baptistry. Reconstruction by O. Brandt. Courtesy Olof Brandt.

the baptistry on its southeast side. Until recently it was thought that little or nothing remained of Constantine's baptistry. But this view has been challenged by Olaf Brandt on the basis of his work in the baptistry between 1995 and 1997.[40]

The baptistry was built on a circular foundation which gave it a diameter of 19 m (fig. 3.18). This ring was inserted into preexisting buildings of the Lateran property. In the center of the ring of the foundations there was a second ring for the font proper. When these two foundations had been prepared, the level was artificially raised and eight steplike foundations were built against the inner side of the main foundation while two others were placed on the exterior. These small foundations were intended to support columns. On the interior these were the same porphyry columns that were reused by Sixtus III for his remodeling. The small foundations were too small to hold columns of this size alone. The upper building, however, was to be not circular but octagonal (fig. 3.19). Placing an octagon on the circle of the foundations meant that where the segments of the octagon came together part of the foundation was not occupied. It is just at these points that the small foundations were placed so that they and the unoccupied surface of the foundations could carry the columns. The two small extra foundations on the exterior would have supported the columns of a porch.

The elevation of the baptistry, as one sees it today from outside, is thus the Constantinian building complete with flat arrises at the meeting points of the segments of the octagon. Of course, there have been changes and repairs. Originally, Brandt believes, there was only one range of windows rather than the two (blocked up) that one sees today. But the overall effect of the exterior is original.

How Constantine's building was roofed is open to conjecture. The porphyry columns set against the interior walls may have carried arches to support a dome.

The font is known in some detail from the passage in the *Liber Pontificalis* recording Constantine's dedication.[41] The font was porphyry covered with silver decoration. In addition:

> In the center of the baptismal font there is a porphyry column topped by a golden basin where a candle is placed. It is of pure gold weighing 52 lb. And at Easter 200 lb of incense is burned by a wick of compressed asbestos. On the edge of the font there is a gold lamb from which water flows and which weighs 30 lb. And on the right side of the lamb the Savior in purest silver, 5 ft. high weighing 170 lb., on the left of the lamb is St. John the Baptist in silver, 5 ft. high, holding a scroll with the message, "Behold the Lamb of God—behold—that which lifts off the sins of the world." It weighs 125 lb. There are 7 silver stags from which water flows, each weighing 80 lb.[42] And an incense burner of purest gold with 48 green gems weighing 15 lb.

These sumptuous arrangements are suggested in Brandt's restoration of the baptistry when new.[43]

The Basilica ad Corpus S. Pietro in Vaticano e S. Paolo Fuori le Mura

With San Pietro in Vaticano we meet for the first time a *basilica ad corpus,* that is, a church raised over the tomb of a martyr.[44] The earlier history of the area and the question of the presence of St. Peter's tomb at or near the place of his martyrdom are questions best reserved for separate treatment.[45] By Constantinian times, however, this valley between the Vatican and Janiculum hills had long since ceased to be the location of the circus associated with the fate of the Christian martyrs of A.D. 64. The land on which the church was built was the site of a pagan cemetery. The large mausoleum which stood to the south of the nave of the Constantinian church, the Chapel of S. Andrea, is a Severan monument which also documents the decline and abandonment of the old circus.[46]

S. Pietro is in some ways the best known and the most poorly documented of the Constantinian churches. This is so despite the fact that the old church remained very little altered throughout the Middle Ages, only to be torn down to make way for the mammoth basilica raised by Michelangelo and his successors down to Carlo Maderno, the creator of the nave and façade. Drawings exist of the old church in various stages of demolition. Perhaps the most evocative is that of Giovanantonio Dosio done shortly after 1574 and showing the porch and nave of Old St. Peter's with the dome of the new basilica rising behind it (fig. 3.20). The section with perspective done around 1605 and found among the drawings in the Vatican Library, two of which are signed "Tasselli," shows the interior of the building and gives an idea of the interior and of the roofing.[47] The basilica fronted on an atrium. It was provided with double side aisles, a full transept, and an apse (fig. 3.21). The columns of the nave carried a flat architrave while those dividing the two aisles were topped by arches. There were twenty-two columns in each of the four rows, a medley of spolia from various sources. As we learn from the sixteenth-century architects Baldassare Peruzzi and Antonio da Sangallo, the columns of the nave were a mixture of granite (gray and reddish) and "onion skin" marble (the so-called Cipollino). The drawing of Cherubino Alberti is especially valuable in showing a base, column, and part of the architrave.[48] The transept was entered from the aisles through openings divided in three parts by two columns in each opening. A grand triumphal arch set off the transept from the nave. The exedrae at either end of the transept were also marked off by a pair of columns. Windows lit the interior from the nave clearstory and from above the transept.

It is impossible to give precise measurements for the building. Relying on the surveys of the Renaissance architects Alfarano and Baldassare Peruzzi, Krautheimer estimates the clear inner length of the nave as 90.78 m and the depth of the transept as 17.07 m, thus giving the length as 360 Roman feet. For the width of the nave and aisles there is also archaeological evidence. It is therefore possible to give the width of the outer aisles as 9.83 m and that of the inner aisles as 9.21 m. In neither of these cases are the measurements of sufficient precision to allow exact conversion into Roman feet.[49] The width of the nave can be estimated to be 63.42 m,

Fig. 3.20 Old S. Pietro in Vaticano. The Constantinian church
and the drum of Michelangelo's dome. Drawing by Giovanantonio
Dosio, Berlin, after H. Egger, *Römische Veduten*.

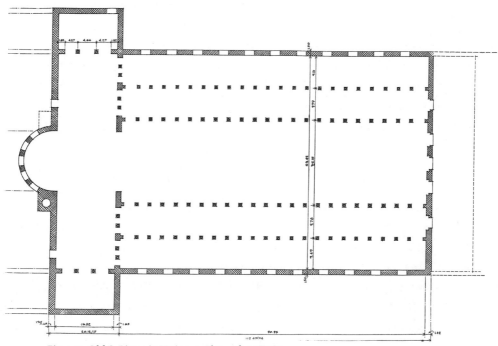

Fig. 3.21 Old S. Pietro in Vaticano. Plan. After *CBCR*.

80 Roman feet. The nave and aisles together make a width of 212 Roman feet. The total width of the transept is 90.95 m. The apse diameter may be estimated at 17.39 m.[50]

S. Pietro was oriented east–west with its apse toward the west. The foundations were made with great care owing to the problems created by the location of the building on a hillside. This required making a substantial cut in the slope of the Vatican hill to the north and creating a platform with deep foundations toward the south, where the Circus of Nero was originally located. It was during this work that the pagan mausolea under the nave of the present basilica were intentionally filled after their tops had been leveled off. Parts of five foundation walls have been uncovered under the nave. They are the south exterior wall, the walls under the two rows of columns in the southern half of the nave and those under the two corresponding rows of columns on the northern side of the basilica, also the west wall of the church and its apse and the wall separating the transept from the nave. A number of walls were also built across the mausolea and passageways of the necropolis underlying the building. These are much thinner than the bearing walls (0.6 m as against 3.5 m). The pavement of the nave was made up of square and rectangular marble slabs and filled out with small, irregularly shaped pieces of the same material.

A revolutionary rethinking of the evolution of the plan of S. Pietro has now been proposed by Carpiceci and Krautheimer.[51] Their argument comes from the observation that the east wall of the transept (toward the nave) had the same carrying capacity as the other walls of the transept and was thus originally intended to be an exterior wall. In its first phase, therefore, the transept was a rectangular building enclosing the apostle's tomb. There was no nave at all. When the nave was built, it had only two side aisles. This additional revision in our thinking about the church is also based on the evidence from the foundations. In fact, the foundations of the colonnade separating the two side aisles of the basilica as it finally came to be are more stoutly built than the foundations under the two colonnades flanking the nave itself. This is because, Carpiceci and Krautheimer suggest, the heavier foundations originally supported an exterior wall. When the basilica was enlarged they were used for the colonnade separating the aisles.

This revision of the history of the plan of the church has important implications for the history of the Christian basilica. S. Pietro is the first basilica with a transept (fig. 3.22). The transept, however, arose from the addition of a nave to a preexisting martyrium. The transept proved useful for the functions of the church and thus became an integral feature of basilica design.[52]

During the building operations of the sixteenth century the nave was divided crosswise by a wall to protect the area where the dome was in course of construction. This wall contains plinths and column bases from the screen that closed off the northern wing of the transept and from the north aisle of the nave of the old basilica.

The honor paid to the apostle's tomb was revealed by the excavations carried out after 1940.[53] The simple niche that had marked the supposed grave of St. Peter was enclosed in a grand white marble casing banded in porphyry (fig. 3.23). This monument stood fully 2.5 m

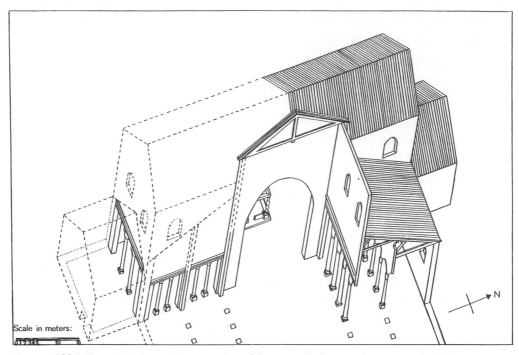

Fig. 3.22 Old S. Pietro in Vaticano. Reconstruction of the west end of nave and transept. After *CBCR*.

high.[54] The marble columns encircled by vine scrolls that flank the niches of the great piers supporting Michelangelo's dome which face inward toward the Papal Altar beneath Bernini's baldacchino appear to come from this tabernacle of the old basilica and are Roman work of the fourth century (fig. 3.24).[55]

Several inscriptions copied in Old St. Peter's bear on its foundation. The first was to be read, though with difficulty, on the triumphal arch until 1506: "Because with You as our Leader the world rose to the stars, Constantine the victor in triumph founded this hall for You."[56] In the apse of the church there was another inscription copied during the Middle Ages: "What you see is the seat of justice, the house of faith, the hall of decorum. It is piety that is the possession of every thing which famously rejoices in the virtues of the Father and of the Son and makes equal its Author with the praises given the Father."[57] This later inscription, which has been used to support the theory that Constantius II rather than Constantine founded the church, should rather be read with reference to the Trinity.[58] To be sure, the record of the foundation attributed to Constantine in the *Liber Pontificalis* is clouded by the possibility of confusion between Constantine and his sons. But an important piece of evidence for the earlier date of the basilica does occur in the *Liber Pontificalis,* in which we read that Constantine donated a gold cross inscribed by himself and his mother with the following inscription: "Constantine Augustus and Helena Augusta. He surrounds this house making / it gleam regal in its splendor with a hall."[59]

Fig. 3.23 Old S. Pietro in Vaticano. Reconstruction of the Constantinian monument around the Tomb of St. Peter. After *Esplorazioni.*

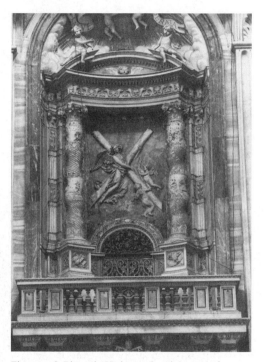

Fig. 3.24 S. Pietro in Vaticano. Surviving spiral columns from the Constantinian monument around the Tomb of St. Peter reused in the Renaissance Basilica. Photo Schwanke, DAI Rome, Inst. Neg. 79.3525. Copyright Deutsches Archäologisches Institut.

The church was endowed with the income from properties in the eastern part of the empire which came under Constantine's control only after the defeat of Licinius in 324.[60] But the building of the basilica could have been started earlier. In any case the evidence of the inscription on the gold cross shows that it must have been finished before Helena's death before 330.[61] In the thinking of Carpiceci and Krautheimer both the martyrium and the basilica were built before 324, although the decoration of the basilica may have been completed only at a later date.[62]

The grand basilica over the tomb of the Prince of the Apostles was, after San Giovanni in Laterano, the major gift of Constantine to Christian Rome. It reproduced and perfected the basilical type introduced at San Giovanni in Laterano. In size it magnified the plan of San Giovanni, being fully one-third larger in every dimension than the seat of the bishop of the city. Almost by accident it created the transept found so widely in subsequent Christian churches. Proof that early Constantinian basilicas in the neighborhood of Rome existed without transepts has now been provided by the recent discovery of such a basilica of Constantinian date at Ostia (fig. 3.25).[63]

During its planning and construction San Pietro remained a work in progress. It is well worth noting the judgment on the building expressed by those scholars who in the twentieth century may be said to have known it best:

> From this study there emerge the two faces of the first Basilica. The first is what makes it one of the most important monuments of western architecture, the true archetype of Christian churches, an organism remarkable for its perfect functionality stamped by the first great Christian community. The second aspect lies in its modest claims to architectural and ornamental distinction in comparison with the important buildings of the period. Indeed, Old Saint Peters was an edifice built on a plan that was not perfectly symmetrical, disjointed in its individual parts and made up of a succession of high and weak walls held up by secondhand columns taken from the leftovers of marble depots with bases and capitals often mismatched or unfinished.[64]

But San Pietro was not a church in the same way that San Giovanni was. Instead of an altar at the focal point of the building where the nave met the transept there stood the porphyry and marble tomb monument of St. Peter. The celebration of the Eucharist was subordinated to the memorial of the apostle and must have been celebrated on portable altars. This building was, first and foremost, a vast covered cemetery.[65] The necropolis on the site continued as a Christian burial ground below the floor of the church. Viewed from the standpoint of pagan Rome, the magnetism of the martyrs and especially of the martyrs' graves for the early Christians is a peculiar phenomenon. True, in distant times the ancient world had known heroes who kept a watchful and beneficent eye on their countrymen from the tomb and who would, on

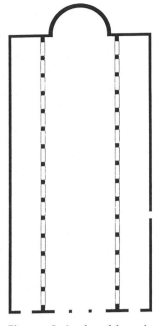

Fig. 3.25 Ostia, plan of the early
Christian basilica. Courtesy
Michael Heinzelmann.

occasion, emerge to fight by their side in moments of critical danger. True, in Latium of the
centuries when Rome was little more than a group of villages on their individual hills the burials of the members of a clan would crowd around the tomb of their progenitor. But such cus-
toms and superstitions had long since lost their force. The cult of the Christian martyrs was
something new.

The Christian fervently believed that death was not a finality. "We shall not all sleep, but
we shall all be changed. In a moment, in the twinkling of an eye, at the last trumpet: for the
trumpet shall sound, and the dead shall be raised incorruptible, and we shall be changed."[66]
Among the Christian dead, the martyrs enjoyed unquestioned sanctity. The martyrs, moreover,
enjoyed a special proximity to divine grace. Their souls awaited the Last Judgment and reunion
with their earthly bodies beneath the altar of Heaven.[67] Christ Himself, furthermore, dwelt
within the martyr.[68] Demons and devils trembled before their remains.[69] Nurtured on the
scriptural reports of the miracles worked not only by Jesus but by the apostles and within the
power of the saints, it is no wonder the Christians assumed that grace would come to them
through these ministers of the Almighty and contact with or proximity to those very earthy remains with which the souls of the martyrs were so soon to be reunited.[70] The windows opening
onto the repositories of the relics—for example, the simple confessional tucked in under the
stairwell of the Christian meeting place under SS. Giovanni e Paolo—served the faithful to

lower charms which by contact with the relics of the saint acquired some of their miraculous power. Cloths were considered especially useful for absorbing potency from contact with the bones against which they brushed.[71] An opening of the kind found at SS. Giovanni e Paolo permitted similar access to the grave below the marble and porphyry monument in the center of San Pietro. Needless to say, burial in the vicinity of a martyr was a much sought after advantage among the Christians.

The cemetery, moreover, was the focus of an important Christian ritual. This was the periodic commemoration of the dead at the tomb accompanied by a feast and by a celebration which frequently reflected the conviviality of the occasion, the *refrigerium*.[72] It was inherited from the pagan commemoration of the dead in which on various occasions through the year the family gathered to eat and drink in a spirit much more that of a holiday than of mourning. These affairs were marked "not [by] sadness or silence, but joyfulness, a carefree tone and dismissal of the enmities and disputes which, then as now, trouble families."[73] And so the Christians, especially after the Peace of 312, made their refrigeria in abundant eating and drinking.[74] And *dignitas* was not always maintained. At St. Peter's there were daily and conspicuous scenes of immoderation.[75] True to the Master's teaching, however, the Christians extended their hospitality to the poor, orphans, and widows. An especially large number of participants gathered at St. Peter's in 397 for the refrigerium in honor of Paulina, wife of Pammachius.[76] Episcopal opposition to this custom, not only at Rome but throughout Christian lands, is understandable. It was responsible, however, for the building of a series of extraurban basilicas at Rome that I shall consider shortly.

As buildings, San Giovanni and San Pietro were the two poles of monumentalized Christianity in Constantine's Rome. One was the seat of the bishop. The other was the justification of that same bishop's primacy, a monument to the succession from Peter himself, the rock on whom Jesus had promised to build His church. San Giovanni was a Christian church as we understand it; San Pietro was a covered cemetery and memorial of the Prince of the Apostles. It was a gathering place for those meals in commemoration of the dead that were so beloved by the Roman Christians. The celebration of the Eucharist appears, from the archaeological evidence, to have been a secondary consideration.

One might have expected similar honor for St. Paul, but the arrangements in Constantine's day for his tomb at the location of his martyrdom on the Via Ostiensis south of the city appear to have been modest in comparison to the monument for St. Peter.[77] The building of the basilica is attributed to Constantine by the *Liber Pontificalis*.[78] The passage, however, has all the indications of an interpretation intended to make San Paolo appear as old and rich as San Pietro.[79]

The early Christian basilica for St. Paul, in the form given it during the reign of Theodosius I in 384, survived almost unaltered until 1823, when it fell victim to a disastrous fire. The old church was extensively documented even before the fire, and following it, in the few years before reconstruction began in 1833, other drawings were made of the building in its ruined state. Like San Pietro, the basilica proper was preceded by a colonnaded atrium and porch.

There were two side aisles on each side of the nave. There was a transept with abbreviated arms and an apse in the rear (east) wall.[80]

The two rows of columns flanking the nave began with a pair of columns with white marble shafts placed just inside the door. Then there followed eleven pavonazzetto columns in the northern row and thirteen in the southern row. The subsequent eight columns north and six south are once again of white marble. Three of the Corinthian capitals were of Severan date. The rest appear to be of the late fourth century.[81]

The transept was raised above the nave. But originally the paving may have been uniform and the columns here cut down at a later date when the paving was raised. There were three round arched windows above each side of both wings of the transept, and above these there were additional round windows (three in the west wall, two or three in the east wall).

This late antique building went through a series of phases, and a key to these is provided by the history of the structures over the tomb of St. Paul below the high altar. These have been significantly reworked. Two blocks of the present upper step of the structure over the tomb have the inscription "Paulo Apostolo Mart." on their upper surface (fig. 3.26). They are not in their original location. They were originally intended to be placed upright with hanging lamps suspended from them (as shown by a number of small holes along their lower edges where the hooks for the lamps were inserted).[82] The other components of this structure are missing and would have carried the name of the donor that preceded the remaining words. The inscription is apparently late fourth century or fifth century in date, making it contemporary with the Theodosian church.[83]

The remains below the level of the two marble courses were uncovered in 1838 and are known only from the sketches made at the time.[84] These show a base of two finished courses and above them a grill protecting a cavity some 0.223 m deep. It is important to note that the grill faces not the Via Ostiensis but the byroad that branched off from it and ran obliquely toward the Tiber. It can be assumed that the church originally faced toward the Tiber too, so that the worshiper entering the building from this direction could approach the apostle's shrine directly and have access to its wonder-working properties through the grilled fenestrella. What this building was like in plan or dimensions it is impossible to say.

The traces of the first apse of the church, however, exposed in 1850, belong to a building that had changed direction so that it now faced away from the river and toward the Via Ostiensis. Finally, when the Theodosian church was built in 384 once more it changed its axis 180 degrees and again faced back toward the Tiber. It is this church that we know as the S. Paolo destroyed in 1823.

The dating of the initial phases of the basilica is extremely difficult. If one discounts the testimony of the *Liber Pontificalis,* there is little to guide one in dating the first phase of the building or its successor facing the Via Ostiensis. Furthermore, the size and plan of these two first shrines to the apostle are a matter of conjecture.

Both S. Pietro and S. Paolo are testimony to the cult of the martyrs in early Christian

Fig. 3.26 S. Paolo fuori le Mura. Inscription to the apostle on structure below the high altar. Photo Fototeca Unione Neg. 5906. Copyright.

Rome. S. Pietro was rapidly enlarged and in addition to the tomb of St. Peter housed a large covered cemetery. In Constantine's Rome far greater energy and expense were devoted to the construction of such covered cemeteries, *coemeteria subteglata,* than to that of churches. The other monuments of this type, to which I now turn, were grand in themselves, and they created another early Christian architectural tradition. But, strange to relate, they had completely vanished from sight (or had been made indistinguishable from churches of more recent centuries) until rediscovered by archaeological investigation.

Coemeteria Subteglata and Mausolea

Via Labicana

Constantine prepared his tomb on the road which issues from Rome just to the north of S. Croce in Gerusalemme through the present-day Porta Maggiore.[85] This is the Via Labicana, and he chose the location at five kilometers (slightly under three miles) outside the city on part of the imperial property known as "ad duos lauros."[86] The tomb, traditionally known as Tor Pignatara, was a brick rotunda standing in the long-established line of gigantic round imperial tombs beginning with the mausoleum of Augustus and perpetuated in the later empire under the influence of the Pantheon (fig. 3.27). The lower drum is preserved for more than half of its circumference. The upper drum was pierced by arched windows which were recessed in tall domical niches on the exterior. The cupola is not preserved, but the height of the structure up to its springing is 21.09 m. The interior diameter of the mausoleum is 20.18 m, and the exterior, 27.74 m. The walls of the interior were covered with incrustation, of porphyry as well as of colored marbles, as shown by the clamp holes still visible on the wall faces. These were

Fig. 3.27 Via Labicana, Tor Pignattara (Tomb of St. Helena). Photo Fototeca Unione Neg. 1126. Copyright.

applied to a wall articulated by a series of niches around the lower drum answered by the arched openings of the windows above. The niches were fitted with mosaics, some parts of which could still be made out in the sixteenth century, as was the interior of the dome.[87] The exterior was plastered.

According to the *Liber Pontificalis*, it was not Constantine but his mother, the empress Helena, who was buried in the mausoleum ad duos lauros.[88] Her porphyry sarcophagus still survives in the Vatican (figs. 3.28, 3.29). The sarcophagus, decorated with masculine scenes of a victorious battle with barbarians, offers the clearest evidence that the mausoleum was prepared as Constantine's own tomb before he decided to transfer the capital of the empire to Constantinople and make a resting place for his earthly remains in the Church of the Holy Apostles.[89]

The imperial mausoleum does not stand alone. It is connected directly to a long apse-ended structure, the basilica of SS. Marcellino e Pietro. Constantine, according to the *Liber Pontificalis*, provided handsomely for both, although twice as much gold and silver was lavished on the mausoleum as was given to the other.[90] By the sixteenth century almost nothing was to be seen of the basilica, and aside from Antonio Bosio's plan of the apse made in 1594,[91] what we know of it comes from the excavation carried out since 1940 by Friedrich Wilhelm Deichmann and Arnold Tschira and then by Jean Guyon. The basilica is 65 m in length and

Fig. 3.28 Sarcophagus of St. Helena. Vatican Museum. Photo Como, DAI Rome, Inst. Neg. 63.2339. Copyright Deutsches Archäologisches Institut.

29 m in width (figs. 3.30, 3.31). The apse and ambulatory are features which characterize this building and the others of the same type erected, often in connection with mausolea, in the Constantinian period. The apses of churches in the tradition of San Giovanni are clearly conceived as an addition to the flat rear walls of churches, but in these buildings the side walls continue to form the apse end, thus giving them a full ambulatory including the side aisles.[92] The side aisles are 6.5 m in width; the nave is 13 m wide. The narthex of the basilica, 6.5 m deep, is attached directly to the mausoleum.[93] In the foundations of the walls, which consisted of a rubble fill in trenches cut in the tufa bedrock, there were found blocks apparently coming from mausolea of the Republican period in the neighborhood, notched bricks frequently found in mausolea of the imperial age, and many fragments of stelae belonging to the tombs of the Equites Singulares, the force suppressed by Constantine whose cemetery had been located here.[94] Fragments of painted plaster from the interior of the building show that the walls were painted.[95]

South of the basilica, between it and the Via Labicana, there was a large portico. This was

Fig. 3.29 Sarcophagus of St. Helena. Vatican Museum. Photo Como,
DAI Rome, Inst. Neg. 63.2340. Copyright Deutsches Archäologisches
Institut.

matched by a similar enclosure to the north, which, however, seems to have had no more than
a perimeter wall. Guyon, the most recent investigator of the remains, reconstructs the outer
wall of the southern portico and the perimeter wall of the northern enclosure as forming the
original boundary of a single enclosure. This he identifies as the cemetery of the Equites
Singulares.[96]

The complex of basilica and mausoleum was entered from the Via Labicana through a
doorway at the southeast corner of the south portico. The visitor proceeded along the covered passage of the portico to the southeast corner of the nave of the basilica. Entering the
building at this point, he was a few steps from the openings to the narthex. To his right was
the narthex and beyond it the rotunda of the mausoleum, to his left, the nave of the basilica
and its apse. It is clear, therefore, that the mausoleum was never a freestanding building but
always part of the basilica complex. Both monuments are Constantinian in brickwork and are
mentioned together in the *Liber Pontificalis*.[97] The brick stamps from the mausoleum are
generically Constantinian. A coin found in the mortar of the marble revetment of the interior

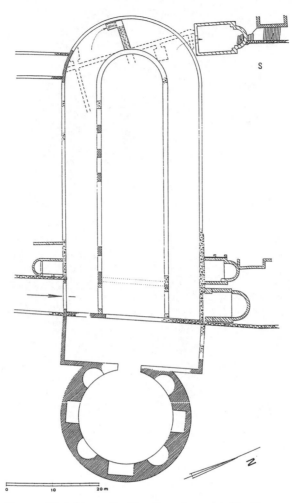

Fig. 3.30 Via Labicana, Tor Pignattara. Apse-ended basilica and mausolea. Plan. After *Felix Temporis Reparatio.*

belongs to the series of 324–26. Its presence in the mortar must represent a very late stage of work.[98]

The area within the portico and northern enclosure was one large graveyard. Burials in simple cist graves, *formae,* were also crowded into the covered passages of the southern portico. In addition, six small mausolea were built in these enclosures, five of them abutting the walls of the basilica or portico. Four other mausolea have been identified to the west of the enclosed area. All were packed with burials in the floor. Niche burials under arched openings in the walls, *arcosolia,* are also documented, and there are also two fragmentary decorated marble sarcophagi. Considering the depredation that these cemeteries had suffered, there were once certainly many others.

The basilica was also a covered cemetery. The tombs found during the excavations are

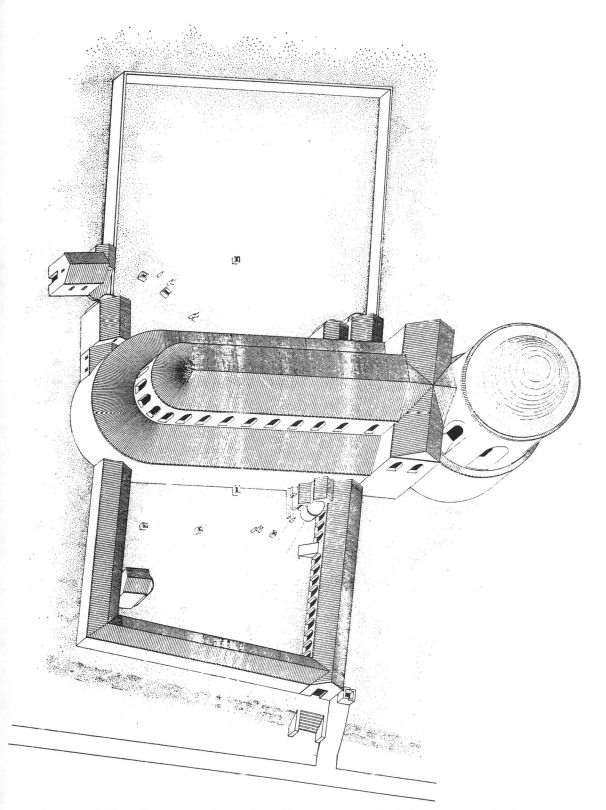

Fig. 3.31 Via Labicana, Tor Pignattara. Apse-ended basilica and mausolea with adjoining porticoes. After Guyon, *Le Cimetière aux deux lauriers.*

medieval (covered with masonry vaults) and seem to have been made when the church was already abandoned and roofless.[99] The find of fragments of Constantinian gravestones, however, shows that burials were made inside from the beginning.

Finally, the catacombs of SS. Marcellino e Pietro were actively used and expanded during the Constantinian period. The aboveground structure located at the north corner of the apse of the basilica may be interpreted as the chapel of the martyrs who gave their names to the cemeteries. In the catacombs just below this room, which might easily be mistaken for another mausoleum were it not for the lack of burials inside, there is a large chamber reinforced with brickwork walls and arches. On one side there are two loculi, and a graffito nearby hails the martyrs Marcellinus the deacon and Petrus the exorcist. The cemetery ad duos lauros was alive with martyrs, some fifty in all.[100] The history of the relation of Marcellinus and Peter with the cemetery (to which their remains were moved at some unspecified date) is complicated, but the archaeological evidence shows that they were venerated here from Constantinian times and before.[101]

Guyon estimates that approximately eight thousand burials, or half the total number in the catacomb, were made after 325. There were possibly another one thousand in the basilica, the same number under the porticoes of the southern enclosure, and five hundred or so in the mausolea plus an indeterminate number in the open spaces of the north and south enclosures. These numbers include all burials made throughout the life of the cemetery, which continued in use until the early ninth century. It is interesting to observe that there were no graves beyond the imperial mausoleum east of the old enclosure wall of the cemetery of the Equites Singulares with one exception, and that a grave placed immediately beside the enclosure wall.

The complex at SS. Marcellino e Pietro seems both impressively planned and curiously irregular. Neither the southern porticoed court nor the northern enclosure have strictly parallel sides, although this is due to the form of the enclosure for the cemetery of the Equites Singulares. And although its narthex is centered on the imperial mausoleum, the basilica is canted at an odd angle to it.

Yet obvious circumstances caused these irregularities. The axis of the imperial mausoleum through its doorway is oriented perfectly in respect to the Via Labicana. But the front wall of the nave of the basilica (or rear wall of the narthex) employed the old enclosure wall of the cemetery of the Equites Singulares for its foundation. This wall ran at a slightly obtuse angle to the perpendicular from the Via Labicana. The basilica was set farther askew with regard to the same perpendicular which governed the siting of the mausoleum. The reason for this additional divergence from the orientation of the mausoleum must lie in the position of the martyrium of Saints Marcellino and Pietro. For obvious reasons the builders of the basilica were concerned not to run the line of the apse foundation too close to the large underground shrine of the martyrs.

Fig. 3.32 Via Nomentana, S. Costanza and adjoining apse-ended basilica. Photo Felbermeyer, DAI Rome, Inst. Neg. 41.2588. Copyright Deutsches Archäologisches Institut.

But to the visitor to the imperial mausoleum and its adjacent buildings, the basilica, the portico, or the catacombs these variations from strictly axial planning made no difference at all. His progression through the south portico to the basilica or mausoleum was controlled by interior spaces which gave the impression of axiality while they displayed the sumptuous honor accorded to the mother of the emperor and to the martyrs.

Via Nomentana

On the Via Nomentana, well beyond the gate in the Aurelian walls of the same name, was the catacomb associated with the tomb of St. Agnes. The small basilical church of the early seventh century is well known, as is the round church of Santa Costanza nearby. What was not realized until the excavations of the 1950s was that the massive structure to the north of Santa Costanza was in reality the apse of an apse-ended basilica to which the church was attached about halfway along its western side (fig. 3.32).[102] The apse itself is a mighty construction placed at the edge of the terrace it shares with Santa Costanza and therefore requiring deep foundations beneath it. It is preserved to a height of two stories. The interior was illuminated by large windows in both side walls and apse proper. The building is known only in its barest outlines. It measures 98 m in length and 40 m in width. The plan is the same as that of the basilica of the Via Labicana with the addition of an atrium before the entrance. There are also foundations for a second apsidal enclosure within the curve of the ambulatory colonnade.

The church of Santa Costanza in the parklike setting of the Via Nomentana, two miles outside the Aurelian walls of Rome, seems to be a virtually unchanged survival of the Constantinian age (fig. 3.33). The round building is complete save for what was supported on an outer ring of foundations. It is connected to the apse-ended basilica by an elliptical fore chamber. On the interior, the ambulatory with its barrel vault carrying its famous mosaics opens to the center through a series of arches supported by pairs of columns rather than by piers (fig. 3.34). The columns have carefully chosen but not matching Corinthian capitals. The ring of arches supports the drum, which gives a spacious height to the interior and light through its large windows. The interior diameter is 22.5 m, and the drum rises to a height of 19 m above the floor (fig. 3.35). Here, if anywhere, is a taste of an interior of Constantinian Rome alive with the color and the interlacing designs of its mosaics in the vault over the ambulatory. The shadow of the corridor makes a sensible contrast with the openness and light-filled volume of the drum, whose weight is carried so easily by the arches and small columns separating them. Finally, in the rectangular niche directly across from the entrance, there stood the grand porphyry sarcophagus adorned with cupids tramping out the vintage. Briefly removed in 1467–71, it has since the eighteenth century been preserved in the Vatican Museum (figs. 3.36, 3.37).[103] There are seven other niches on either side of this rectangular niche. The center of each group is occupied by a larger semicircular niche.

Yet the idea that Santa Costanza is an unchanged treasure of Constantinian times should not be accepted without reservation and without realizing that a tangle of problems surround this monument and its interpretation. First there is the question of the mosaics, both those of the ambulatory admired by every visitor to the building and those of the upper part of the drum which had deteriorated badly by the early seventeenth century when they were removed.[104] Even the mosaics in the vault of the ambulatory are not precisely as they were when originally installed. What we see is a nineteenth-century restoration carried out between 1836 and 1843. A close study of the accounts of the work has shown that no more than 30 percent of the original surface was intact when the project began.[105] Naturally the symmetrical and repetitive nature of the designs as well as the care with which the work was carried out means that the overall effect is consistent with what originally existed.[106] But the restorers' work in some cases led to a simplification of the original design.[107]

The sequence of panels is symmetrical on either side of the panel immediately above the door (I) and can be summarized as follows:

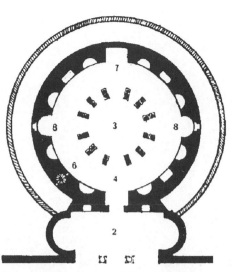

Fig. 3.33 Via Nomentana, S. Costanza. Plan.
After Cecchelli, S. Agnese fuori le Mura.

Fig. 3.34 Via Nomentana, S. Costanza. Interior.
Photo Bartl, DAI Rome, Inst. Neg. 57.1201.
Copyright Deutsches Archäologisches Institut.

Fig. 3.35 Via Nomentana, S. Costanza. Section. After Donati, *Profilo a Roma*.

Fig. 3.36 Sarcophagus of Constantia or Helena. Vatican Museum. Photo Como,
DAI Rome, Inst. Neg. 63.2342. Copyright Deutsches Archäologisches Institut.

Fig. 3.37 Sarcophagus of Constantina or Helena. Photo Como,
DAI Rome, Inst. Neg. 63.2343. Copyright Deutsches Archäologisches
Institut.

I—geometric designs (fig. 3.38)

II, XI—lozenges and stars (fig. 3.39)

III, X—cupids, winged female figures, birds in an intertwining frame pattern (fig. 3.40)

IV, IX—vintage (fig. 3.41)

V, VIII—circles with floral and figurative designs (fig. 3.42)

VI, VI—birds, boughs, and greenery, randomly arranged vessels, doves perched
on bowl (fig. 3.43).

These mosaics have all the complexity and clarity of high quality design and are consistent
with the long traditions of Roman mosaic and stucco work.[108] Only two of the panels have
narrative elements, and these are the grape harvesting scenes that appear on the sides of the
IV and IX. Most of the surface of these panels is occupied with a vine arbor filled with small
figures. At the center of each there is a bust.[109] The total effect, however, is one of the most
glorious to be had from any surviving Roman building, a carpeting overhead, fresh, bright,
and skillfully made—and traditionally and thoroughly pagan. The design of the mosaic which

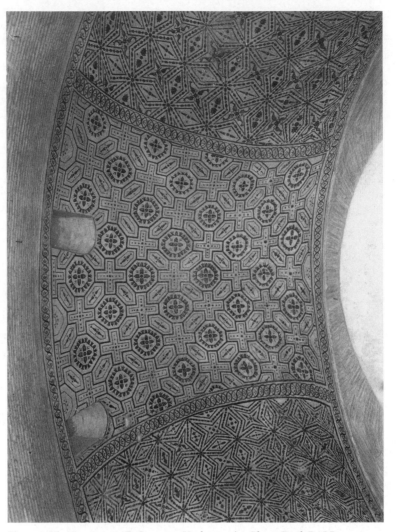

Fig. 3.38 Via Nomentana, S. Costanza. Vault mosaics. Photo Bartl, DAI Rome, Inst. Neg. 57.1257. Copyright Deutsches Archäologisches Institut.

originally occupied the center of the floor was recorded by Pier Sante Bartoli in the seventeenth century.[110] Its subject is a silenus on his donkey preceded by a satyriscus and surrounded by vines, altars, a pipe, and shepherd's crook.

The second point at issue is the name Santa Costanza. Costanza evidently comes from the confusion of the names Constantina and Constantia, the feminine forms of Constantinus and Constans. No member of the imperial family is mentioned directly in connection with the building. The *Liber Pontificalis,* however, says that Constantine acceded to the wishes of his daughter Constantina by erecting a basilica for St. Agnes and a baptistry.[111] The same source adds that both Constantina and her aunt of the same name, sister of the emperor, were baptized

Fig. 3.39 Via Nomentana, S. Costanza. Vault mosaics. Photo Bartl, DAI Rome,
Inst. Neg. 57.1249. Copyright Deutsches Archäologisches Institut.

in the baptistry. The role of Constantina in relation to the church of Sant' Agnese is made clear
by an acrostic inscription of which a copy survives and which records that Constantina dedicated the church to the virgin martyr.[112] Krautheimer proposed with reason that Constantina's
dedication was made after she was widowed in 337.[113]

More than one scholar has interpreted Santa Costanza as the baptistry mentioned in the
Liber Pontificalis. But the evidence for a font, supposedly found in the nineteenth century, was
debated from the time it was announced and has not gained favor since.[114] The building, therefore, is effectively divorced from written tradition. By the ninth century it had acquired the
name Santa Costanza and was a church.[115] But if the name is a corruption of Constantina and

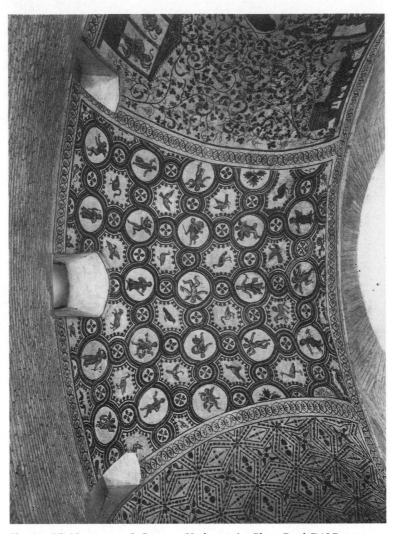

Fig. 3.40 Via Nomentana, S. Costanza. Vault mosaics. Photo Bartl, DAI Rome,
Inst. Neg. 57.1253. Copyright Deutsches Archäologisches Institut.

the building was originally a mausoleum, then the connection of the princess with the building
cannot be easily dismissed, especially since it is known that Constantina was buried with her
sister Helena on the Via Nomentana, presumably in the vicinity of Sant' Agnese.[116]

Artists and scholars of the Renaissance took a marked interest in Santa Costanza. There
is a long graphic record of the decoration of the church beginning in the fifteenth century.[117]
Among the scholars Marliani, Andrea Fulvio, and Gyraldi all were unanimous in considering
Santa Costanza a temple of Bacchus. They saw nothing Christian in a building fitted out with
pagan mosaics and a pagan sarcophagus.[118]

At the end of the sixteenth century this view of S. Costanza changes. The change was due
to Pompeo Ugonio. A lifelong enthusiast for the history of Roman churches, Ugonio was pro-

Fig. 3.41 Via Nomentana, S. Costanza. Vault mosaics. Photo Bartl, DAI Rome, Inst. Neg. 57.1250. Copyright Deutsches Archäologisches Institut.

fessor at the Archigimnasio at Rome. He accompanied his pupil Antonio Bosio, father of the modern study of the catacombs, on his first explorations of subterranean Rome.[119] Ugonio owned a vineyard on the Via Nomentana, and, as he tells us in the manuscript describing the first of his visits to the church, on the first of October 1594, during the grape harvest he left his servants and relations at work and betook himself to the church.[120] At Santa Costanza the Counter-Reformation cleric was faced with a church whose pagan character was so notorious that a fraternity of artists from the Netherlands resident in Rome conducted initiations there before the porphyry sarcophagus, which they had baptized the Tomb of Bacchus.[121] Some relatively recent frescoes (including one with Saint Francis) decorated the outer wall of the ambulatory. But looking up above the level of the large windows into the dome, Ugonio saw

Fig. 3.42 Via Nomentana, S. Costanza. Vault mosaics. Photo Bartl, DAI Rome,
Inst. Neg. 57.1251. Copyright Deutsches Archäologisches Institut.

the remains of mosaic decoration which he interpreted as having biblical subjects, Elias, Tobias,
Susannah, and Noah. The primary evidence for their identification disappeared in 1620 when
a restoration of the church was made by Cardinal Veralli. But Ugonio and the drawings made
before the restoration work have served to promote the Christian or at least semi-Christian
interpretation of the decoration.[122] Such studies are inevitably made "laboriously but with no
conviction," to quote the opinion of Charles Rufus Morey.[123] Certainly groups of figures—
often indistinguishable as to sex—in scenes where there is no clear attribute present can be
juggled into biblical story lines.[124] But the effect of these efforts loses further credibility when
one considers that the decorative borders of the scenes are adorned with panthers and cary-
atid maenads. The marine panorama at the base of these scenes, cupids engaged in fishing, is

Fig. 3.43 Via Nomentana, S. Costanza. Vault mosaics. Photo Bartl, DAI Rome,
Inst. Neg. 57.1236. Copyright Deutsches Archäologisches Institut.

no less equivocal, being a scene possibly admissible as Christian but thoroughly at home as
part of a pagan scheme of decoration.[125]

   Two other mosaics are located over the semicircular niches in the ambulatory. In the first
Jehovah gives the law to Moses. In the other Christ passes His law to Peter and Paul. On the
frame of the niches there were mosaic bands, one of them with stars and the Chi-Rho. This
mosaic work is an addition to the original decoration of the building but not a late one. The
two mosaic scenes have been compared to the apse mosaic of Christ and the apostles in Santa
Pudenziana, and consequently, they may have been added within a century of the erection of
the building.[126]

   In 1955, Karl Lehmann took up the question of Santa Costanza and argued forcefully that this was a pagan mausoleum. In doing so he raised the possibility that the mausoleum was connected with Julian, the nephew of Constantine who renounced Christianity publicly when he became emperor in 361.[127] Recent archaeological discoveries have connected Julian even more closely with Santa Costanza. In 1992, David J. Stanley made a small excavation in the antechamber of Santa Costanza. He found, first, that the walls of the antechamber were not bonded into the walls of the large apse-ended basilica. Second, he discovered that below the antechamber there were the remains of a small triconch structure the walls of which did tie into the exterior wall of the basilica (fig. 3.44).[128] The first question that emerges from this important discovery is, What was the lower building, a tomb or the baptistry of the *Liber Pontificalis*? Judging by the disposition of mausolea at other apse-ended basilicas, especially the triconch mausoleum on the south flank of San Lorenzo, the lower building at Santa Costanza appears to be a tomb. One may even hazard the guess, though a guess it must remain, that Constantina was buried here in 354. But when Helena, Julian's newly deceased wife, came to join her what happened? That Julian built Santa Costanza for Helena and her sister Constantina has been argued by G. Mackie.[129] One can second this opinion without, however, believing, as Mackie does, that Julian authorized a half-Christian, half-pagan decorative scheme. It was a tomb flooded with the blessings of Dionysus, not with the grace of Christ, in which Constantina and Helena were finally buried, though still in the place Constantina had chosen beside the apse-ended basilica of the Christians. It appears that both ladies were buried in noble sarcophagi because in addition to the well-known sarcophagus with Dionysiac decoration, a second porphyry sarcophagus from S. Costanza is preserved in the Basilica of S. Pietro in Vaticano.[130]

Via Praenestina

The third apse-ended basilica connected with a mausoleum is found in the complex on the Via Praenestina (Tor dei Schiavi). Here again the mausoleum, the identity of whose builders and occupants remains unknown, as is that of the proprietors of the grand villa which the complex adjoins, has long been a well-known monument of the Roman Campagna. The basilica disappeared, and its plan has been recaptured only by excavation (fig. 3.45).[131]

The mausoleum, however, is a pre-Constantinian structure dating to the period of the tetrarchs. Its walls show no trace of the block and brick construction that becomes common in Constantinian times and already appears in the touches given by Constantine's masons to the Basilica Nova.[132]

The date of the basilica, however, to judge from its brickwork, should lie between the major Constantinian structures and the Theodosian basilica of S. Paolo fuori le Mura.[133] It measures 66 m in length by 28 m in width. It was a covered cemetery. But it is a later follower of the Constantinian coemeteria subteglata, and it was an addition to the architectural landscape of pagan villa and mausoleum of third century and tetrarchic times. There can be no question of the mausoleum and basilica having been planned as a functional unity.

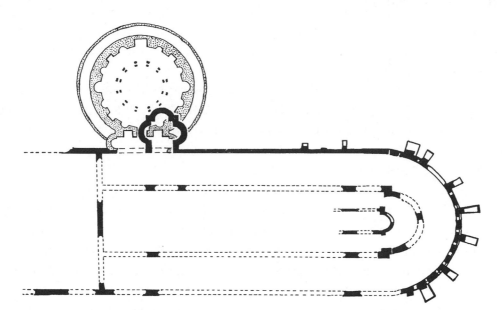

Fig. 3.44 Via Nomentana. Apse-ended basilica, mausoleum, and S. Costanza. After Mackie in *Byzantion* 67.

Via Appia

Certainly of Constantinian date and a key monument in the history of the cemetery basilica is the Basilica Apostolorum, also known as S. Sebastiano, set in a shady dip of the Via Appia within a short distance of the large catacombs of S. Callisto and of Domitilla (fig. 3.46). The church is screened from the road by the wall of the courtyard before it and almost hides against the rising ground behind. S. Sebastiano is the only Constantinian basilica to survive intact, but the Constantinian structure can be glimpsed only from outside. The interior is masked by the remodeling of the beginning of the seventeenth century. Despite the patronage of Scipio Borghese the work shows a simplicity dictated by economy, except for the handsome paneled ceiling. Excavation and probing through the baroque overlay at various times have made it possible to gain a clear idea of the original basilica.

The ancient name of the church, Basilica Apostolorum, comes from the Apostles Peter and Paul, who were venerated here before the removal of the remains considered to be theirs to the Vatican and the Via Ostiensis. The discussion of the important vestiges of the prebasilica period will be taken up in relation to the Tomb of St. Peter (see chap. 4).

In length the basilica is over 65 m with a width of 30.5 m (fig. 3.47). The aisles are separated from the nave by rows of masonry piers. These form an ellipse in the apse as against the arc of a circle of the exterior wall. Consequently the width of the aisle varies from 5.5 to 5.7 m. A spring within the area now occupied by the basilica was made accessible from there by a flight of stairs. It is now reached by a new stairway from outside. In its original state the nave may be estimated to have been 58.3 m long and 13.5 m wide, 200 × 45 Roman feet. The aisles and ambulatory had a width of 7 m, not quite 24 Roman feet. The total inner length of 73.4 m approximates 250 Roman feet.

The outer east wall of the Constantinian church has disappeared. But the inner wall between nave and narthex is preserved, although hidden from view. It has openings for three large clearstory windows. In the nave piers carry arches setting off the side aisles. The clearstory had one window above each of nine arcades on each side while in the apse windows and blank spaces alternated above the eight arcades.

S. Sebastiano, like the other apse-ended, extramural basilicas of Rome, was a single great cemetery. The aisles and nave were packed with graves. The inner face of the outer walls, except for the opening to the narthex at the east, was lined with tiers of burial loculi arranged in arcosolium-like embrasures: three tiers above and up to five tiers below the present floor, reaching to a depth of 3 m below the present paving. One may, therefore, envisage the original floor as having been lower than the present paving. Many of the tombs in the floor, moreover, can be dated by their accompanying inscriptions, the earliest, in the eastern part of the south aisle, to 349 and the latest, in the western part of the nave, to 357. Below its floor the church also contained the remains of the portico—in which some 190 graffiti salutations to Sts. Peter and Paul were discovered—known as the *triclia* (portico), and the general area associated with the structure, referred to as the *memoria*. The original basilica seems to have served to keep alive the memory of Peter and Paul on the Via Appia, just as the tomb of St. Peter in the Vatican was memorialized in the Constantinian martyrium. Krautheimer discusses this situation as follows:[134]

> To explain these seemingly irreconcilable factors we have to assume that the basilica was built expressly as a burial site and originally had no common level and obviously no pavement. It consisted only of walls and arcades, with roofs covering the area of the memoria complex, the adjoining valley to the west and the higher terraces toward the Via Appia to the east. Within this area the ambulatory and the west portions of the nave and aisles occupied a level corresponding to the lowest tier of loculi and to the stylobate of the nave arcades. On this level, the remains of the triclia were left standing over two meters high, while the memoria courtyard may have been filled in level with the stylobate. On the other hand in the east portions of the nave and aisles, presumably from the outset, the level corresponded closely to the present one, which in turn is roughly that of the old terrace east of the memoria complex. One would like to think that the two levels in the nave were linked by stairs. . . . When the tomb of the boy Panigyrius[135] and a number of other graves in its close vicinity were placed on the present level, high above the memoria complex but within its area, burials within the low-lying portions of the graveyard had apparently risen four or five layers.[136]

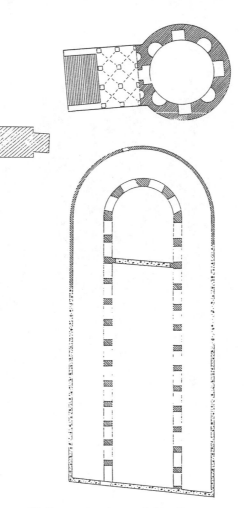

Fig. 3.45 Via Praenestina. Apse-ended basilica.
After *Felix Temporis Reparatio.*

In any case, in a brief time the original two levels in the nave gave way to one. Since the later datable graves were fitted in among earlier burials it is safe to assume that this had already happened by 340–50. Of course it is equally possible that the lower loculi in the walls and graves under the floor were all occupied at the time of the covering of the church and for this reason there was never a difference in floor level.

The building of the basilica destroyed various funeral monuments. Others were erected, especially along the south side, as soon as the basilica was built. At the end of the fourth century mausolea were also added to the north side of the basilica. Others, detached from the building, were built northward in the direction of the Via delle Sette Chiese.

In all likelihood the crypt of St. Sebastian already existed when the basilica was first built

Fig. 3.46 Via Appia. S. Sebastiano. Photo Bartl, DAI Rome, Inst. Neg. 59.1309. Copyright Deutsches Archäologisches Institut.

(fig. 3.48). In the southeast corner of the nave a double stair leads to a crypt, later called the Platonia, which had been formed by widening a catacomb gallery in order to provide for a gathering at the martyr's tomb.

The date of the basilica of S. Sebastiano is uncertain. The church is not mentioned in the list of Constantinian foundations included in the section of the *Liber Pontificalis* devoted to Pope Sylvester or his successors Mark and Julius.[137] But the silence of this document is hardly grounds for excluding a Constantinian date for the building, especially if it was not an imperial project. Largely on the basis of its absence from the *Liber Pontificalis,* scholarly opinion has flirted with the possibility of dating the building even before Constantine. To support this idea there is only one piece of concrete evidence, the use of elliptical window arches in both the basilica and in the Tomb of Romulus, son of Maxentius, whose mausoleum formed part of the grandiose villa of Maxentius directly across the Via Appia from San Sebastiano. Krautheimer connects this detail with the work of a single architect.[138] But surely this detail is just as likely to have been imitated by one group of builders working on S. Sebastiano from the work of a completely different master builder and his men who had worked on the Mausoleum of Maxentius. And even allowing this slender evidence as a valid criterion for dating, there is no way of determining whether San Sebastiano was built in 310, 320, 330, or even later.[139]

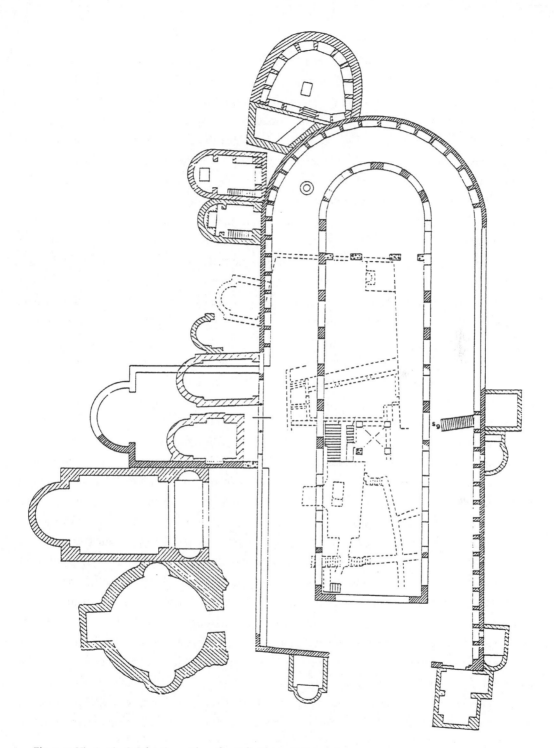

Fig. 3.47 Via Appia. S. Sebastiano. Plan after *Felix Temporis Reperatio*.

Via Tiburtina

The basilica of S. Lorenzo fuori le Mura adjoins Rome's largest cemetery, the Campo Verano, a short distance along the Via Tiburtina, which leaves the city through the gate of the same name on the Esquiline plateau. The Via Tiburtina at this point is a wide thoroughfare, occupied partly by the meeting place of several trolley lines. But the space around the basilica and the cypress trees in the background of the Verano, which occupies the high ground behind and to the sides of the church, create a peaceful setting. San Lorenzo was the only historic monument damaged by the Allied air raid on Rome of July 19, 1943. But apart from shattering the roof, the bombs destroyed only some modern restoration on the interior. This interior, composed of a lower nave and a vast raised presbytery, is one of the most majestic of any surviving Roman churches built before the Renaissance. This is not the Constantinian church. The presbytery was constructed by Pelagius II (579–90), and the nave and porch added by Honorius III (1216–27).

The Constantinian basilica is another of the ghosts of early Christian Rome. It was located immediately south of the existing church, but its remains were brought to light by excavations only in 1950 and 1957 (figs. 3.49, 3.50).[140] This is an area of catacombs, which are found on either side of the Via Tiburtina in the vicinity of the basilica. The catacomb which is around and under the basilica (the Cymiterium Cyriaces of the *Liber Pontificalis*) forms a single unit.[141] It was entered at a point north of the basilica through an opening into the hillside. These catacombs have been little explored except below the present basilica.

The excavations revealed an apse-ended building with ambulatory and nave flanked on each side by an aisle. Its total width is 35.5 m (120 Roman feet). The two aisles and nave, measured along the outer flank of the north wall, are 81.59 m, or 276 Roman feet. The width of the north aisle could be measured and is 8.75 m, or 30 Roman feet. The nave is 17.2 m from center to center of the columns flanking it. This measurement does not translate easily into Roman feet.[142] The total length can be estimated as 333⅓ Roman feet, or 98.6 m.[143] One column from the interior is partly preserved. It is made of green cipollino marble. Other fragments found outside the building suggest that there were gray cipollino and red granite columns as well. The distance from the center of one column to another (the intercolumniation) can only be estimated at between 3.0 and 3.4 m. A slight indentation of the apse from the line of the nave colonnades is suggested by the observed indentation of the apse where it meets the north outer wall of the building. The arrangement of the façade and entrance is hypothetical. As is to be expected, the interior was one large graveyard.

There are remains of four mausolea against the north wall at the apse end. Only the ends of the walls where they meet the wall of the basilica were excavated. The one farthest to the east was partly built over what seems to be a mausoleum antedating the basilica.

The *Liber Pontificalis* credits Constantine with the erection of a basilica in honor of St. Lawrence.[144] But the bulk of the report there has to do with arrangements made for the mar-

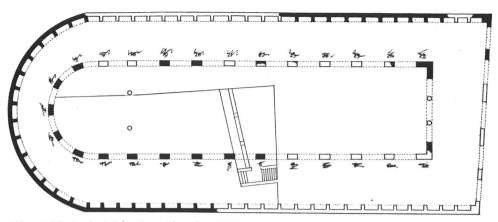

Fig. 3.48 Via Appia. S. Sebastiano. Plan after *CBCR*.

tyrium of the saint. Before the discovery of the apse-ended basilica this passage appeared hope-lessly confused. Now, however, it is clear that the martyrium was located outside the basilica. The masonry of the basilica fits with a Constantinian date. The basilica was called the *basilica maior* in an epitaph of the late fourth or early fifth century.[145]

Via Ardeatina

The most recent addition to the group of apse-ended basilicas of the Roman Campagna is the building discovered on the Via Ardeatina in 1990 and published in 1999.[146] Its location is six hundred meters distant from S. Sebastiano and lies in an area rich in catacombs, San Callisto and Domitilla among others. The basilica is possibly that built by Pope Mark in 336, but the identification is hypothetical.[147] The discovery is an achievement of aerial observation. But on this occasion no aircraft or aerial photography were involved. A member of the Salesian house of S. Callisto nearby, looking out an upper window, saw the outline of the basilica in the differential growth pattern of the vegetation in the neighboring field. The following exca-vation, which, naturally, has been limited in extent, revealed a building 66 m long and 28 m wide. Pilasters created a three-part opening into the presbytery contained within the horseshoe of the ambulatory, as at San Sebastiano. The nave and aisles were packed with tombs, as was a portico behind the apse. In the church the burials were stacked two deep, but along the walls this increased to three or four. One tomb, in the middle of the apse, was a focus of attention. It contained a marble sarcophagus under a masonry arch, and other tombs crowded around it. The deployment of the tombs followed a rational pattern proceeding from the door toward the apse. The aisles and apse were packed to capacity, the nave less so. The interior was appar-ently decorated with frescoes on a red background and areas of marble (cipollino) revetment. At the rear of the basilica there is a small portico, and tucked in between the portico and apse end there is a mausoleum with cist graves and arcosolium tombs.

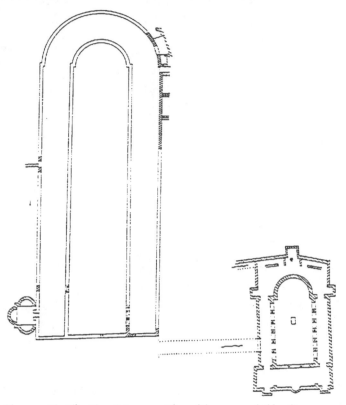

Fig. 3.49 Via Tiburtina. S. Lorenzo. Plan of the apse-ended basilica
and later church after *Felix Temporis Reperatio.*

The inscriptions accompanying tombs on the interior of the basilica were level with the
floor. The dated epitaphs begin with one of 368. The latest was inscribed in 445. One must remember, however, that only a portion of the interior of the building has been excavated.

Discussion

The discovery of the six apse-ended basilicas of the Roman Campagna have led to an intense
discussion as to their origin and purpose. These are huge buildings. The largest of them is the
length of a football field. The smallest is two-thirds that size. They are also huge covered cemeteries with no permanent clergy attached to them.[148] Except for the basilica of the Via Praenestina,
they were built in the neighborhood of Christian catacombs and surface cemeteries. But though
close to the resting place of martyrs, they were not usually built over a martyr's grave, and only
one has what may be a martyr's grave as a focus of its plan.[149] They represent a spectacular
but transient phase of Christian architecture. They were all built within two generations of
the beginning of Constantine's rule.

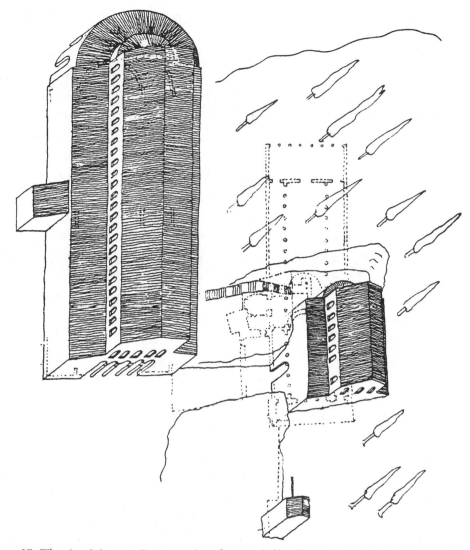

Fig. 3.50 Via Tiburtina. S. Lorenzo. Reconstruction of apse-ended basilica and later church after *CBCR*.

In 1960, Krautheimer tentatively considered (but did not accept) the idea that the apse-ended church could have been derived from the Roman circus.[150] It would thus mirror the comparison made by Tertullian between the race in the circus and the Christian life.[151] More recently confirmation of this suggestion has been found in the oddly canted façades or entrances of the basilicas of the Via Labicana, of San Sebastiano, and of the Via Praenestina. This feature of the three basilicas reproduces, it is held, the angulation of the starting gates of the Roman circus.[152] These observations have led to the formulation of a theory whereby the mausoleum and circus basilica are a continuation of the combination of circus and mausoleum represented in the Villa of Maxentius on the Via Appia, with all the overtones of heroization implicit in this complex.[153]

As J. B. Ward-Perkins noted, however, the Christian discovery of symbolic values in architecture is a phenomenon of the end of the fourth century.[154] And as far as the starting gates of the circus are concerned, as many of the apse-ended basilicas of the Roman Campagna fail to show evidence of this characteristic as have it. In the case of the Via Labicana, as discussed above, it arises from the fact that the execution of the building project utilized preexisting walls. So only two basilicas, if those, would in any way conform to this pattern. Furthermore, who would have been aware of such a deviation from the symmetry of the entrance to any of the basilicas? The same may be said of the circus apse. Viewing the interior of the basilica with a line of columns or pillars on each side of the nave and the same screening the far end of the building, who would have thought of a circus, especially under the roof of a basilica? The same visual interference of the columns or pillars should make one cautious about any comparison with secular basilicas.[155] Krautheimer's words of caution concerning such speculations are well worth repeating: "Archaeologists, accustomed to looking at plans, have fallen time and again into the trap of such pseudo-resemblances."[156]

The apse-ended basilica of the Via Labicana complex has a good claim to be the earliest of these buildings. As we have already seen, San Sebastiano, though frequently dated early, has no certain chronology. And none of the other basilicas of this class has a claim to be older than the building on the Via Labicana.

As emphasized already in the discussion of the basilica of the Via Labicana it was only one part of a funeral complex that included both mausoleum and basilica. The two were entered from the same door in the south portico. They were inseparably united. The question is, therefore, Why did Constantine and his architects unite a basilica with the mausoleum? and why did they give it its unusual form? The basilica extended burial within the walls of the imperial funeral structure to individuals not of the imperial family. This is not an act to be expected from a pagan. It is an act of Christian charity. As he opened his purse to the poor, orphan children, and women in distress, Constantine opened his door to his Christian brothers and sisters in a way unknown to the pagan, for whom the tomb and the household were inseparable.[157] He housed them in the tomb complex intended for himself and occupied by his mother. He was not deaf to the words, "Thou shalt not turn away from him that is in need, but shalt share with thy brother in all things, and shalt not say that things are thine own; for if thou are partners in what is immortal, how much more in what is mortal?"[158] Perhaps even at this time the pontifex maximus was contemplating the Christian road to salvation.

What was this apse-ended basilica but an amplified mausoleum? A domed building can only be made so large. To exceed what can be covered by a dome it would only be natural to open one side and extend it, thus making a nave and an apse. This kind of architectural invention seems to me far more likely as an explanation of the genesis of the complex of mausoleum and basilica than any symbolic gesture to pagan architecture or pagan thought.

Thus, in my opinion, the apse-ended plan has nothing to do with the circus. It is not a copy of any Roman secular basilica. Neither is it a reminiscence of circus gardens, and far less a partial recreation of the ambulatories of pagan circular tombs or adaptation of the combination of circus and mausoleum. Rather, it was developed as an essential part of the imperial mausoleum on the Via Labicana and was then imitated by other coemeteria subteglata. The type was short-lived, but it was revolutionary.

The Catacombs

In the past the vast underground burial places of the early Christians of Rome have seemed almost synonymous with the early Christians themselves. There are catacombs in every direction along the highways radiating from the city. Underground, their corridors extend for miles in narrow darkness, faintly illuminated from time to time by a light shaft open to the sky above. The galleries of one level lie above those of another below it. Their world today is full of the same gloom that set St. Jerome's teeth on edge when he descended into the catacombs in the fourth century.[159]

Along the main corridors simple burial recesses cut into the side walls (the loculi) are stacked five, six, ten high. The small rooms (the *cryptae* or *cubicula*) opening off the corridors can be single chambers or part of a multichambered family tomb belonging to a long pre-Christian tradition of such underground burial suites in the Mediterranean. It is in these tomb suites that fresco decoration is most often found. Occasionally a wider space has been created, generally to form a chapel at the tomb of a martyr. Following the Constantinian age semi-subterranean basilicas were built for the same purpose.

The lore of the catacombs has been infused with fantasy: that Christians used them as refuges during the persecutions; that their church services were conducted in the passages of the catacombs; and that the catacombs themselves were as old as the Christian community in the city.

The catacombs, rather, testify to the consolidation of the Christian position in Rome and to the Christians' growing membership at the end of the second century. The Christians felt a responsibility to insure that all the brothers and sisters, no matter how poor, escaped the fate that awaited the indigent pagan and slave, whose remains were consigned to open refuse pits.[160] We hear of the Christians' sense of obligation in the third century from Tertullian and Hippolytus.

The African bishop puts the Christians' responsibilities succinctly:

A moderate donation on a certain day of the month, as and how the common fund wishes it and if it can arrange it, so it appoints. For no one is forced but makes a contribution spontaneously. For [our funds] are not wasted on banquets and drink and eating houses but are used to feed and bury the poor, to care for boys and girls and such of these that are orphaned, for old servants and the victims of shipwreck and those condemned to the mines or imprisoned on islands or in confinement, so long as they are imprisoned for their faith and they acknowledged it openly.[161]

And Hippolytus makes the arrangements at Rome in the mid–third century quite clear: "Let there be no heavy charge for burying people in the cemetery for it is for all the poor; except they shall pay the hire of a workman to him who digs and the price of the tiles. And the bishop shall provide for the watchman there who takes care of it from what they offer at the assemblies, so that there be no charge to those who come to the place."[162] Finally to quote Lactantius: "That last and greatest office of piety is burial for foreigners and the poor."[163]

Faced with the need to bury ever more Christians, the community was also faced with the problem of finding space for the purpose. Tunneling below ground was more economical than finding large areas above ground for cemeteries.[164] At the same time the Jews of Rome were adopting the same expedient for their cemeteries.[165]

There was at least one Christian catacomb by the beginning of the third century, when Callixtus was put in charge of it by Pope Zephyrinus.[166] This was surely the complex on the Via Appia that bears Callixtus's name to this day. Like many of the other catacombs, the complex of the Via Appia was developed where a quarry for pozzolana stone had been located. This provided the initial galleries for the purpose. Elsewhere sandstone deposits were also exploited. Preexisting hypogea could be enlarged, and corridors extended from them. And in other circumstances preexisting cisterns and water channels were pressed into service, such as those used in the area of the catacombs on the Via Labicana (SS. Marcellino e Pietro) and at the Catacomb of Priscilla. Callixtus's appointment and Hippolytus's statement make it clear that already in his day the bishop was the controlling authority.

The excavation of the catacombs was carried out by a specialized corps of workmen, the *fossores*. Picturesque images of these catacomb excavators armed with their picks and working by the light of a lamp hung on a movable hook survive in the catacombs.[167] It appears that in the expansion of the catacombs in the fourth century the fossores became entrepreneurs, selling loculi directly to their clients, but that papal control was subsequently reestablished.[168]

The planning of the original sections of the catacombs, such as Area *I* of S. Callisto, shows that the corps of the fossores was directed by full-fledged architects. The plan of this catacomb and others like it was developed from straight major galleries with secondary galleries between them (the so-called fish skeleton plan).[169] Subsequently, there was introduced the system of a long major gallery with secondary galleries crossing, such the lower level of S. Priscilla.[170] The precision and regularity of such planning are difficult to appreciate in the general plan of Roman catacombs, which include the various superimposed levels of galleries and the accumulation of two centuries of activity.[171]

During the third century the catacombs retained an egalitarian character. The martyrs' tombs were not significantly distinguished from those of their brethren. The tombs of the popes in Area *I* of San Callisto were also plain loculi. Only Sixtus, also a martyr, was buried in a larger cavity covered by a stone slab (the so-called *mensa* tomb).

With the rapid increase in conversions to Christianity in the years following 312, whole sections of catacombs seem to have been laid out, the catacomb of Praetextatus, of Domitilla, of S. Ermete, the catacomb of the Giordani and of Sant' Agnese among others.[172] These galleries were crowded with the simplest kind of loculus burials. It is at the end of the Constantinian age and the decades following, beginning around 330, that the introduction of elaborate family tombs is seen. The apse-ended basilicas also exercised a magnetic effect. On the Via Labicana (SS. Marcellino e Pietro), where it is estimated that some eight thousand tombs were added to the catacomb after 312, the area of expansion is below and around the basilica.[173] The same was true at the catacombs of Sant' Agnese, which developed under the new semisubterranean basilica located to the east of the basilica and mausoleum of S. Costanza, and at S. Sebastiano, where stairs led down to the enlarged catacombs from the church. The same development is also noticeable at S. Callisto.

Pagans felt the same pressures of finding space as the Christians. They too went underground in the third century. Such family hypogea were often enlarged into catacombs and today stand at the heart of the vast Christian networks. One such is the Hypogeum of the Flavii, quite possibly of pagan origin, in the Catacomb of Domitilla.[174] One of the most richly decorated hypogea, that of the Via Latina (Via Dino Compagni), also shows a clear tension between pagan and Christian decoration. This complex of six clusters of chambers was certainly in use in the Constantinian period. Its first phase may be earlier. It was used over a long period of time, and elements of its decoration have been dated into the fifth century.[175]

Chronology, in fact, is a weak point in our knowledge of the catacombs. It is secure only when there is epigraphical evidence. Despite their general brevity, the tomb inscriptions of the catacombs occasionally include beside the name of the deceased a specific date registered by the names of the consuls of the year. Even when such evidence is lacking, the letter forms of the inscription and its phraseology can be helpful. The occasional finds of coins, especially those set in the mortar in which the tiles closing a loculus were secured, provide a good basis of dating, while lamps, gold glasses, and other material offer a less good one. There are still, however, wide differences of opinion, especially as regards the chronology of the fresco decoration of tombs. One subject of dispute concerns the Constantinian age in particular, since a sizable number of frescoes can be dated before the Peace of the Church.[176] In the opinion of the most recent investigator of the Via Labicana catacombs, which are distinguished for the relatively high number of paintings in their aedicula, the great age of catacomb painting is pre-Constantinian.[177]

The frescoes of the catacombs are difficult to treat as major art. The fundamental purpose in painting those chambers that received decoration was to make a light-colored surface that would reflect the lamplight by which the tombs were visited. The white background is frequently subdivided by a lattice of lines in red. Elaborate framing motives and architectural details are less common. Only rarely are there successive bands across the walls or ceilings covered with floral decoration. Within the fields thus formed there is figure decoration. These figures are small and isolated, and most often the scenes are simple. The execution is often hasty, and it is all too obvious that economy, as well as the noxious working conditions, encouraged haste. The fundamental repertoire is drawn mainly from the Old Testament, emphasizing episodes that can easily be interpreted as harbingers of resurrection and salvation. So we find numerous scenes of Jonah, of the three Hebrew brothers surviving in the fire, Daniel in the lions' den, the sacrifice of Isaac. Similar scenes from the New Testament were used, for example, the raising of Lazarus and Jesus and the Samaritan woman at the well. The Good Shepherd and his lamb appear frequently, and there is more than one instance of the saints reclining at the refrigerium of paradise. Any suggestion of the Passion is avoided; the emphasis is on the resurrection of the faithful. Naturally, there are atypical subjects, some pagan, such as Medusa or Orpheus, others unusual but easily interpreted, such as the crossing of the Red Sea by the Israelites or an occasional scene showing the occupation of the deceased. One must wait for a later moment in the history of catacomb painting, at the end of the fourth century, to encounter monumental images, for example, the scene of the widow Turtura with saints, the Virgin and Christ Child from Domitilla, or the enthroned Christ with saints from the Catacomb of the SS. Marcellino e Pietro. Much of the more common catacomb painting is more amuletic than monumental. These pictures are strangely reminiscent of the miniature landscapes and isolated figures that appear in panels of Roman wall painting of the Julio-Claudian age. Like them, and like the various isolated figures that decorated Roman walls in other centuries, these images appear to be intended for encouraging whispers at the time of burial and commemoration rather than riveting the attention.

Painting belongs to the wealthier tomb clusters of the catacombs. One must not forget that overwhelmingly the tombs of the catacombs belong to persons who could not afford decoration. The cubicula with paintings are certainly representative of a step up the economic scale from the burials of the loculi. But how far up the ladder are they? They are clearly below the level of the mausolea attached to apse-ended basilicas that arose in the same suburban belt around Rome where the catacombs were located. But one cannot simply set up a downward sequence from imperial mausoleum to smaller mausoleum to cubiculum to loculus because there are the cist graves inside and outside the basilicas that must be taken into consideration. Such cemeteries of surface tombs are common in other parts of the Christian Mediterranean. The densely packed tombs around the basilicas of the Via Labicana and the Via Ardeatina provide the most important documentation of this kind in Rome, and they raise the question of how many other cemeteries *sub divo* have escaped attention because the reluctance of the Christians to put grave goods in the tomb makes them difficult to distinguish unless an inscribed tomb marker is found. Do these burials represent a separate social class? One may doubt that the situation is so simple. In fact the basic grave both above and below may have belonged to the same stratum of society. A stone sarcophagus, whether in the catacomb or in the aboveground cemetery, is an indicator of superior status, as is the decorated cubiculum below ground. But why some Christians were interred in catacombs and others above ground is a question that is not easy to explain.

IV   The Tomb of St. Peter

S. PIETRO IN VATICANO today is a church brought into being by an accumulation of genius. The colonnades, which replaced the atrium of the ancient and medieval basilica and curve around the square before the present basilica, are the work of Gian Lorenzo Bernini (1656–57). Of course Bernini was given some assistance and some direction. Carlo Maderno's façade was in place when he began work, and the obelisk that once adorned the median divider of Nero's Circus situated slightly south of the basilica was reerected in its present location in 1586. The new church itself, begun in 1506, was completed as a Latin cross, with a long nave by Maderno ending in the crossing covered by Michelangelo's dome. But the original plan of Bramante and then Michelangelo was a Greek cross. The Latin cross design was introduced by Pope Julius II relying on Raphael and Giuliano da Sangallo. Then over the course of the sixteenth century the Constantinian basilica was torn down, while a series of master architects struggled over the final design. The basilica faces east onto Piazza S. Pietro. Its apse is turned toward the west.

St. Peter's is also a church built for pilgrims (fig. 4.1). It offered them a magnificent setting in which to approach the tomb of the apostle and, thanks to Maderno's nave, offered space sufficient for the crowds that came from near and far for the great feast days. Like all great Christian churches of the Middle Ages and later centuries, it gave the pilgrim some intimation of the glories of paradise to which the Christian life would surely lead. Everything about the interior is gigantic. The cherubs supporting fonts of holy water along the nave dwarf whomever approaches them. The bronze baldacchino of Bernini which towers over the papal altar below the dome has none of the canopy-like delicacy of medieval ciboria. It is an imperial monument

Fig. 4.1 S. Pietro in Vaticano. Nave. Photo Center for Old World Archaeology and Art, Brown University.

worthy of Solomon himself, whose temple, and from it the Column of the Flagellation, was evoked by the four spiral columns that are its most prominent feature. (The bronze for the baldacchino was acquired by stripping the Pantheon porch of the sheathing of its roof beams, not without some satirical comment from Romans comparing the Barberini pope [Urban VIII, 1623–44] to the barbarian looters of ancient Rome.) Finally, surrounded by an explosion of alabaster, one sees the dove of the Holy Ghost in the apse. All around papal tombs and colossal saints are overshadowed by their setting.

At the base of the dome, in dark letters on a gold mosaic background, there run the words of Jesus in St. Matthew's Gospel, "You are Peter and upon this rock I shall build my church."[1] It is St. Peter, the first bishop of Rome, who justifies the primacy of the Roman Church, a claim enunciated forcefully by Rome since the time of Leo the Great (440–61). The basilica that bears St. Peter's name was erected over the place where Constantine and the Christians of his day believed the apostle's tomb was located, and the archaeological investigation of this site led to one of the most courageous, difficult, and disputed excavations of modern times.

In the basilica immediately before the papal altar one can look down over a balustrade into a lower level (fig. 4.2). This is the confessional of the basilica, given its present form by

Fig. 4.2 S. Pietro in Vaticano. Confessional. Photo Center for Old World Archaeology and Art, Brown University.

Maderno, illuminated by ninety-five lamps kept burning day and night and decorated with marble and intarsia work.

At the west end of the confessional behind a gold door made by Benvenuto Cellini there is the Niche of the Pallia (figs. 4.3, 4.4). The pallium is a narrow band of white wool trimmed with black silk worn by the pope and archbishops and occasionally conferred on bishops as a special mark of favor. Today the pallia, which are consecrated once a year in a service at San Giovanni in Laterano, are kept here. Throughout the Middle Ages each pallium was lowered through an opening (a fenestrella) down a shaft (a cataract), where it remained overnight in proximity to the relics of the apostle.[2]

The simple pilgrim, too, could approach the tomb with the expectation of participating in its wondrous grace. Gregory of Tours (ca. 530–94) describes the experience of visiting Peter's tomb as follows:

> His tomb is located beneath the altar and certainly is a thing of rarity. But one who
> wishes to pray having opened the gates that enclose the tomb, reaches a point
> above it. There a small window makes an opening and putting his head inside the

Fig. 4.3 S. Pietro in Vaticano. Niche of the Pallia. Photo Center for Old World Archaeology and Art, Brown University.

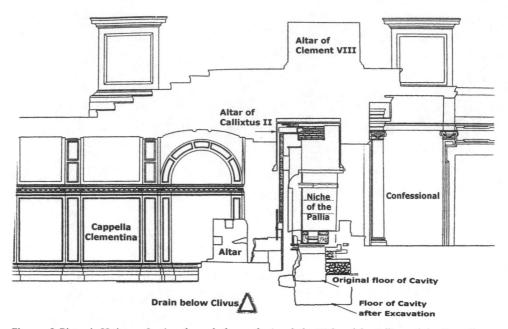

Fig. 4.4 S. Pietro in Vaticano. Section through the confessional, the Niche of the Pallia, and the Cappella Clementina. After *Esplorazioni*.

supplicant asks what he needs. Nor is there delay in answering his prayer if it is just. And should he wish to take away some talisman, he lowers a bit of cloth that he has weighed before. Then keeping vigil and fasting, he prays most earnestly that the apostolic power may assist his devotion. Wonderful to relate! If his faith prevails, the cloth emerges from the tomb so imbued with divine power that its weight is increased beyond what he found it weighed before. Then he who lowered it knows that together with it he has raised the grace he sought.[3]

The tomb, however, was very much of a mystery. In 1615 graves were discovered during the work undertaken around the papal altar, and another group came to light during the laying of foundations for Bernini's baldacchino in 1626. These were apparently both pagan graves and burials of Christian ecclesiastics.[4] At the end of the nineteenth century Hartmut Grisar, S.J., attempted to study the cavity of the tomb through the opening in the rear of the Niche of the Pallia.[5]

The full-scale exploration of the apostle's tomb would have to wait another four decades. The credit for undertaking the excavations belongs to Pope Pius XII (fig. 4.5), who was elected to the throne of St. Peter in 1939. He lost no time in making clear his intention of investigating the last resting place of the apostle by thorough excavation. It was a decision requiring both courage and faith, but Pius XII was prepared to attempt to establish once and for all the reality of Peter's tomb and the primacy of the Roman Church.

Fig. 4.5 Eugenio Cardinal Pacelli in 1938 shortly before his election as Pope Pius XII. Photo by Ernest Nash. Copyright Ernest Nash Archive Seminar für Griechische und Römische Geschichte, Abt. II, J. W. Goethe Universität, Frankfurt am Main.

The excavations, beginning in 1940 and continuing in their first phase through 1949, were entrusted to distinguished students of Christian archaeology, Engelbert Kirschbaum, S.J., and Antonio Ferrua, S.J., and together with them the eminent collaborators Bruno M. Apollonj-Ghetti and Enrico Josi. The directional oversight of operations was held by Mgr. Ludwig Kaas, Segretario della Congregazione della Reverenda Fabbrica di San Pietro, that is, the administrator of the basilica.[6] The results of their work in two handsome volumes were presented to Pius XII just before Christmas, 1951.[7] After 1949 the excavations were extended by Adriano Prandi.[8] The most recent excavations were carried out in 1979 in mausoleum *N* of the pagan sector of the necropolis.[9]

The excavations of the 1940s were made under difficult circumstances. The Second World War was hardly a favorable time for such exploration, even in the relative safety of Vatican City. But the topography of the excavations created even greater problems. This was to be an investigation carried out by burrowing under and around the substructures of the existing church and those of Constantine's basilica. The opportunities for exposing the pre-Constantinian remains would always be limited. In some cases, notably in that of the surroundings of the apostle's tomb, the possibility of observation would be reduced to a minimum. Excavation was most often a one-man operation in a cramped space. The removal of earth must always have been a slow and awkward business. Furthermore, the work was to be done without publicity. Consequently, little could be accomplished in the open setting of the confessional. Fortunately, the inner wall of the confessional, with the Niche of the Pallia, was approached within feet from the opposite side by the Cappella Clementina (Clement VIII, 1592–1605). The latter is, as it were, a tunnel running east–west, on the same axis as the confessional but under the papal altar. The chapel could be closed off to permit the archaeological work to go on undisturbed. When work had to be carried out in the confessional, it was done at night.[10]

The official excavation report is a magisterial, flowing account of the labors of the excavators to recover the resting place and relics of St. Peter. Appreciation of its persuasiveness, however, must be tempered by the realization that the authors tend to gloss over those aspects of the excavation in which the evidence remained incomplete and difficult to interpret. The excavation drawings, in particular, often give the impression of fact even when they represent hypothesis. This emerges clearly from Father Kirschbaum's debate with the early critics of the excavations. Yes, he admits, there are misleading drawings in the publications, but the assertions of the excavators are supported by other—and, he emphasizes—more accurate drawings in the same publication.[11]

There were two main parts of the investigations. The first was the actual probing of the traditional location of St. Peter's tomb. The second was a by-product of the undertaking but physically the more extensive of the two parts. This was the excavation of two lines of Roman masonry tombs of the second century that extend eastward from the confessional toward the main doors of the basilica (fig. 4.6). The alignment of these tombs continues that of another of the same date that was excavated earlier underneath Piazza S. Pietro.[12] The tombs below St. Peter's were preserved because the ground level around them was artificially raised to create a terrace against the hillside to the north when the Constantinian basilica was built. Yet this important discovery of a necropolis of prominent Romans of the Antonine period is of only marginal importance to the study of St. Peter's tomb and Constantinian Rome.[13]

As the street of the tombs goes westward, however, the ground level rises toward the Vatican hill, and just as the ancient ground surface rises it encounters the sunken level of the confessional (fig. 4.7).[14] Thus, while the visitor to the street of the tombs can be standing in a deep excavation surrounded by masonry structures that reach above his head, in the area of the confessional the ancient level is separated from the floor above by a mere crawl space. Indeed, between the west end of the confessional and the eastern end of the Cappella Clementina the excavators were to encounter pre-Constantinian remains that had been trapped in the space between the end walls of these two sunken parts of the Renaissance basilica. Below the floor of the confessional immediately in front of the Niche of the Pallia and thus just before the narrow space between the chapel and the confessional, there was the hidden cavity venerated

Fig. 4.6 Roman tomb beneath S. Pietro in Vaticano.
Photo Sansaini, DAI Rome, Inst. Neg. 54.618.
Copyright Deutsches Archäologisches Institut.

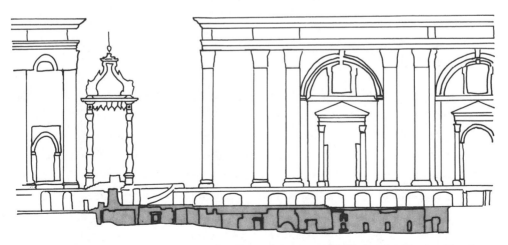

Fig. 4.7 S. Pietro in Vaticano. East–west section. Excavations 1940 and following tinted in gray. Drawing
by A. Walsh.

Fig. 4.8 S. Pietro in Vaticano. Cappella Clementina,
view toward the east showing the Constantinian
monument of marble and porphyry. Photo
Moscioni, DAI Rome, Inst. Neg. 54.514. Copyright
Deutsches Archäologisches Institut.

as the Tomb of St. Peter. My use of the term *the tomb* in what follows is merely one of convenience reflecting a tradition of belief as old as Constantine and is not intended to prejudice
any assessment of the archaeological results.

The excavation in the area of the tomb began by the making of an opening in the east
wall of the Cappella Clementina. The excavators found themselves face to face with a surpris-
ing discovery. Immediately behind the Renaissance structure there appeared the facing of
another wall, intact and as well preserved as the day it had been set in place. Two large slabs
of marble were set above a dado of porphyry while an upright band of porphyry separated
them (fig. 4.8). The large, beautifully encased construction had risen 2.34 m above the floor
of the Constantinian basilica. One could immediately see how it occupied the focal point of
the basilica, placed on the centerline of the nave before the apse and extending slightly into
it. It was too high to be an altar. It was, therefore, immediately recognized as part of the regal
monumentalization of the tomb.

Fig. 4.9 The Samagher Casket. Venice, Archaeological Museum. Photo Angiolini, DAI Rome, Inst. Neg. 68.4788. Copyright Deutsches Archäologisches Institut.

This was the porphyry monument that Constantine had raised over the tomb according to the *Liber Pontificalis*.[15] Naturally, there was a grave question how to proceed. The direct route to the tomb was obstructed by the marble- and porphyry-covered monument. So the rear wall of the Cappella Clementina was opened both to north and south of the original breach. In the meantime it had been possible to observe the walling to which the marble and porphyry surface had been added. It was distinctive in that it was covered with a red plaster, and this same red surface was to be found later in the excavations on the opposite face of the wall. From its red coating this wall was named the Red Wall (frequently abbreviated *MR* for *Muro Rosso*).[16] It was to play a significant role in the further investigations. To the south, observation through a narrow opening found the actual return of the Constantinian monument running toward the east from the southwest corner of the monument. The Red Wall had originally extended beyond this point further toward the south. But here it had been cut down to the level of the paving of the early basilica by Constantine's workmen, as was the case to the north of the Constantinian monument.

Fig. 4.10 S. Pietro in Vaticano. Reconstruction of the
Memoria over the Tomb of St. Peter and the apse of
the Constantinian basilica. After *Esplorazioni.*

The further removal of the east walls of the Cappella Clementina revealed two blocked-up spaces that had been left when the chapel was installed. In both, fragments of the marble paving of the Constantinian basilica were still in place. In both, moreover, there were marks on the pavement showing that something had rested there, presumably the bases of columns. A fencing of some kind had run from column to column. Apparently temporary at first, like the wooden barriers of San Giovanni in Laterano, the arrangement was made permanent in marble at a later date. Here, then, were traces of the position of "vine scroll columns" mentioned in the *Liber Pontificalis.* Subsequently, three appropriate bases and the setting marks for two columns in line with those found behind the walls of the Cappella Clementina were discovered farther east. An enclosure could thus be reconstructed. The columns of the enclosure, carved with spiral shafts and floral decoration, apparently survive, having been reused by Bernini to decorate niches on the piers below the cupola of the present basilica. With the aid of the design on the ivory casket from Samagher in Istria, which shows not only a monument enclosed by four such columns, but also an architrave over the columns continuing to right and left to reach two additional columns, the excavators have suggested a reconstruction for the monument,

Fig. 4.11 S. Pietro in Vaticano. Column built into
wall subsequent to wall *s*. Photo Center for Old
World Archaeology and Art, Brown University.

or Memoria (figs. 4.9, 4.10).[17] It is on this basis that they restore additional columns left and right at the very beginning of the apse and on line with the western columns of the enclosure. The enclosure on the casket is open, but suspended from two arching beams that meet over its center there is a large lamp. This is presumably the lamp recorded as one of Constantine's gifts to the basilica in the *Liber Pontificalis*: "a gold crown in front of the body, which is a chandelier, with 50 dolphins, weighing 35 pounds."[18]

At this point in the development of the investigation beneath the confessional, the work was still focused on the Constantinian era. But what came before? and especially what was the Red Wall? To look further into this mystery the excavators removed the upright band of porphyry between the two marble facing slabs. They were now looking at the back of the Red Wall at the point where today it carries (on its other side) a mosaic of Christ facing into the confessional. The mosaic is the facing of a niche which was to become known as *N2* in the reports of the excavation. It had been hollowed out of an earlier depression in the wall, *N3*, which carried a "small wall surface with a coating of smooth plaster, running back diagonally, which must constitute the remains of a small rectangular window aperture that had been inserted here."[19] Quite apart from the limited opportunity afforded the excavators to examine them,

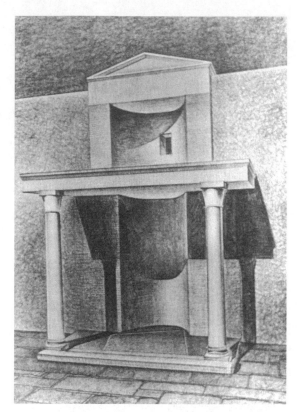

Fig. 4.12 S. Pietro in Vaticano. Reconstruction of the
Memoria over the Tomb of St. Peter. After *Esplorazioni.*

there are two aspects of these features of the Red Wall that should be emphasized. The first is that the character of *N3* is more than a little unclear. Its existence could be hypothesized only from what could be seen through the sill of the small plastered opening. Second, any detailed examination of *N2* was impossible because of the mosaic on its eastern side facing into the confessional. And one must keep in mind what excavators found as they began probing from the Cappella Clementina onto the far side of the Red Wall: "The general impression here is one of chaos and it is eloquent of repeated destructions."[20]

Probing continued. A bit of marble facing was exposed on the east side of the Red Wall. Clearly at some time the Red Wall had presented an embellished face toward the east which was hidden by the construction of the Constantinian monument. With small pick and penknife the explorers dug further into the space to the east of the Red Wall. And now they were greeted by a column shaft of white marble that had been built into a small spur wall (fig. 4.11).[21] The wall enclosing the column that one sees today is a secondary structure built on the stump of an earlier wall. This earlier wall is wall *s.* Above the column, resting horizontally in the fill, was a travertine slab broken into two pieces. The travertine slab and the column (with fragments of the second, similar column), together with *N2* and *N3,* are the basic elements of the re-

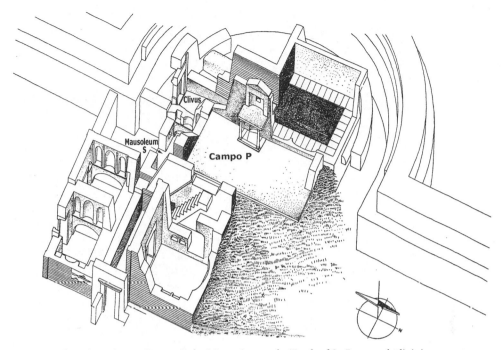

Fig. 4.13 S. Pietro in Vaticano. Campo *P,* the Memoria over the Tomb of St. Peter, and adjoining structures. After *Esplorazioni.*

construction of the Memoria, which the excavators restore against the Red Wall (figs. 4.12, 4.13). Yet just as *N2* and *N3* are incompletely known, so the travertine slab and the column present their own problems. The travertine slab that is restored as the shelf of the Memoria is fragmentary; it was not resting on the column that is supposed to have carried it.[22] The excavators noted with satisfaction that there could have been just room for a capital, now lost, to fit between the top of the column and the travertine slab.[23] But how are we to imagine that the slab remained perfectly in position when the capital was removed from below it? Surely no antigravitational force was present to sustain it in midair. The slab would either have slipped onto the top of the column or, more likely, would have fallen to the ground.

The marble column itself cannot have been part of any memorial structure such as proposed by the excavators (see fig. 4.12). The key to this fact is the marble facing found on wall *s.* The facing covered a small U-shaped alcove formed against the Red Wall by wall *s* and another wall, wall *g,* which I shall consider presently. The Red Wall between walls *s* and *g* (including *N2*), the alcove side of wall *g,* and the side of wall *s* opposite it all had marble facing (see fig. 4.16). Wall *s* was something of an afterthought in the creation of the alcove, as shown by the fact that it was built up against the marble facing on the Red Wall. The column, moreover, is certainly an afterthought in respect to Wall *s* because the marble facing of that wall runs tight behind it, so tightly that it could not have been wedged into place behind a column that

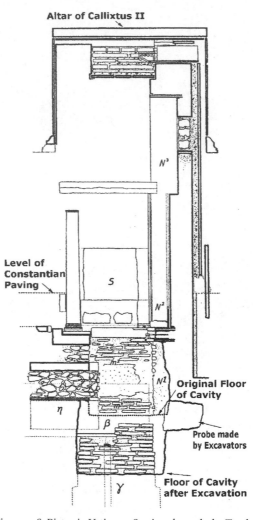

Fig. 4.14 S. Pietro in Vaticano. Section through the Tomb
of St. Peter and surrounding remains. After *Esplorazioni.*
Note that the insertion of the horizontal slab into the
lower part of *N3* is hypothetical.

was already in position. One is left to conclude that the column was simply a piece of stone,
unsuitable for reuse (the side facing into the wall was badly damaged), that belongs to the next
phase of construction after the marble-faced alcove.[24]

In the fill beneath the column there was another flat piece of travertine on which the excavators assumed that the column had been positioned, although again their possibilities of
observation were extremely limited, and they may well have exaggerated the size and importance
of this element (figs. 4.14, 4.15, 4.16).[25] The excavators further assumed that this element would
originally have been long enough to have supported a matching column on the other side (the

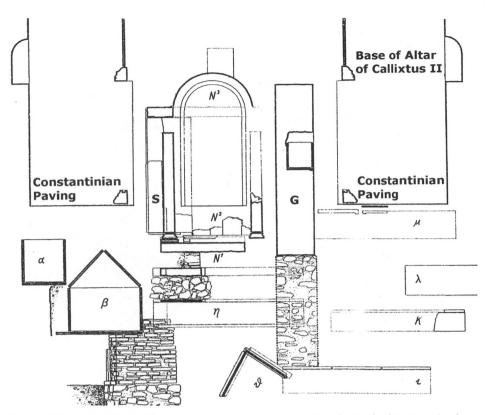

Fig. 4.15 S. Pietro in Vaticano. Section through the remains surrounding the Tomb of St. Peter. Greek letters indicate tombs. After *Esplorazioni.*

north side) of the niches. When the investigation reached that point, however, the excavators found that the travertine slab did not extend so far. The lower part of a column was there, standing loose in the fill. This column is not quite the mate of the southern column because its base was made separately from the shaft.[26] Its precise location was never recorded. There was no support below it. The northern column was thus left, as it were, hanging in air (fig. 4.17).[27] The expression is not completely fanciful. The fragmentary column was in a position directly above the cavity of the tomb, which the excavators soon entered. Their probing in the soil surrounding the cavity resulted in the unsupported column's crashing down into the open space below it.

A further problem connected with the travertine piece under the southern column arises when one examines the plans published in the major report of 1951. In the original state of the Memoria the southern column sits at the edge of the travertine foundation. In the second state of the Memoria, after the construction of walls *g* and *s,* the column has been moved toward the north, but it is still at the edge of the same piece of travertine, which seems to have shrunk conveniently to fit the new position. It is all too clear that the excavators never saw the edge

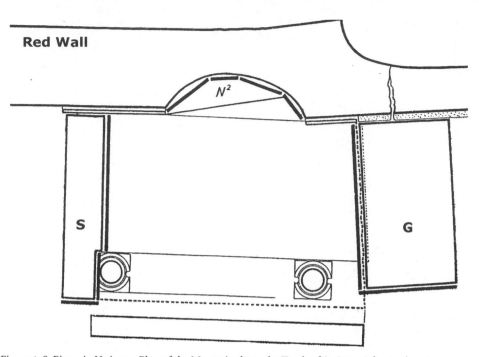

Fig. 4.16 S. Pietro in Vaticano. Plan of the Memoria above the Tomb of St. Peter. After *Esplorazioni*.

of the travertine element lying below the southern column in the fill and altered its dimensions to suit the convenience of their restoration.[28] In fact, it seems they were able to observe very little of this piece of travertine, and, as already suggested, they may have unduly exaggerated its size and importance. It may have been no more than a fragment that never played a role in any structure. In the following discussion I shall continue to follow the excavators' line of reasoning in their work, but one must keep in mind that the evidence for the Memoria as they restored it is insufficient to support their reconstruction.

Wall *g* derived its name from the graffiti that covered its northern side, that is, its long side away from the alcove. Its foundations reach to a much deeper level than those of wall *s*. In wall *g* there was a small, boxlike cavity 77 × 29 × 31.5 cm. lined with marble. Originally its only opening was a small slot that gave out onto the north face of the wall, but at the time of discovery part of its side was missing. When found, according to the excavators, it was empty save for some slivers of bone, a bit of lead, a few threads of silver cloth, and a coin of the Counts of Limoges datable to the tenth/twelfth centuries.[29] This marble box and its contents were to become a point of great contention in the later history of the interpretation of the excavations.

There is an apparent fissure in the Red Wall exactly behind the end of wall *g*. Prandi's subsequent observations showed that at this point the Red Wall comes to an end and that what was thought to be its continuation northward is a completely separate structure which he

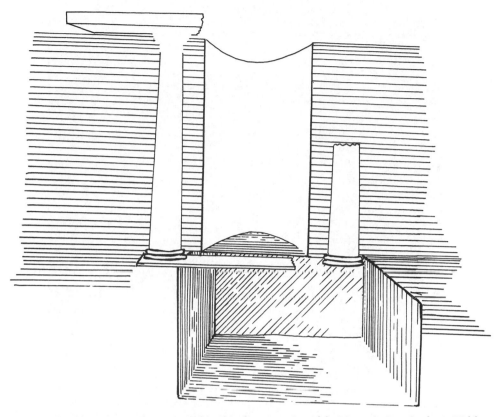

Fig. 4.17 S. Pietro in Vaticano. Elements combined in the restoration of the Memoria. Drawing by A. Walsh.

termed *Muro Q*, or *MQ*. Wall *g*, furthermore, does not touch the juncture of *MR* and *MQ* and therefore cannot be, as the original excavators supposed, a buttress made in an effort to repair a crack.[30]

Now for the first time an opening was made in the Constantinian pavement in the northern chamber of the pair that been created behind the east wall of the Cappella Clementina. As Father Kirschbaum describes the result, "The breach was made close to the Red Wall, just large enough for us to push a man through it. Lying flat on his back, he was able to light up a very irregular little space, about 80 cm. square and nearly as high."[31] This cavity, no larger than a good-sized cupboard, is in the very location venerated for so long as the Tomb of St. Peter. Overhead could be seen a reused marble inscription of one P. Aelius Isidorus, thought to be the owner of one of the mausolea in the street of the tombs nearby, from where the marble slab with the inscription would have been taken (fig. 4.18).[32] The marble slab was placed face down to cover the cavity. It is broken and there is a small section missing toward the Red Wall. The former tombstone, however, was only the lowest covering over the cavity. Above it there

Fig. 4.18 S. Pietro in Vaticano. The Tomb of St. Peter. The cover slab with the inscription of Publius Aelius Isidorus is visible above the cavity. After *Esplorazioni.*

was another marble slab and cut into it a rectangular aperture which matched the opening in the Isidorus tombstone. Finally, there was a thick layer of mortar and above that again the remains of three sections of lead sheeting which originally seem to have covered the upper marble slab and what lay below. The shaft down to the Isidorus tombstone was lined with green porphyry. On the side of the shaft there was a nail, from which, in medieval times, a censer may have been suspended. On the south side of the cavity there are two bits of walling, one above the other, labeled *m2* and *m1,* respectively.[33] The excavators believe that *m2* could have served to hold one side of a removable cover for the cavity at a time before the arrangement with the Isidorus slab was installed.[34] This is a hopeful interpretation of these slender remains, and it assumes that *m2* at one time formed part of a subterranean enclosure related to St. Peter's tomb (*m1* is below the level considered by the excavators to have been the original floor of the tomb). These two fragments of walling were undoubtedly part of something or of two successive "somethings." Any other elements of walling that went with them disappeared before the covering using the Isidorus inscription was made.

On the eastern side of the cavity the Red Wall has been hollowed out at its base, and the resulting depression is known as *N1*. From photographs it gives all the appearance of a heavy-handed attempt to get at something under or protruding from below the wall. This was the opinion of the original excavators, who believed that the niche had been hacked out of the wall and then patched up as well as possible. Prandi, however, viewed the patching as original construction.[35] The fact that at this point the foundations of the Red Wall were not carried to the depth found elsewhere along its course was given great importance by the excavators, who saw in this a deliberate attempt by the builders of the Red Wall to avoid a now-vanished tomb on the spot.[36] It was on the floor of the cavity under the opening of *N1* that a group of bones was recovered. These bones play a vital part in the discussion of the tomb and that will be considered in due course.

Coins, 1,418 in all, were also found on the floor of the cavity. Although in date they are spread over more than ten centuries, the only coins before 270 are a worn coin of Augustus, one of Antoninus Pius, and three of Claudius Gothicus.[37] The coins of Claudius Gothicus were issued only after 268 and so were current in 270. The coin of Augustus was worn by long years in circulation, and the single coin of Antoninus Pius is no indication of any reverence for the cavity before the consistent record of coin offerings begins in the third quarter of the third century. The logical interpretation of the evidence is that the deposition of coins in the cavity began around 270. Thereafter the record is one of heavy accumulation through the third, fourth, and fifth centuries, 573 coins in this period, and a steady rate of accumulation in later centuries.

Further proof of the honor accorded whatever had originally been deposited within the cavity was a gold ex-voto, a plaque 3.5 by 6.1 cm. which Father Kirschbaum pried out of the south side of the cavity. Two eyes peer out from its surface, and between, in place of a nose, there is a cross (fig. 4.19). It was this operation that dislodged the column that had been hanging precariously in the fill over the cavity.

From the vantage point of the cavity the excavators could see more of *N2*, which as noted is largely hidden by the mosaic in the Niche of the Pallia. The flooring at its base was badly damaged toward the north side, where the excavators had entered through their opening in the Red Wall.

Next, an attempt was made to examine the east side of the Red Wall from the confessional. The work lasted only two nights. On the north side the removal of the walling of the confessional revealed medieval paintings on a wall built in front of wall *g*. To the south more could be seen of the travertine slab in the fill. In the center the mosaic of Christ blocked the way, but the excavators could make out something of the upper niche, *N3*, which had been so

Fig. 4.19 S. Pietro in Vaticano. Gold ex-voto. After *Esplorazioni.*

hypothetical when the first traces of its fenestrella had been discovered on the other side of the Red Wall. The excavators believe that this was the original niche and that N2 was set into it. The section published in the *Esplorazioni,* however, does not support this view. There, N3 is more deeply embedded in the wall than N2, suggesting that N2 was made first and that N3 represents a further hollowing out of the wall. And as always, one must keep in mind that the higher one goes on the Red Wall, the more hypothetical the section becomes. Certainly the part within the medieval altar of Callixtus II could not be examined.[38]

To summarize: in the excavators' opinion, above the tomb there had been a small structure reminiscent of the arrangement made to emphasize some groups of ash urns in pagan cemeteries. This they termed the Memoria.[39] In essence they restored a travertine "table" supported on two small columns and let into a niche in the Red Wall. I have already called attention to the tenuousness of the evidence for this restoration. Sometime after the original Memoria was built, again in the opinion of the original excavators, two walls were added perpendicular to the Red Wall, the graffiti wall *(g)* and its companion to the south *(s).* The excavators believed that wall *g* had to be built as a buttress against the crack in the Red Wall and that wall *s* was added for symmetry. But wall *g,* as noted above, was not a buttress. I prefer to hold that the first monument on the spot consisted solely of the alcove formed by wall *g,* wall *s,* and the part of the Red Wall between them, including the newly made niche N2. The walls of this alcove were covered with a marble veneer. Below the floor of this memorial, covered by the Isidorus slab and reinforced by the marble pieces and the lead sheeting between the two, there was the cavity honoring the resting place of St. Peter and kept accessible by means of a shaft through the flooring through which strips of cloth and other objects such as the gold ex-voto, the coins discovered in the excavation, and finally the pallia themselves could be lowered into contact with the relics. The burial on this spot of the bones venerated as the remains of the apostle did not take place, as we shall see below, until 251.

The Isidorus inscription presented a serious problem for the view of the excavators that

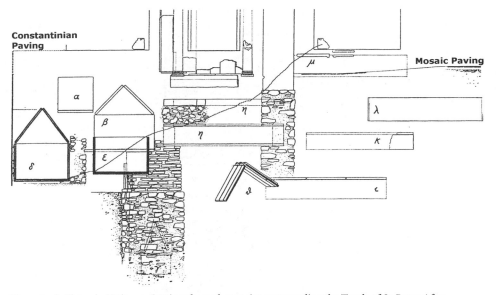

Fig. 4.20 S. Pietro in Vaticano. Section through remains surrounding the Tomb of St. Peter. After *Esplorazioni* with ground line ascending from south to north added following Tolotti in *MEFRA* 91.

their hypothetical Memoria was built in the second century over a preexisting tomb. They too admit that this inscription from a neighboring pagan tomb could not have been reused as a floor slab until possibly as late as Constantinian times.[40] And the second marble slab above it is part of the same flooring meant to seal and protect the tomb.[41] The only alternative to admitting a very late date for the entire group of features connected with the tomb was to suggest that the Isidorus slab had been put in place as a repair to the Memoria well after the time of its original erection.

The further theory, accepted by the excavators, was that the original tomb of the apostle, dating from the time of his martyrdom and thus in place long before the Memoria was created, had left traces in the irregular shape of the base of the Red Wall. But this theory was dealt a serious blow by the results of Prandi's work on the site. The new director of the excavations pointed out that wall *m2* made a poor boundary for the tomb since only the south side of the tomb was protected by it.[42] He surveyed the tomb where his predecessors had envisaged a no-longer-surviving burial running obliquely under the Red Wall and shook his head. "In our opinion," he concluded, "there was never that obliquely placed tomb under the Red Wall."[43] This observation, of course, refers to a normal inhumation for a newly deceased individual. There is ample space in the tomb for a container with bones moved to this location long after their original burial, as I shall argue below.[44]

In the area east of the Red Wall, where the tomb was located (Campo *P* in the excavators' terminology), the ground originally sloped upward both from the south to the north and from

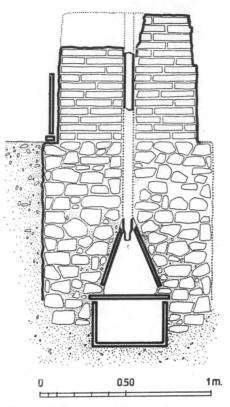

0   0.50   1m.

Fig. 4.21 S. Pietro in Vaticano. Tomb gamma.
After *Esplorazioni*.

the east to the west. As the cemetery of mausolea grew larger, dirt from the excavation needed to build them into the hillside or to clear their foundations was dumped into Campo P, until the slope became less pronounced. In fact, just north of the tomb a terrace wall (of which only meager traces remain) was built to hold back the earth of the slope in that direction, and the Red Wall as well seems to have been a terrace wall protecting the alley (the *clivus*) west of Campo P from the dirt pile. This dump soon became the site of a modest graveyard.[45]

The tombs themselves are anonymous (fig. 4.20). Three of them, gamma, theta, and iota, immediately adjoin the cavity. Gamma was the tomb of a child (fig. 4.21). This tile-lined burial was only 1.26 m long. The tile coffin supported a sloping roof of tile, and from this a tube, through which liquid offerings could be poured, led to the surface. The grave and the tube were enclosed in a masonry structure. This has the appearance of a pagan burial, although an argument can be made for the persistence of liquid offerings among the Christians.[46] The original excavators wish to date this tomb to the first century, but Prandi found a brick stamp of about 120 in its masonry and concluded that all of the graves in Campo P dated after ca. 135.[47] Grave iota also lies partially under the Red Wall.

The burials in the southern part of Campo P took place long after the last loads of earth

Fig. 4.22 S. Pietro in Vaticano. Reconstruction
of the *clivus*. To the right, the Red Wall. After
Esplorazioni.

from tomb building in the neighborhood had been dumped in Campo *P.* These burials, in
large marble coffins, were made under the floor of the Constantinian basilica. They include
tomb beta, which together with epsilon overlies the upper structure of gamma. Tomb beta
appears to have belonged to an ecclesiastic of the Constantinian or post-Constantinian era.
Fragments of gold thread were found in it, and a fragment of an inscription from one of the
pagan masonry mausolea nearby, the Tomb of the Valerii, was used in its construction.

On the western side of the Red Wall there was an alleyway that separated Campo *P* and
its neighbor mausoleum *S* to the south from two mausolea farther west, *R* and *R'* (fig. 4.22).
It led up, by a flight of stairs, to mausoleum *Q*, which begins at the point of the juncture of
the *MR* and *MQ*.[48] The stairway has two sections. The older, with steeper rises to its steps, is
to the north. The foundations below these steps are footed well below the base of the foundations of the Red Wall. The stairway is therefore earlier than the Red Wall.[49] There was a
drain under the clivus (fig. 4.23 center). Among the tiles covering this drain there were five
bearing the same stamp. On it Marcus Aurelius is designated as Caesar, meaning that the tile
was produced before 161, when he became emperor. His wife, however, is already Augusta, a
title she received in 147. The tiles, therefore, were made after 147 and before 161.[50]

The relation of the drain to the clivus and of the clivus to the Red Wall is a matter of great

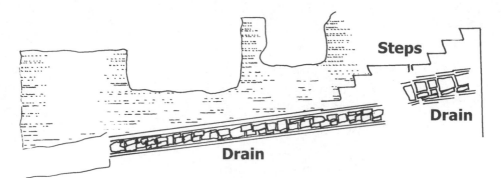

Fig. 4.23 S. Pietro in Vaticano. The *clivus* with stairs and drains. Drawing by A. Walsh after Prandi.

importance for the question of the burial of St. Peter within the confines of Campo *P.* For the authors of the official publication there was no question that the drain dated the clivus, which in turn dated the Red Wall, which in turn dated the wall monument attached to it, which therefore dated the use of the cavity below it to before 160. Each step in this chain of reasoning, however, is open to question. The drain belongs to an early period in the development of this area of the Vatican necropolis. It is interrupted before reaching the southern end of the Red Wall and of mausoleum *R* across the clivus from it.[51] In the opposite direction it breaks off under the steps leading up to *Q.* The date of the tiles covering the clivus drain is simply a terminus post quem for the later buildings. There may, however, be some validity to Prandi's argument that because the dumping of building spoils into Campo *P* belongs after ca. 135, the Red Wall, serving as a retaining wall along the clivus, should belong to the same time.[52] At one time a drain led out of *Q* southward, but this drain is not the beginning of the drain under the clivus. It is larger, it could not connect with the clivus drain (in fact, its floor is at the level of the top of the latter), and it too is broken off, leaving a length of only about 1 m.

But the crucial question is whether the hypothetical Memoria was erected at the same time as the Red Wall. This relation hinges on the niches. The original excavators stated that *N2* is an integral part of the original structure of the Red Wall. The confidence of these scholars, whose opinion must be accorded great weight since they alone (and Prandi) have had the opportunity to examine the evidence at firsthand, was based on very limited observation. *N2* could not be seen from the east, that is, from the Cappella Clementina. Toward the confessional its base retains its marble veneer, and its upper part is covered by the mosaic figure of Christ. The most recent student of the question considers *N2* a later feature and falls back on *N3* as the original marker of the Tomb of St. Peter belonging to the original state of the Red Wall.[53] *N3*, however, is also poorly documented, and, as pointed out already, it is a secondary feature. Initially its existence was little more than a guess, and the observations made subsequently from the east side of the Red Wall are far from complete. More to the point, one must ask with Theodore Klauser why a niche should have been made as part of the original construction in the weakest point of the Red Wall just before it joins *MQ*.[54]

To repeat: almost everything about the Memoria and the tomb below it as reconstructed by the original excavators is conjecture. The uncertainties include not only the upper parts of *N2* and *N3*. As noted above, the travertine slab restored as part of the shelf of the hypothetical Memoria is fragmentary; it was not resting on the column that is supposed to have carried it. The column itself was a damaged piece reused in the wall that succeeded wall *s*. The recess in *N2* meant to receive the shelf exists only as a hypothesis. Of the two columns supposed to have supported the shelf, the northern member of the pair was found loose in the fill with no possible support to stand on. The southern column, as stated, was incorporated in the fabric of the wall that succeeded wall *s*. Its relationship to the piece of travertine observed below it in the fill was never properly observed. On the basis of this evidence, one might advance the theory that the southern column came to its present location only when it was used as building material in the new wall *s*. Its northern counterpart was even more certainly not in its original position as part of a structure, having been found loose in the fill between the Cappella Clementina and the confessional. Although we have become used to the restoration of the Memoria offered by the excavators, it would be well to keep in mind that there may have been nothing of the sort on the spot and that the first and only Memoria consisted of walls *g* and *s* and the marble facing along their inner sides and along the portion of the Red Wall between them, including *N2* (fig. 4.24).

As noted, however, a group of bones was found lying below *N1* on the floor of the cavity. These bones had a period of notoriety, when it seemed that just possibly they might be relics of the apostle. But analysis of the bones, published in 1965, showed that they belonged to three individuals, two men and a woman, as well as to a number of domesticated animals.[55] At this point Prof. Margherita Guarducci, who was engaged in the study of the graffiti found during the excavations, brought forward other bones she claimed represented the relics of the apostle. They were connected with the marble-lined recess in wall *g*. One may recall that this wall was veneered in marble on the side toward the Memoria, but on its far side there were innumerable graffiti scratched on its plaster surface. There were names, but many were simply initials. The deceased were included, identified by the phrase VIVAS IN CHRISTO. The CHRISTO was always written as Chi-Rho joined together, the ligatured abbreviation which appears first in the Constantinian period. Notably missing from the graffiti was any mention of St. Peter. But Peter's name was identified by Father Ferrua on a fragment of plaster of the Red Wall. It is a Greek text which reads PET (followed by an upright staff which could belong to a Greek *R*) EN (followed by another upright staff of an incomplete letter). Prof. Guarducci proposed the restoration PETROS ENESTI, meaning "Peter is within."[56]

Prof. Guarducci entered the orbit of the Vatican excavations in 1953 when she began studying the graffiti of wall *g*. She enjoyed not only her reputation as one of the world's foremost authorities on Greek epigraphy but also easy entrée to both Popes Pius XII and Paul VI. As

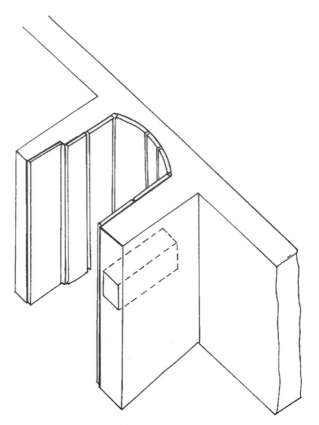

Fig. 4.24 S. Pietro in Vaticano. Reconstruction of the Memoria above the Tomb
of St. Peter. Drawing by A. Walsh.

she has recounted on various occasions, Prof. Guarducci happened one day, while engaged on
her epigraphical work on wall *g,* to express her curiosity concerning the material discovered
in the boxlike cavity in the same wall. A Vatican workman who was nearby overheard her re-
mark and recalled that there should be something else stored away. He soon produced from
the Vatican ossuary a wooden box complete with a ticket specifying that the bones came from
wall *g.*[57] Some, notably Father Ferrua, declared the ticket to be illegible.[58] And the ticket alone
does not clarify the problem because the excavators had found the boxlike cavity almost empty.
The Vatican workman and Prof. Guarducci maintained that Mgr. Kaas was responsible for
having collected the bones and having them deposited in the ossuary without the knowledge
or permission of the excavators. Given such uncertainty surrounding the provenance of the
skeletal remains in the box, it is difficult to accept the claim that among them there are the
mortal remains of St. Peter.[59]

    The problems of the graffiti wall and of the bones from the excavations beneath the confes-
sional of St. Peter's are inextricably linked to the pre-Constantinian remains below the Basilica
Apostolorum (S. Sebastiano, fig. 4.25). The archaeological situation below the basilica on the

Outline of the Basilica

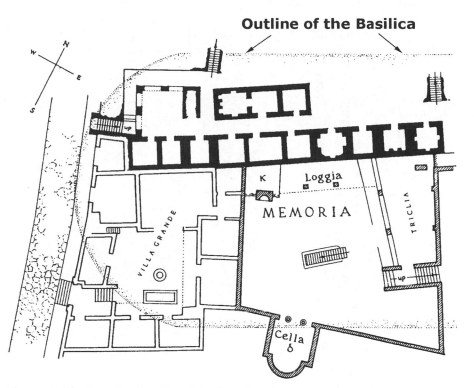

Fig. 4.25 S. Sebastiano. Cemetery beneath basilica. After *CBCR*.

Via Appia is a rich combination of many levels and many uses.[60] Initially, in Republican times, there was a tufa quarry, which later became a burial place. The quarry created a deep pit under what was to become the western part of the basilica. By early imperial times a house (the Villa Grande) had been erected to the west in the area that was later to be largely enclosed by the apse of the basilica. This house remained in use in the third century. Immediately north of the house, beginning in the Julio-Claudian period, there came into being two rows of free-standing tomb chambers flanking a passageway. Entrance to this cemetery was gained by a flight of stairs leading up to it from the road to the west, which also ran along the flank of the villa. The stairs connected first to a small courtyard fronting on the first two tombs. A loculus in its center gave light to another tomb located beneath the floor of the courtyard.[61]

In the area east of the villa and south of the group of tombs just described there was the pit of the tufa quarry. In the second century this was transformed into a cemetery. Three elegant brick façades gave access to burial chambers located at a lower level (fig. 4.26). In the central one beside one of the loculi there is a Greek inscription reading "The two Gordians In. . . ." The final two letters stand for the burial association that owned the tomb, the Innocentii. Two other such inscriptions salute Gordian alone and Pupienus and Balbeinus (Balbinus) together. These names refer to the emperors of the year 238, Gordian I, II, and possibly III, Pupienus,

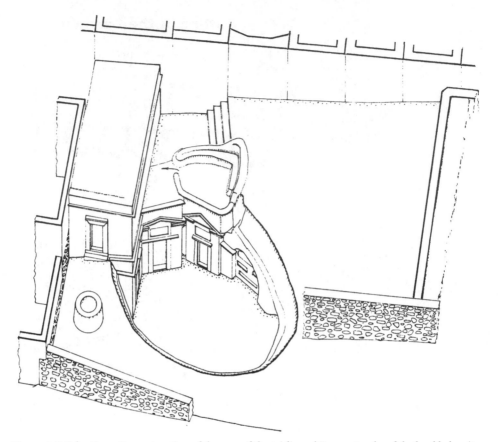

Fig. 4.26 S. Sebastiano. Reconstruction of the area of the *triclia* and Roman tombs of the level below it. After *RAC* 60.

and Balbinus. The tomb, therefore, was in use in that year. At the same time (beginning in the third century) the old galleries of the quarry began to be used for burial. The occupants of the tombs are an interesting group including imperial freedmen of eastern origin. There is no clearly Christian presence among them.[62]

At some time after 238 the pit was filled in, and the three impressive tomb façades disappeared from view. On the new level that was created above the old quarry and cemetery there appeared a motley group of structures (fig. 4.27). It is unclear whether these structures were built for the Christian refrigeria they came to serve or whether originally they had a purely secular purpose. In the center of a paved court a stairway led down to a well. At the east side there was a portico known in the literature as the *triclia* (variant of *trichila*, a summer house).[63] It had a lean-to roof supported by four masonry pillars. It was raised above the level of the courtyard and was furnished with a bench against its back wall. There was a similar, but smaller and less elaborate portico against the outside wall of the complex on the north and a bench in front of it. Beyond it a small niche had been created out of the ruin of a

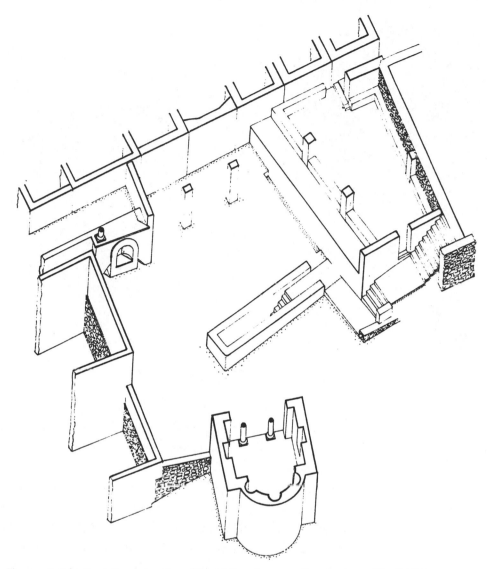

Fig. 4.27 S. Sebastiano. Reconstruction of the *triclia* and surrounding structures. After *RAC* 60.

vaulted substructure originally attached to the villa to the west. Finally, there was an apse-ended isolated chamber entered through a façade with two columns. If not originally a mausoleum, it quickly became one. Four sarcophagi were found in it, and loculi had been cut out of the walls.

It is the first portico, raised above the courtyard on its eastern side, that is the focus of interest in this complex. Its rear wall was decorated with frescoes of birds, animals, and flowers. Scratched into these are 190 graffiti recording Christian refrigeria held here, almost always acknowledging the presence of Saints Peter and Paul (other Christian graffiti were found on its

Fig. 4.28 S. Sebastiano. Reconstruction of the *triclia*. Drawing by A. Walsh after *CBCR*.

stairway leading down to the well, figs. 4.28, 4.29). The messages of the graffiti are spontaneous and touching. On the wall of the triclia Tomius Coelius recorded that he made his refrigerium for Peter and Paul. A man whose name ended in . . . *sinum* asks Peter and Paul to have him in mind while he makes his refrigerium. Sozomenus asks Peter and Paul to remember him and you too who read his wish. Primitivus confesses he is a sinner and asks the saints to come to his aid. And an anonymous Christian prays that Peter and Paul keep us all in mind.[64] To stand before this wall, as one can today below the floor of the Basilica of the Apostles, is to hear the faint voices of those long-departed souls who gave their faith to Christianity in decades sometimes of indifferent tolerance, sometimes of danger, but always with the comfort of the presence of Peter and Paul in this place.

One graffito has a consular date of 260.[65] Obviously, this marks neither the beginning nor the end of the series but has considerable importance in showing that the refrigeria were in full swing on the Via Appia in the third quarter of the third century.

The problem of the double cult of Saint Peter in the Vatican and at San Sebastiano is complicated by the type of evidence found in the two locations. The Tomb of St. Peter that was honored in Constantine's time in the Vatican was reduced over the centuries to that scene of chaos and repeated destructions which greeted the excavators in 1940. The evidence of graffiti in the immediate neighborhood of the grave is controversial. At San Sebastiano there is a

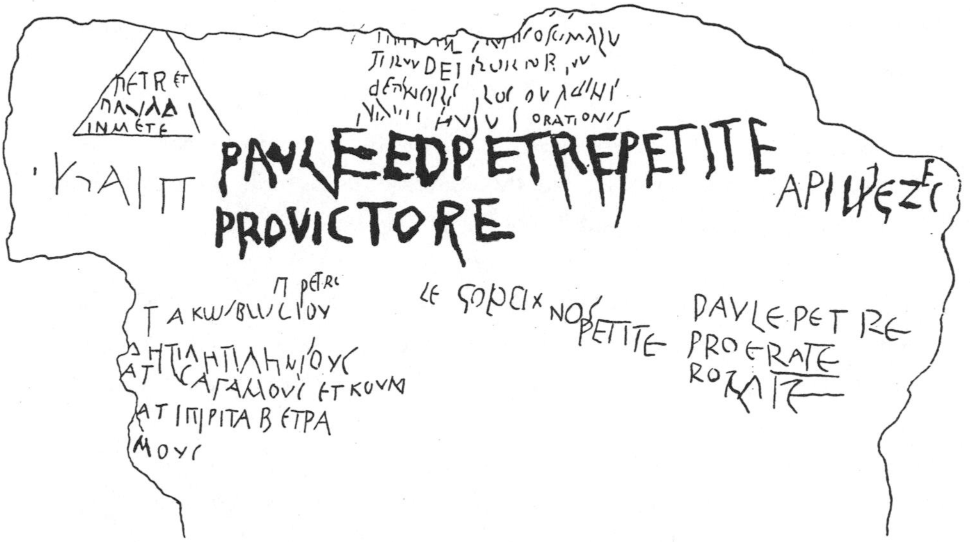

Fig. 4.29 S. Sebastiano. Graffiti from the rear wall of the *triclia*. After *RQ* 29.

chorus of graffiti invoking the apostle and his relics but no evidence of a tomb. Fortunately, there are testimonia that clarify the problem.

The first is the report in the *Liber Pontificalis* in its entry for Pope Cornelius (251–53): "In his time, at the request of a certain matron Lucina, he took up the bodies of the holy apostles Peter and Paul from the catacombs by night; first of all the blessed Lucina took the body of St. Paul and put it on her estate on the Via Ostiensis close to the place where he was beheaded; the blessed bishop Cornelius took the body of St. Peter and put it near the place where he was crucified, among the bodies of the holy bishops at the temple of Apollo on the Mons Aureus, in the Vatican of the palace of Nero on the 29th of June."[66]

This entry in the *Liber Pontificalis* has been curiously neglected. The objections to it were formulated by Paul Styger, the first excavator of the remains below S. Sebastiano.[67] First, the story is legendary and does not fit with historical reality. Second, the date of 251 contradicts the date 258 given elsewhere for the establishment of the observance on the Via Appia. Third, the remains at S. Sebastiano are not as early as the mid–third century. The first and second objections are conjecture. Historical reality and chronology are well served by accepting this account, as we shall see. And the triclia is known to have been in use by the year 260.

The second piece of evidence comes from the Deposition of the Martyrs contained in the Calendar of 354, which was compiled by Furius Dionysius Filocalus, the amanuensis of Pope Damasus (366–84).[68] This calendar lists the feast days of the martyrs and in three cases, including those of Peter and Paul, the year that the feast was instituted: "Month of June, the 29th. Of Peter in the Catacombs, of Paul at the Via Ostiensis, in the consulship of Tuscus and Bassus [that is, 258]."

The notice in the Filocalean calendar is actually an abbreviation of the full entry given in the *Martyrology* of St. Jerome:

June 29th, at Rome the anniversary of the Holy Apostles Peter and Paul, of Peter in the Vatican, Via Aurelia, of Paul on the Via Ostiensis, of both in the catacombs, who suffered under Nero; consulship of Tuscus and Bassus.[69]

Finally, there is the inscription of Pope Damasus originally displayed at the Basilica Apostolorum. Only fragments of the original survive, but the text was copied by a pilgrim of the seventh century and is preserved in a manuscript of the eighth century at Einsiedeln:

> Here you must know there dwelt
> Peter and Paul alike whom by name you seek.
> The East disciples sent them, we say.
> By Christ's blood's power they followed the stars
> And sought ethereal regions where the pious reign.
> Citizens Rome can claim them hers.
> Damasus gives praise to you new among the stars.[70]

To these testimonia pertaining to the third century we must add one further item, the much-debated statement of Gaius (ca. 200) quoted by Eusebius: "I can show you the trophies of the apostles. If you wish go to the Vatican or to the Via Ostiensis, you will find the trophies of those who founded this church."[71]

What these trophies may be has been long a matter of dispute. They may be the tombs of the apostles. They may be monuments to them, and the excavators of the remains below the confessional of St. Peter's were not slow to identify Gaius's trophy with their Memoria. And it is not impossible that the places where they won their crowns of martyrdom were in themselves the trophies of their victory.[72] Other testimonia belong to the elaboration of the traditions concerning St. Peter at a later time.[73]

Discussion of the problem of St. Peter's tomb in the Vatican and his presence on the Via Appia has led to various conclusions. In the time of Pope Callixtus II (1119–24) the testimony of the *Liber Pontificalis* was believed. Sts. Peter and Paul were buried at the catacombs. Their remains were moved by Pope Cornelius.[74] In the fifteenth century, Maffeo Vegio held that the apostles were buried on the Via Appia and only subsequently translated to the Vatican and the Via Ostiensis. He believed that the translation was carried out by Constantine.[75]

Since the appearance of the report on the excavations of the 1940s, there have been four major treatments of the problem in addition: those of Theodor Klauser, Armin von Gerkan, Hans Georg Thümmel, and José Ruysschaert.[76] Before reviewing them, however, it may be useful to recall the position taken by the excavators of the work between 1940 and 1949, in the words of Father Kirschbaum: "We set ourselves the objective of seeking whether the tomb of the apostle lay in the place which had been a centre of honour for centuries and what remains might be discovered and what conclusions drawn. We found the marble-ornamented tomb, erected by the first Christian Emperor. This precious shrine contained, as though it were a hidden relic, the Tropaion of Gaius in the Red Wall. This second-century monument shelters in its bosom traces of the original grave of the apostle."[77]

Von Gerkan was convinced that Peter was buried in the Vatican. But he was not convinced that the burial took place where the Memoria (which he accepts as Gaius's tropaion) was erected. Possibly he lay in a mass grave for the victims of Nero's revenge on the Christians? The Christians were not sure. The Memoria, however, was built to mark the place of Peter's martyrdom. Around the middle of the third century the Christians rifled the area below the Memoria looking for bones but probably did not find what they were looking for. In 258 bones now believed to be those of Peter and Paul were deposited at S. Sebastiano and venerated there until taken back to the new basilicas in the Vatican and on the Via Ostiensis. In the meantime the old Memoria had been repaired with walls *g* and *s* and a marble revetment.[78]

Klauser put forward the "two traditions" theory. The early Christians were divided in their notion of where S. Peter was buried. The Martyrium entry with the date 258 shows this. The tradition of the martyrdom of Peter in Rome is genuine. The reference of Gaius to a tropaion is accurate. But from the mid–third century there was a second tradition centered on the Via Appia. Constantine honored both places. Just where the grave in the Vatican was is unsure. The date 258 presents problems, but it may be interpreted as the date of the first liturgical celebration on the Via Appia. Klauser ruled out any translation hypothesis.[79]

Thümmel believes that the Memoria is much later than the Red Wall but that N3 was part of the wall from the beginning. This marked the tomb. At the Via Appia there was no grave, merely a cult. The grave under the Memoria has been destroyed.[80]

Ruysschaert followed the idea first put forward in modern times by Louis Duchesne: that there was a translation for a period of time of the apostles' remains to the Via Appia that gave rise to the cult there. Ruysschaert saw the damage to and repair of the Memoria in Campo *P* as an indication of the hurried transfer of the bones from the original tomb in the Vatican to the Via Appia under the threat of the Valerian persecution and then of their return to the Vatican.[81]

None of the positions outlined above is in agreement with all of the ancient testimonia. Pope Cornelius's translation of 251 was hardly given consideration except by von Gerkan and Ruysschaert (and before him by Duchesne). But the notice of the *Liber Pontificalis* does make sense in the light of the archaeological evidence. I propose to accept the account of the *Liber Pontificalis* and reconstruct the events as follows. Until 251 the relics that were venerated as those of Saints Peter and Paul rested in graves on the Via Appia. If they were in fact the bones of Saints Peter and Paul, they had come there under the normal provisions of Roman law regarding the bodies of the condemned, to wit, anyone present at the execution who claimed the body could arrange burial at his own convenience.[82] Then Pope Cornelius moved the bodies. Although a persecution had begun, his decision is not likely to have been connected with concern for the safety of the bones. The Christians had no cause to fear the pagans' violating their tombs and stirring up ghosts, but habitual Christian gathering places were best to be avoided. The tradition of the victory won in martyrdom by Peter at the Vatican and Paul by the Ostian highway, and reflected in the boast of Gaius some half century before, was strong enough to give a pope, in a moment of crisis, the inspiration of rallying Christian sentiment around the field of martyrdom of the two apostolic saints. Very possibly Cornelius did not release all the relics to their new graves. In any case, a full-size grave was not required for the disarticulated bones of the apostle at the Vatican. Under the pressure of the persecution and due to Cornelius's death, possibly as a martyr, in 253 the new cults were not inaugurated until some years later, just after the outbreak of the Valerian persecution, which began in 257. The next year, in 258, the Christians, again in need of mutual encouragement, rallied at the Tomb of St. Paul on the Via Ostiensis, at the Tomb of St. Peter in the Vatican, and for both saints at their original resting place, the Via Appia, and this at the very time that Cyprian was calling on the faithful to take up spiritual arms in the face of persecution and fortify themselves with spiritual and heavenly safeguards.[83] The graffito of 260 in the triclia on the Via Appia and the numismatic evidence from the tomb in the Vatican, where coins began to be deposited just at this time, tell the same story. Furthermore, the mass of graffiti in the triclia beneath San Sebastiano is eloquent proof that in the later third century Christians flocked to the celebration there. They would not have done so had not some relics of the apostles remained secretly behind, although the fate of these is uncertain, even that of the supposed skulls of the apostles, whose presence at the Lateran, where they reside today, is not documented before the late eleventh century.[84] The basilica that was raised on the same spot was known, significantly enough, as the Basilica Apostolorum. And Pope Damasus, a half century later, confidently asserted that once the apostles had been lodged there.

Valerian's edict, it is true, barred the Christians from access to their burial grounds.[85] But the grave against the Red Wall in Campo *P* was not in the midst of a Christian graveyard. The same would have been true of St. Paul's grave on the Via Ostiensis. And if the agents of the emperor found gatherings in the triclia at S. Sebastiano, the participants could well have dared them to find any clear sign of a Christian grave. Even though Peter and Paul had been buried nearby—relics of them were possibly still concealed on the spot—and even though the catacombs of San Callisto and Domitilla were at hand, a search for Christian graves would have had little success among the buildings that Richard Krautheimer described as having the appearance of "a rustic trattoria."[86]

At the Vatican what is sure is only that an open enclosure formed by walls *g, s,* and the Red Wall, all appropriately veneered in marble, was set up after 251 and apparently some time after that date. The flooring of this shrine was devised to provide maximum security for what was buried below, and possibly from the beginning there was an opening through it to assist the pious veneration of what were surely believed to be the remains of Saint Peter. The lower marble slab was spolia from a nearby pagan tomb. It is not unlikely that this modest memorial was made only after 312 because the graffiti cut on the surface of the wall *g* uniformly use the Constantinian Chi-Rho. Constantine then encased the tomb made by Pope Cornelius in porphyry and marble, making it the focal point of the martyrium and then of the basilica in the Vatican. In the process a second wall into which a loose column shaft was built took the place of wall *s*. The tomb was violated possibly during the sack of Rome by the Saracens (846) or by the Normans (1084). But some part at least of the precious relics of the Prince of the Apostles was thought to have survived, and lowering of the pallia and brandea[87] through a fenestrella into the cavity below continued long afterwards.

The study of the tomb below the confessional of San Pietro in Vaticano has been clouded by a desire on the part of those engaged in it to document the burial place of the apostle in the Vatican and to document its existence there since the moment of his martyrdom, or, lacking such proof, to document its existence there from the earliest possible time. The alternative hypothesis regarding Peter's burial, that the apostle was initially buried in an unknown grave on the Via Appia and that his bones were only later moved to the Vatican, has had far less appeal. It is the Vatican grave as a physically proven fact that is important because no other evidence will suffice to overcome the opposition of those who, following in the footsteps of Martin Luther, refuse to believe that Peter ever came to Rome.[88] For the Roman Catholic Church only the Resurrection has more historical importance than this because the denial of Peter's presence in Rome is the denial of the supremacy of Rome over all Christian communities. For the Protestant nations no question was more central to their liberation from foreign control of religion.[89] Archaeology cannot settle the so-called Petrine question. It does, however, show how Peter was honored in the third century and how those remains that were venerated as his were employed by Pope Cornelius to sustain the resolve of Christians, threatened by persecution but trusting that Peter and Paul would grant them aid in their time of need.

Notes

CHAPTER I. *Constantine and the Christians*

1. The bronze portrait of Constantine the Great in the Capitoline Museum, illustrated here, is one of three pieces preserved from the original heroic statue. The other fragments are the left hand and a globe surmounted by a spike. It has recently been suggested that the figure was a reworking of the Colossus of Nero that originally stood in the atrium of the Golden House, see Ensoli, "I colossi di bronzo."

2. Namely, Constantius Chlorus and Maximian. Both were dead, Constantius of natural causes in 306, Maximian by suicide, it was said, as a prisoner of Constantine's in 310. Diocletian lived on in retirement until 313, having emerged only briefly in 308 to add his authority to the creation of the reconstructed tetrarchy. Galerius, the fourth partner in the original tetrarchy, died in 310 after suffering a wasting illness that Christian writers took pleasure in seeing as the judgment of God on a persecutor of the faith.

3. The text continues (beneath the foliage), "Sixteen centuries having passed, under the auspices of the Supreme Pontiff Pius X, The Catholic World held a solemn commemoration of the event and enhanced the place by this inscription." The Latin text reads CONSTANTINUS MAGNUS IMPERATOR V KAL NOVEMB A CCCXII HEIC AD SAXA RUBRA DIVINITUS DEBELLATO MAXENTIO VEXILLUM CHRISTI NOMINE INSIGNE IN URBEM INTULIT AEVI FELICIORIS AUCTOR GENERI HUMANO. XVI POST SAECULA AUSPICE PIO X PONTIFICE MAGNO ORBIS CATHOLICUS SOLEMNEM REI COMEMORATIONEM EGIT LOCUM TITULO HONESTAVIT.

4. Burckhardt, *Age of Constantine.*

5. The bibliography is staggering. To cite only a selection of works in English, Barnes, *Constantine and Eusebius;* Jones, *Constantine;* MacMullen, *Constantine;* A. Alföldi, *Conversion.* Among recent additions mention may be made of Pohlsander, *Constantine;* Elliott, *Christianity of Constantine;* Curran, *Pagan City;* and Drake, *Constantine and the Bishops.* Of course the serious student will not neglect the fundamental works in other languages.

6. *Life of Constantine* I, 28–31. Eusebius makes much of the cross-shaped standard, a pole with a cross-piece from which the banner was hung. But such cross-shaped standards were the common form of

battle flags in antiquity. For a coin image of such a Constantinian standard, issued in 327, see Mattingly, *Roman Coins,* pl. LXIII, 7; Bruun, *Constantine* (London, 1966), pls. 18, 19, and for the date p. 572. For a recent, lengthy discussion of the question of the vision, see Leeb, *Konstantin und Christus,* 127–42.

7. Kraft, "Silbermedaillon." For the origin of the ligature, Bruun, *Victorious Signs.*

8. In the words of Bruun, *Constantine,* 61, "The coins give no positive evidence of any conversion but only of a gradual changing attitude toward the old gods." And that change of attitude is far less an announcement of Christian faith than the exaltation of the "heaven-inspired ruler vested with a diadem." See also Bruun, "The Christian Signs."

9. *On the Deaths of the Persecutors,* 44. A Latin panegyrist of the year 310 suggests that Constantine had had a vision of Apollo, *Latin Panegyrics* VII (VI).

10. Neither of these authors can escape the charge of putting rhetoric and devotion to their cause before veracity. Burckhardt's judgment on Eusebius, *Age of Constantine,* 249, is telling: "Constantine's historical memory has suffered the greatest misfortune conceivable . . . he has fallen into the hands of the most objectionable of all eulogists, who has utterly falsified his likeness." On Lactantius we may refer to the word of Paulinus, *Letters,* LVIII, 10, "If only Lactantius, almost a river of Ciceronian eloquence, had been able to uphold our cause with the same facility that he overturns that of our adversaries."

11. *Acts,* 9.

12. Plutarch *Sulla* 9, 6. This is not to deny that instantaneous conversion seized pagans attracted by cults like that of Isis and Christians alike; see Nock, *Conversion.*

13. Livy XXXIX, 8 ff., CIL I ed. 2, 581.

14. Tacitus *Ann.* II, 85, Josephus *Jewish Antiquities,* XVIII, 72, Suetonius *Tiberius* 36.

15. Josephus *Jewish Antiquities,* 18.5, Suetonius *Tiberius* 36, *Claudius,* 25.4, Dio LXVII, 144 ff. Flavia Domitilla and her husband, Flavius Clemens, who suffered under Domitian. Their "Jewish superstitions" may, in fact, have been Christian.

16. The pagans caricatured Christ by giving him the head of an ass, as we see in the graffito preserved from the Palatine palace in Rome, Testini, *Archeologia Christiana,* fig. 1. The taunt is mentioned by Tertullian *Apologetic* 116, 11.

17. Tacitus *Ann.* XV, 44 and Suetonius *Nero,* 16, 38–39.

18. *Letters* X, 96, and Trajan's rescript 97.

19. Lyons: *The Martyrs of Lyons* and Eusebius *Ecclesiastical History,* V, 1–3, Polycarp *The Martyrdom of Polycarp,* and Eusebius *Ecclesiastical History,* IV, 14, 10.

20. Isaiah 64, 4.

21. Romans 8, 18.

22. Cyprian *Letters,* LV (LVIII), 9, *http://www.ccel.org/fathers2/ANF-05/anf05–80.htm#P5796_1806406. Christian Classic Ethereal Library.*

23. *The Passing of Peregrinus.* Lucian's Christians support their own in prison, even to the extent of bribing the guards for permission to share their confinement through the night, just as in *The Martyrdom of Saints Perpetua and Felicitas.*

24. Celsus from Origen *Against Celsus* and Porphyry from the *Apocriticus* of Macarius Magnus.

25. *To the Nations,* 1, *http://www.ccel.org/fathers2/ANF-03/anf03–15.htm#P1202_489126, Christian Classic Ethereal Library.*

26. See Osborn, "Apologists."

27. For the question of burial, see Bodel, *Dealing with the Dead,* 126–51. The study of the human remains from Roman cemeteries of the empire is just beginning. An important first step in this direction is represented by Catalano, Minozzi, and Pantano, "Le necropoli romane," 127–37. These studies of seven cemeteries occupied by people who were at least able to afford a tomb shows a rather early age at death (between thirty and forty years of age), somewhat high juvenile mortality, and evidence of heavy work performed by both men and women.

28. The διδάσκαλοι and, more colorful still, the ἐθελοδιδάσκαλοι, Hermas 22.

29. *On the testimony of the soul*, 1, *http://www.ccel.org/fathers2/ANF-03/anf03–20.htm#P2512_816125. Christian Classic Ethereal Library.*

30. *On the True Doctrine*, trans. R. J. Hoffman, 73.

31. Chap. 17. For the nature of late antique paganism, its syncretism, the intrusive eastern cults, and the ascendancy of astrology there is no better short account than that given by Burckhardt, *Age of Constantine*, chaps. 2, 4, 5.

32. Eusebius *Ecclesiastical History*, VI, 43, 11.

33. *Apology* 39.

34. Ibid., 43.

35. "An independent and increasing state in the heart of the Roman empire," Gibbon, *Decline and Fall*, chap. 15. On the economic challenge of Christianity, see Mazzarino, *L'impero romano*, 2:451–558.

36. *On the Lapsed*, 6. *http://www.ccel.org/fathers2/ANF-05/anf05–113.htm#P7009_2277176 Christian Classic Ethereal Library.*

37. Ep. 52. Cf. the same charges in the letter of Pope Cornelius in the Cyprian collection no. 50.

38. *Elenchos against all heresies* or *Philosophoumena*; on its authorship, see P. Nautin, *Encyclopedia of the Early Church*, 1:383–85, s.v. "Hippolytus."

39. *Elenchos against all heresies*. IX, 6. *http://www.ccel.org/fathers2/ANF-05/anf05–13.htm#P2186_684202 Christian Classic Ethereal Library.*

40. The situation is complicated by the fact that Callixtus was faced with an antipope, that same Hippolytus to whom the *Elenchos against all heresies* is often attributed, and that insults were flying in all directions at the time. The activities of Paul of Samasota, originally a financial official in the administration of Queen Zenobia and then bishop of Antioch who enriched himself through extortion, belong to a somewhat later period (he was convicted of heresy by a church council in 268), Eusebius *Ecclesiastical History*, VII, 30, 6 ff.

41. *Ecclesiastical History*, VII, 30, 19.

42. Kraeling, *Dura Europos*.

43. On the period, see now Southern, *Roman Empire*.

44. See Syme, *Historia Augusta*.

45. The Christians had long been accused of being the cause of any calamity, Tatian, *Address to the Greeks*, 9. For this and the subsequent persecution of Valerian, see Selinger, *Persecutions*.

46. Eusebius's explanation that Decius acted to spite his predecessor Philip the Arab could make sense only if one believes that Philip was a Christian or quasi-Christian himself, the evidence for which comes only from the tale of Philip and his empress Otacilia Severa forced to do public penance by the bishop of Antioch, Eusebius *Ecclesiastical History*, VI, 34.

47. Eusebius *Ecclesiastical History*, VII, 10, 6–9.

48. Ibid., VII, 10, and Cyprian *Letters*, 77–81.

49. Eusebius *Ecclesiastical History*, VII, 10, 4. quoting a Roman source. The Greek for Macrinus's office is vague, ἐπὶ τῶν καθόλου λόγων, a translation of the Latin *a rationibus*.

50. *Letters*, 81.

51. Harl, *Coinage*, 313–39. The Antoninianus was initially a coin worth two denarii.

52. Rostovtseff, *Social and Economic History*, 449.

53. Lactantius *On the Death of the Persecutors*, 11.

54. Ibid., 12.

55. In the tetrarchy there were two major rulers (Augusti) and two lieutenants (Caesares).

56. See the discussions of Sordi, *The Christians*, chap. 8, and Williams, *Diocletian*, chap. 13.

57. See Corcoran, *Empire of the Tetrarchs*, 349–53.

58. The following account depends on Wissowa, *Religion und Kultus*, 410–90. For the continued importance of the emperors' role as priests in the later empire, see Gordon, "Veil of Power."

59. II, 29, 1. For Zosimus, Constantine is the darkly superstitious tyrant whose conversion to Christianity was only a last resort when the pagan priests refused him purification for the murders of Fausta and Crispus, his wife and his son by a previous marriage. The same accusation against Constantine is implicit in the emperor Julian's *Symposium,* trans. W. C. Wright, Loeb Library, 2:413, a work written in 361.

60. It is far from certain that he neglected to make the proper sacrifices on the Capitol on this occasion, Zosimus II, 29, 5. See the commentary in *Zosimus,* ed. Ridley, 157. The motif of neglected sacrifice was a standard motive of propaganda, Curran, *Pagan City,* 74–75.

61. Turner, *Gallant Gentlemen,* 85.

62. It was the art historian Richard Krautheimer who understood Constantine and the demands of his position better than most; see his *Three Christian Capitals,* chap. 1. For the background of ceremony in the early and high empire, see A. Alföldi, "Zeremonials," 1–118.

63. "Ille quasi Majestatis Tuae comes et socius," Latin *Panegyric* VIII, 14, of the year 311. For the relation of Constantine to the pagan cults, see the masterful treatment of Maurice, *Numismatique Constantinienne* 2:xxi–xciii, and more recently Leeb, *Konstantin und Christus,* 9–28.

64. M. R. Alföldi, *Goldprägung,* ca. 118.

65. *Chronicon Paschal,* Monumenta Germaniae Historiae IX, Chron. Min. I, p. 233. The column still stands today, Muller-Werner, *Istanbul,* 256–57.

66. Αὐτοκράτωρ ἰσαπόστολος, Zonaras XIII, 4, 20, for the tomb Eusebius *Life of Constantine,* IV, 60, and for the remains, Dark and Özgümïs, *New Evidence.*

67. Athanasius *Letter on the Decrees* 19. Constantine was hardly a theologian despite the fact that he enjoyed subjecting his court to tedious expositions of the Christian religion as he understood it. In these debates, he "was quite beyond his depth" (MacMullen, *Constantine,* 169).

68. SOLI COMITI AVGN, M. R. Alföldi, "Sol Comes," 10–16.

69. Eusebius *Life of Constantine,* IV, 24. ἐγὼ δὲ τῶν ἐκτὸς ὑπὸ θεοῦ καθιστάμενος ἐπίσκοπος. "ὑπὸ θεοῦ καθιστάμενος" I take to be a Eusebian gloss.

70. On Constantine's favor of the Christian clergy, see Salzman, "Conversion," who comments, "Granting exemptions from public service to Christian clergy insured that their public and social status would, at least, be equivalent to that of the pagan priests."

71. *Life of Constantine,* II, 47–50, IV, 25. Measures against the haruspices were directed against the private use of such informants. One must treat the documents cited by Eusebius with caution because they are never free from suspicion that they may be forgeries. And one must not be influenced unduly in his estimate of Constantine by phrases extolling Christianity and debasing paganism that may have been interpolated by its editors into the text of the *Codex Theodosianus,* for example, the redundant "sanctissimae legi" at XVI, 2, 5, the unnecessary "sanctissima" at XVI, 2, 4. The same is true, only more so, for the Constantinian citations of the *Corpus Juris Civilis.*

72. At Hispellum, CIL XI, 5283.

73. On Maxentius's buildings, see Cullhed, *Conservator Urbis Suae,* 50–60.

74. A recent attempt to make the baths a Constantinian initiative, Curran, *Pagan City,* 85, does not take account of the fact that brick stamps are of tetrarchic date, Steinby, "L'industria laterizia," esp. 142.

75. This too may have been a reworked image of Maxentius, see F. Coarelli in LTUR, s.v. "Basilica Nova." On the basilica, Kultermann, *Maxentius-Basilika.* The Circus Maximus was restored, Aur. Vic., 40.

76. See Barnes, *New Empire,* 68–76; also Bruun, *Studies.*

CHAPTER II. *The Arches*

1. The most important element of any Roman triumphal arch is the dedicatory inscription. In fact a Roman commemorative arch, potent assurance of favorable omens in its form alone, could have dispensed with sculpture, but not with a direct commemorative statement. See my comments in "Arch of Titus." Despite criticism from various quarters I find Holland, *Janus and the Arch,* a fully convincing treatment of the original significance of these structures as markers of places of dangerous

passage (over water particularly) where favorable omens were made permanent by a Janus (the god who was himself an arch). The Arch of Constantine remains one of those intensively studied but imperfectly published monuments. The arch was 70 Roman feet high and approximately 85 Roman feet wide, P. Cicerchia "Considerzioni metrologiche sull'arco," in Conforto and Melucco Vaccaro, *Adriano e Costantino,* 61–77. Giuliani, "L'Arco di Costantino come documento storico," gives height as 21 m., width 25.7 m., and length on the short sides 7.4 m.

2. "Imp. Caes. Fl. Constantino Maximo / P.P. Augusto S. P. Q R. / quod instinctu divinitatis mentis / magnitudine cum exercitu suo, tam de tyranno quam de omni eius / factione uno tempore iustis / rem publicam ultus est armis arcum triumphis insignem dicavit." CIL VI pars VIII, II, 1139 and 3145, p. 3778, 4328. The date is given by the inscriptions of the north façade VOTIS X VOTIS XX and on the south SIC X SIC XX, referring to Constantine's self-promoted entry into the tetrarchy in 305, which would have marked its tenth anniversary in 315 together with the good wishes for the next decade of his rule. For the relative bibliography, see LTUR s.v. and de Maria, *Gli archi onorari,* n. 98. Coins, the latest an issue of Licinius of 312, were found during the recent restoration of the arch in the mortar of Constantinian repairs to the western passageway of the arch; B. Davide, "I rinvenimenti monetali," in Conforto and Melucco Vaccaro, *Adriano e Costantino,* 58–60.

3. There are still elements of the porphyry slabs remaining in place. The frieze above the freestanding columns is blank today and has been ever since the first modern drawings of the arch were made. But only the frieze backers are in place. It is more likely that the missing frieze itself was another band of colored marble than that it carried sculpture. Colored stone was prized in medieval building and while the sculpture of the arch has remained intact, the porphyry revetment was robbed. So probably the frieze, unless, of course, the stonework intended for it was never put in place. The westernmost column of the north front is a restoration. The pilasters behind the columns were of *giallo antico* marble too. Only one of them survives, the easternmost pilaster of the north front. The others have been restored in marble.

4. For the Arcus Novus, see LTUR s.v. On the phenomenon with specific regard to Constantine, Kinney, *Spolia;* Wohl, *Spolia.* Another arch on the Via Flaminia decorated with spolia is usually placed after Constantine, but E. La Rocca in La Rocca, ed., *Rilievi storici,* attributes it to Gallienus, and Torelli, *Arco di Portogallo,* argues for Aurelian.

5. Calza, *Problema;* Rohmann, *Konstantinsbogen;* and Smith, *Licinius I* prefer Licinius.

6. Compare EAA s.v. "Neoatticismo."

7. Meyer, *Antinoos,* 131 (VI, 7) for discussion. The same identification has been made for the figure leading the horse in the departure scene, Giuliani, *L'arco di Costantino,* text to fig. 9.

8. Most recently by Grenier and Coarelli, *La tombe d'Antinoüs,* and Giuliana Calcani "La serie dei tondi da Adriano a Costantino," in Conforto and Melucco Vaccaro, *Adriano e Costantino,* 78–102. For interpretation as part of a season cycle, see Calcani, *I tondi adrianei,* with ample bibliography of interpretive discussions.

9. He is identified as Tiberius Claudius Pompeianus, general in the wars which occupied Marcus on the Danubian frontier.

10. The pairing of reliefs with similar subjects in this series might suggest that both Constantine and Licinius were represented as protagonists, Coarelli in LTUR 1:89, but this would be mere speculation.

11. LTUR s.v.

12. Inscription, CIL VI, pars VIII, 1014, cf. 31225, p. 842, 3777, 4316. Reliefs, Ryberg, *Panel Reliefs,* and LTUR s.v. "Arcus Marci Aureli."

13. P. Mingazzini, "L'arco Marcaurelio."

14. Amelung, *Vaticanisches Museum,* nn. 9 and 127. Restoration of the figures on the arch in the Forum of Trajan is favored most recently by Packer, *Forum of Trajan.* The head of the barbarians of the arch are modern restorations as is one of the figures of the south front, Pensabene and Panella, "Riempiego," figs. 29 and 30.

15. Maischberger, *Marmor in Rome.* For the Cancelleria Reliefs, see Magi, *I rilievi flavi.*
16. Pensabene and Panella, *Arco di Costantino.*
17. Pallottino, "Il grande fregio."
18. Gauer, "Dakerdenkmal," esp. 336. As the title suggests Gauer sees the frieze as a monument to Domitian's, rather than Trajan's, Dacian war.
19. Packer, *Forum of Trajan,* 445. He believes that the frieze could have adorned the attic of the east colonnade of the Basilica Ulpia facing the Column of Trajan.
20. Forum of Peace, Pallottino, "Il grande fregio," 39. Forum Julium, Gauer, "Dakerdenkmal." For a summary of views on the subject, S. Stucchi "Tantis virtutibus, l'area della colonna nella concezione generale del Foro di Traiano," *AC* 41 (1989): 237–92, esp. 263 n. 95.
21. Vermeule, *Roman Imperial Art,* chap. 6; Liverani, "Il monumento."
22. Holloway, "Spolia."
23. See Camp, *Athens.*
24. L'Orange and von Gerkan, *Bildschmuck.*
25. L'Orange and von Gerkan's work was repeated in the context of a corpus of historical reliefs in Rome by Koeppel, "Historischen Reliefs."
26. Similar use of the leftover space beyond the end columns occurs on both façades.
27. For the interpretation of the troops and their distinguishing equipment, see L'Orange and von Gerkan, *Bildschmuck,* 46.
28. I fail to see that Eusebius's comparison of Constantine's victory with the destruction of Pharaoh's army in the Red Sea, *Ecclesiastical History* IX, 9, 8, written in the 330s, is of any use in interpreting the scene of the arch as an implicit presentation of Constantine as Moses, as McCormick, *Art and Ceremony,* 38.
29. Constantine's victory in a civil war did not entitle him to a triumph in the strict sense of the term, and thus he avoided the two-wheeled triumphal car and the attendant holding the triumphator's crown over his head.
30. I have seen an almost identical system in use for settling accounts with paperboys in Providence, R.I., in the mid-1970s.
31. Berenson, *Arch of Constantine,* 38–39. Dissatisfaction with the Constantinian sculpture of the arch is as old as the sixteenth century, Vasari, *Le vite,* 224; Baldassare Castiglione, *Le Lettere,* no. 409 to Pope Leo X, 1519.
32. Lietzmann, "Spätantike."
33. The seminal study is that of Rodenwaldt, "Kunstströmung," also "Römische Reliefs." This viewpoint was developed in a Marxist framework by R. Bianchi Bandinelli in various studies and at the end of his career in *La fine dell' arte antica,* 73–83. Bianchi Bandinelli saw the fusion of provincial art, favored by the tetrarchs and their sons, and the plebeian art of Rome leading directly to the art of the Middle Ages. The influential work of A. Riegl, *Spätrömische Kunstindustrie,* put forward the theory of a changing approach to the visual field in the artistic reprojection of space in late antique art and found evidence of this phenomenon on the Arch of Constantine, 90–94. For a modern, balanced view of the problem, see Elsner, *Art and the Roman Viewer.*
34. For both bibliography, Torelli in LTUR s.v. "Arcus Constantini."
35. L'Orange, *Art Forms,* 94.
36. Much of this will depend on important recent work, Pensabene and Panella, *Arco di Costantino,* and Conforto and Melucco Vaccaro, *Adriano e Costantino,* both with full bibliography. Special note should be taken of the twin contributions of these authors to *RendPont* 66 (1993–94), Melucco Vaccaro and Ferroni, "Chi costruì?" and Pensabene and Panella, "Riempiego," as well as Melucco Vaccaro, "L'arco dedicato a Costantino."
37. Conforto and Melucco Vaccaro, *Adriano e Costantino,* claim that these sculptures were carved after the erection of the structure, but this does not mean that they are Constantine's. We may agree with her

and her coauthors that the tondos were installed in the first stage of construction of the arch, although dating that first stage of construction to Maxentius rather than Hadrian.

38. Giuliano, "L'Arco di Costantino come documento storico," 442, mentions en passant and without further reference a fragment of an inscription honoring Romulus the son of Maxentius used in the attic.

39. On the north front above the tondos, VOTIS X to the left and VOTIS XX to the right; on the south front in the same position SIC X to the left and SIC XX to the right; within the main passage on one side LIBERATORI URBIS and on the other FUNDATORI QUIETIS.

40. Magi, "Coronamento."

41. Cirone, "I risultati." The deposits (US 66 and 81) result from efforts to recover building material from even earlier structures on the site connected with the Domus Aurea of Nero. A third deposit (US 86), found in contact with the foundation of the south end of the east side of the central passage of the arch, produced fewer sherds but tells the same story.

42. Melucco Vaccaro and Ferroni, "Chi costruì?" 49–52, suggest that this hypothetical monument could have been an arch of Domitian's.

43. S. Zeggio, "La realizzazione delle fondazioni," in Pensabene and Panella, *Arco di Costantino,* 117–13.

44. Thus Constantine had the Senate usurp the arch as he did other buildings of Maxentius. So much we learn from Aurelius Victor, *On the Caesars* XL, 26–27, "Adhuc cuncta opera quae magnifice construxerat [i.e., Maxentius] urbis fanum atque basilicam Flavii [i.e., Constantine] meritis patres sacravere." The motive for the erection of the arch by Maxentius is uncertain; his victory over the revolt in North Africa, Zosimus II, 14, comes too late (311). The theory that Maxentius was the builder of the arch was advanced in a paper by S. E. Knudsen presented to the 94th meeting of the Archaeological Institute of America in 1992, Knudsen, "Arch of Constantine." In previous papers at the same annual meetings Knudsen announced her opinion that the reliefs of the column podia of the north and south façades and the small Constantinian frieze were also spolia, also "Arch of Constantine." Only these short summaries of this work are available at present.

45. As have often been attributed to it. For the appropriate bibliography, see Coarelli in LTUR 1:90. Most recently Elsner, "Culture of Spolia."

46. There are two major studies of the arch, that of Töbelmann, *Malborghetto,* and Messineo, *Malborghetto.*

47. *On the Deaths of the Persecutors,* 44.

48. As in both the Arch of Constantine and the Quadrifrons of the Forum Boarium, on which see below.

49. CIL XV, 1, 1564, Messineo, *Malborghetto,* 57.

50. The drawing of Giuliano da Sangallo was made before 1491, when the arch had been a farmstead for some centuries and would long before have lost its decorative panels and sculpture. These circumstances, together with Sangallo's reconstruction of a conical structure above the arch, suggest that the ornament and other elements of his drawing are imaginary, cf. Hülsen, *Giuliano da Sangallo,* fo. 36v.

51. Confirmed by investigations made in 1993, Tedone, "Roma, Arco di Giano." I am grateful to Prof. L. Lancaster for calling my attention to this reference. On the construction in general, see Pensabene and Pannela, "Riempiego II."

52. Richardson, *New Topographical Dictionary,* s.v., holds that the niches were too shallow for sculpture.

53. In Töbelmann, *Römische Gebälke,* 132, fig. 104, on the model of L'Aiguille at Vienne in France, for which Crema, *Architettura romana,* fig. 789.

54. Lugli, *Itinerario.*

55. In LTUR 3:94.

CHAPTER III. *Basilicas, Baptistry, and Burial*

1. For the foundation, LP XXXIII (Duchesne 1:172–74), *CBCR* 5:9–10. The estates whose income was settled on the church by Constantine, LP cit., were all situated in Rome or in its neighborhood or in Campania, which proves that the foundation was made early in his reign. Later foundations enjoyed

incomes from lands captured on the defeat of Licinius in 324. The Lateran palace, however, remained in private, nonimperial hands for some time after 312. Therefore, the church should really be referred to as the Basilica Constantini juxta Lateranensem, Liverani, "Aedes Laterani."

2. Colli, "Il palazzo sessoriano."

3. For the rest of his reign Constantine had no qualms about managing church affairs, but in 312 he also had no intention of spending more than was necessary on a new church for the Christian bishop or on a martyrium for St. Peter in the Vatican. Despite the parade of donations ticked off by the *Liber Pontificalis* the construction costs of these buildings were held to a minimum. The Christians could do without the cement vaults that covered Maxentius's unfinished baths and basilica on the Forum. A basic hall and a roof supported on wooden beams would suffice.

4. *CBCR* 5:24 ff. and fig. 57. The length must be estimated because the exact position of the façade is unknown. The width measurement is also an approximation because the exact measurement, taken on the foundations, is some 25 cm. wider than 180 Roman feet, but a foundation may be expected to project beyond the upper wall it carried, *CBCR* 5:29 ff. For a recent summary, see also de Blaauw, *Cultus et Décor,* 109–16.

5. Shown in the fresco of the interior of the church in S. Martino ai Monti, which attempts to render it as it was before Borromini's transformation, *CBCR* 5, fig. 77.

6. *CBCR* 5, figs. 68, 69.

7. LP XXXIII (Duchesne 1:172). A hypothetical restoration of the fastigium of the Constantinian basilica was made by Nilgen, "Fastigium."

8. An *ama* is a large vessel.

9. *Encyclopedia of the Early Church,* 1:494–503, s.v. "liturgy."

10. *CBCR* 5:87.

11. Hoffmann, "Die Fassade."

12. Kraeling, *Dura Europos,* 1967. For the so-called titulus churches of Rome, those bearing names of donors postulated to have established churches already in the third century, see Saxer, "Charles Pietrí" with references to the appropriate passages of Pietrí, *Roma Christiana.*

13. *CBCR* 1:293–300.

14. *CBCR* 1:278.

15. Both of these latter images would have been protection against the evil eye (see Elworthy, *The Evil Eye*). The early Christians, like so many of their modern spiritual progeny, were not above seeking protection outside of strictly Christian imagery against such a potent danger as that of the evil eye, although the Christian fish was also pressed into service for the same purpose. Dölger, *Ichthys,* 239–58. There are other so-called decorative paintings (which may also have apotropaic significance) on the walls of the anteroom and of the corridor and the exterior wall to the rear of the house.

16. Brenk, "Microstoria."

17. *CBCR* 1:300–03.

18. *CBCR* 1:284–85.

19. *CBCR* 1:285.

20. Brenk, "Microstoria."

21. *CBCR* 1:296. The account given here is simplified and does not go into the details of various other modifications of the houses.

22. So Duchesne on LP p. cvii, Favez, "L'invention de la Croix."

23. Homilies in PG LXXVII, p. 469, 688, 766.

24. LP XXXIII (Duchesne 1:179). On such confusion in the LP, see Caspar, *Papsttum,* 126, and Duchesne on LP I, p. cxlix ff. Krautheimer, *CBCR* 1:167 inclines toward this view.

25. *CBCR* 1:165–95.

26. *CBCR* 1:64–69; Sapelli, "Basilica di Giunio Basso."

27. CIL VIII, pars VI, 41341.

28. CIL VI 1737, cf. p. 3173, 4747.

29. *CBCR* 4:1–36.

30. For other suggestions as to date, see *CBCR* 1:133.

31. The evidence comes from a slave collar inscribed "Victori acolito a(d) Dominicu(m) Clementis" (CIL XV no. 7192) of the first half of the fourth century discovered in the excavations under the church.

32. Such churches are rare in Rome although known in northern Italy and north of the Alps, see *CBCR* 1:160 n. 3.

33. An exception, of course, is Santa Balbina, but there is no evidence of this being a church until 595, *CBCR* 1:83.

34. The side aisles of S. Giovanni in Laterano and S. Pietro in Vaticano have been interpreted already in relation to the segregation of the catechumens by Carpiceci and Krautheimer, "Nuovi Dati 1996," esp. 9–11.

35. Carpiceci and Krautheimer, "Nuovi Dati 1996," 79 n. 19. Carpiceci and Krautheimer believe there were curtains in the nave of the Lateran and that S. Pietro must have been similarly provided. Alexander, "Studies," arguing from Eusebius *Ecclesiastical History* X, 4, 63, suggests that the catechumens remained in the church atrium. However, in the passage of Eusebius those in the atrium are there throughout the service. They do not withdraw from the church to the atrium at the end of the Mass of the Catechumens.

36. And possibly from S. Pudenziana, where the church is the hall of what had been a bath, *CBCR* 3:299. There is no guarantee that the large hall adjoining S. Martino ai Monti was used for Christian purposes before about 500, ibid., p. 123.

37. On the history of the apse, see Krautheimer's remarks in *CBCR* 1:92 n. 1.

38. As Krautheimer comments in "Building Program," *basilica* simply means large hall. The desire to see overt references to preexisting pagan buildings and equally overt architectural expressionism is, however, strong. See, for example, Pensabene, "Riempiego e nuove mode." For earlier discussions of the problem, see Süssenback, *Christuskult,* and now Lorenz, "Überlegungen."

39. For baptism at Rome in the fourth century, see Pietrí, *Roma Christiana,* 1:106–11.

40. "Il battistero." For earlier work, see Ristow, *Baptisterien,* nos. 404 and 998.

41. *Liber Pontificalis,* 172–75.

42. "As the hart panteth after the water brook, so panteth my soul after thee, O God." Psalm 42, 1. This reference was pointed out to me by my learned wife.

43. The place of this design in early Christian architecture is explored by Brandt, "Il battistero lateranese."

44. In addition to the treatment in *CBCR* 5, see Carpiceci and Krautheimer, "Nuovi Dati." There is a recent general summary of uncertain aspects in the restoration of the basilica in de Blaauw, *Cultus et Décor,* 451–92.

45. See chapter 4.

46. The adjoining rotunda, S. Petronilla, was built following the erection of the church and was entered from the south transept.

47. The best of the various efforts of the sort, although "unreliable in detail, impossible in proportion and awkward in execution," Krautheimer, *CBCR* 5:221.

48. *CBCR* 5:238, fig. 219.

49. Although Krautheimer hazards 33⅓ Roman feet for the exterior aisles and 31 Roman feet for the inner aisles, *CBCR* 5:240.

50. Slightly different measurements are suggested by Arbeiter, *Alt-St. Peter.*

51. Carpiceci and Krautheimer, "Nuovi Dati 1995," 6, 7.

52. See the circulation pattern suggested by Carpiceci and Krautheimer, "Nuovi Dati 1995," p. 10, fig. 12. The reconstruction of Carpiceci and Krautheimer will certainly become standard. For earlier efforts, see Arbeiter, *Alt-S. Peter,* chap. 4.

53. For full discussion of the evidence, see below.

54. In turn, it was covered by an elaborate baldacchino from the center of which a great lamp was suspended, see chap. IV, figs. 4.8, 4.9. For the covering of the monument and its relation to the apse of the basilica, see below figs. 4.9, 4.10.

55. Of the five column shafts recovered during the excavations in the basilica two cannot be placed with certainty; three gray granite shafts are attributed by Krautheimer to the columns that were placed in the entrances to the transept from the nave, *CBCR* 5:200–01, 253.

56. *CBCR* 5:171–72. "Quod duce Te Mundus surrexit in astra triumphans hanc Constantinus victor Tibi condidit aulam" (capitalization supplied).

57. Found in the *Sylloge Einsiedelensis, CBCR* 5:172. "Iustitiae sedis fidei domus aula pudoris haec est quam cernis. Pietas quam possidet omnis quae Patris et Fili virtutibus incluta gaudet Auctoremque suum Genitoris laudibus aequat" (capitalization and punctuation supplied).

58. See Ruysschaert, "Le tableau Mariotti."

59. LP XXXIII (Duchesne 1:176). "Constantinus Augustus et Helena Augusta hanc domum regalem simili fulgore corruscans aula circumdat."

60. Ibid.

61. The hiatus in the series of altars dedicated in the nearby shrine of the Mother of the Gods after 319 has suggested this date for the beginning of work on the basilica but hardly constitutes proof, see *CBCR* 5:171.

62. Carpiceci and Krautheimer, "Nuovi Dati 1996," 18. Doubts persist, however, concerning the Constantinian date, e.g., Guyon, *Deux lauriers,* 250, and more recently Bowersock, "Peter and Constantine."

63. This building measures 51.45 × 23.30 m. It has two aisles and an apse. See Bauer et al., "Untersuchungen," and Bauer and Heinzelmann, "Bishop's Church."

64. Carpiceci and Krautheimer "Nuovi Dati 1996," 64.

65. It was only the occasional seat of papal ceremonies. And the papal residence did not adjoin it as it does today, Pietrí, *Roma Christiana,* 1:114–15.

66. Corinthians 1, 15, 51–52.

67. Apocalypse 6, 9. H. Delehaye, *Les origines,* and Testini, *Archeologia Christiana,* 125–39.

68. "Christus in martyre est," Tertullian *On Modesty,* 22.

69. Delehaye, *Les origines,* 142–48.

70. Μάρτυρες γοῦν ἐκαλοῦντο καὶ διάκονοί τινες καὶ πρέσβεις τῶν αἰτήσεων παρὰ τῶν θεῶν, observed the fourth-century pagan Eunapius a propos of the Christian devotion to the cult of the martyrs in *Lives of the Philosophers and Sophists,* 472. The emperor Julian also noted the contemporary Christian veneration of tombs, *Against the Galilaeans,* 335C.

71. "Brandea," cf. Testini, *Archeologia Christiana,* 232.

72. Schneider, *Refrigerium;* Parrot, *Refrigerium.*

73. Testini, *Archeologia Christiana,* 141.

74. Augustine *Letters* XXIX, 11, "in abundantia epularum et ebrietate."

75. Ibid., 10, "De basilica beati apostoli Petri quotidianae vinolentiae proferebantur exempla."

76. Paulinus *Letters* 13, 11.

77. For the circumstances of the creation of the tomb, see below.

78. LP XXXIII (Duchesne 1:178).

79. See Krautheimer's note in *CBCR* 5:97.

80. The measurements from surveys of the church before 1823 are not in full agreement, but the dimensions of the building can be made out approximately. The nave was 300 Roman feet in length. Adding the width of the façade foundations and those of the transept, one obtains a total length of 310 Roman feet. Also adding the depth of the transept brings the total length to 400 Roman feet. Such round figures depend, of course, on including the width of the foundations in the measurement. The width of the nave if measured foundation wall to foundation wall is 80 Roman feet, but 82 Roman feet at floor level. The church is almost the same size as San Pietro.

81. Are the pavonazzetto columns the original ones and the white marble columns additions from the restoration by Leo the Great after the earthquake of 442–43? Surely not. Either Leo introduced the pavonazzetto spolia to repair the damage—the colonnade having been of the same date as the original church with marble shafts and capitals—or this is the way it was from the beginning. Krautheimer, *CBCR* 5:162–63, accepts the idea of repair because of traces of earthquake found in the repair of bases and capitals with metal clamps. There was no perceptible damage to the aisles. Among the fragments of column shafts from the building there are also some of pink granite.

82. An opening has been bored through the block with the word "Paulo" to permit lowering of charms (or merely simple strips of cloth) to touch the relics.

83. See *CBCR* 5:98, 162.

84. *The Tombs,* 172–73.

85. Deichmann and Tschira, "Das Mausoleum." Photographic coverage Caporicci, *Torpignattara.*

86. LP XXXIII (Duchesne 1:182).

87. Deichmann and Tschira, "Das Mausoleum," 58.

88. LP XXXIII (Duchesne 1:182). Helena's remains were later transferred to the church of S. Maria in Ara Coeli on the Capitoline. On questions surrounding her burial, Pietrí, *Roma Christiana,* 1:32, with bibliography.

89. The sarcophagus is much restored.

90. LP XXXIII (Duchesne 1:182).

91. Bosio, *Roma Sotterranea,* 323.

92. Bosio's drawing shows eight pilasters forming the inner side of the ambulatory around the apse and a doorway through the back of the apse, on center, to the exterior.

93. In the reconstruction of Deichmann and Tschira, "Das Mausoleum," there are two phases of the porch. During the first the clearstory of the basilica did not reach as far as the porch; in the second it was joined to it. Guyon, *Deux lauriers,* 215, believes that the clearstory was joined to the porch from the beginning. A chapel and presbytery of the eighteenth century within the mausoleum mask the remains of the junction between the mausoleum and basilica and those of the porch of the mausoleum joining the narthex of the basilica.

94. Speidel, *Kaiserreiter.*

95. Guyon, *Deux lauriers,* 211.

96. Ibid., 219–30. The walls of the basilica are built up to and over the walls of the south enclosure. See ibid., fig. 30, p. 33, and Deichman and Tschira, "Das Mausoleum," fig. 9, p. 50.

97. LP XXXIII (Duchesne 1:182). Deichmann and Tschira, "Das Mausoleum," suggest that the basilica was built first. In part this conclusion rests on the mistaken notion that the open court north of the basilica and the portico south of it are later additions when in fact they derive from the enclosure wall of the cemetery of the Equites Singulares. According to Deichmann and Tschira, the mausoleum, lying outside the enclosure, would be later still. But even they recognized the unitary nature of the complex, 64.

98. Brick stamps CIL XV 395 f. and 1569 generally Constantinian and a coin obv., CONSTANTINUS IUN NOB C; rev., PROVIDENTIAE CAESS. Guyon, *Deux lauriers,* 238 n. 66.

99. Their date is very unsure because they contained no grave goods.

100. Marcellinus, Petrus, Gorgonius, Tiburtius plus thirty or forty other martyrs beside the Quattuor Coronati.

101. Guyon, *Deux lauriers,* chap. 6. According to tradition, Marcellinus and Peter were martyred early in the reign of Diocletian. Clement, an original member of the Quattuor Coronati but later superseded by Castorius or Simplicius, is also saluted in a graffito.

102. Perrotti, "Recenti ritrovamenti."

103. It is, of course, far from certain that the sarcophagus originally occupied this niche. For its two displacements, see Cecchelli, *Sant' Agnese,* 24–25.

104. Stern, "Sainte-Constance," 192.

105. Matthiae, *Mosaici.*

106. An impression reenforced by the graphic record, especially by the Portuguese painter of the sixteenth century Francesco d'Ollanda, in his perspective drawing of the interior in Madrid, Escorial 28–1-20 f 22r, Amadio, *I mosaici,* p. 30, no. 6.

107. Compare the drawing of the sixteenth-century architect Hugues Sambin in Berlin, Kunstbibliothek 4151 f 74r, Amadio, *I mosaici,* p. 42, no. 15, and the same panel as it exists today. The comparison may be made in adjoining figures of Stern, "Sainte-Costance," figs. 28, 29.

108. Dunbabin, *Mosaics,* 248–51.

109. These have been restored and cannot be identified with confidence.

110. Illustrated by Cecchelli, *Sant' Agnese,* 20, and Frutaz, *Sant' Agnese,* 172. Frutaz, however, does not accept the mosaic as belonging to Santa Costanza. For such denials, cf. Lehmann, "St. Costanza," 195 n. 18 (the mosaic is also illustrated as his fig. 3).

111. *CBCR* 1:16.

112. Ibid.

113. Ibid., pp. 34–35.

114. Mackie, "A New Look," 388–89, reviews the problem.

115. LP CVII: 16 (Duchesne 2:163), Nicholas I. It may have been a church since the fifth century if the mosaics of Jehovah and Moses and Christ with Peter and Paul over the semicircular niches of the ambulatory are any indication.

116. Ammianus Marcellinus XXI. The form Costantia is known in the fourth century, cf. the gold glass in the British Museum, Dalton, *BMCat.,* no. 608, cf. Cameron, "Orfitus and Constantius."

117. Amadio, *I Mosaici.*

118. See Lehmann addendum in "St. Costanza," 291.

119. *Enciclopedia Cattolica,* s.v.

120. Ferrara, Peverati (Angelus) 430 no. 161 NC 6, published by Münz, "Mosaiques Chrétiennes."

121. Cecchelli, *Sant' Agnese,* 25–26.

122. For the more recent development of this position, see Stern, "Sainte-Costance."

123. Morey, *Early Christian Art,* 142.

124. An exception is the man with the fish, Tobias, or possibly one of Dionysus's pirates turning into a dolphin?

125. If the two mysterious figures on the prow of one boat are two souls making the voyage to the next world, it is difficult to make Charon's boat Christian.

126. On these mosaics, see Rasmussen, "Traditio Legis."

127. Lehmann, "St. Costanza."

128. Stanley, "Santa Costanza."

129. Mackie, "A New Look," 383–406.

130. Today it holds the relics of the apostles Simon and Jude. Its provenance is also given as S. Agnese.

131. Gatti, "Una basilica."

132. Rash, *Tor de' Schiavi.*

133. Ibid., 79–80.

134. *CBCR* 4:142.

135. Dated to 357.

136. The reconstruction of the colonnades in the nave of the basilica presents a problem. Only in the eastern part of the basilica can they have stood at their present level. How then was the western part roofed, remembering that there is a difference of more than two meters to be accounted for since the lowest level of graves rests at a level of 3 m. below the present floor in this area? It is difficult to imagine a single colonnade running at two such different levels. A different interpretation of the evidence is offered by Tolotti, "Basiliche cimiteriali." He does not believe there was originally a lower level in

the nave. The tombs "dovevano essere utilizzate dall' alto, non dunque come uno scaffale, ma come uno stretto cassone sprofondato sotto il pavimento," 159.

137. Tolotti, "Basiliche cimiteriali" (with conviction), Krautheimer, *CBCR* 2:145 (without conviction).

138. *CBCR* 2:145.

139. Date post-330, Torelli, "Basiliche circiformi." Date 317–20, La Rocca, "Basiliche cristiane." The monogram cut into the threshold of the doorway giving on to the Via Appia from the courtyard of the church is similarly vague since it can be read Constantinus, Constans, or Constantius.

140. Krautheimer *CBCR* 2:116 ff.

141. This is the Cymiterium Cyriaces of the LP XXV (Duchesne 1:155), where St. Lawrence was buried. His tomb is to be seen today in the eastern (Pelagian) basilica. The crypt is older, although much altered by the work of Cencius Savelli in 1191–92.

142. Quite possibly the width of aisles was determined first and the nave width was what remained.

143. The width of the ambulatory is not known. It is assumed on drawings to match that of the side aisles.

144. LPP XXXIII (Duchesne 1:181).

145. Of one Lucillus Pelio *CBCR* 2:7. Geertmann, "Basilica Maior," dates the excavated basilica at S. Lorenzo to the time of Xistus III (early fifth century). He excluded Constantine as the builder of the church because the donations attributed to him were not suitably lavish for a major basilica, but this is, of course, a subjective argument.

146. Fiocchi Nicolai, "La nuova basilica." Not to be confused with the semisubterranean basilica at the catacombs of Balbina, Nestori, *Basilica Anonima*.

147. LP XXXV (Duchesne 1:202).

148. C. Pietrí, *Roma Christiana*, 1:125–26.

149. Thus the heated debate between R. Krautheimer, who considered them martyrs' shrines, and Deichmann, "Märtyrerbasilika," for whom a church not directly located on the martyr's grave could not be a martyrium.

150. Krautheimer, "Mensa-Coemeterium-Martyrium." The idea seems to have been that of Frank Edward Brown, at the time a vigorous adherent of the symbolic interpretation of ancient architecture movement launched at Yale by Vincent Scully.

151. *De Spectaculis*, 29.

152. Torelli, "Basiliche circiformi"; the observation was originally made by Jastrzebowska *Untersuchungen zum christlichen Totenmahl*, 162, and accepted by Morin, "La basilique circiforme."

153. La Rocca, "Basiliche cristiane," 204–20. For the underlying symbolic interpretation of the circus and Tomb of Romulus in the Villa of Maxentius as an evocation of the Circus Maximus and the presence of Hercules, especially at the Ara Maxima, in its vicinity, see Frazer, "Iconography." Practical motives adduced for the apse-end plan are also far from convincing. Liturgical processions did not require an apse; they seem to have done very well at San Giovanni without one. There are refrigeria shown in catacomb paintings, where the participants seem to recline at a curved table, apparently out of doors, e.g., the Cubicolo dei Sacramenti at S. Callisto, Fiocchi Nicolai et al. *The Christian Catacombs of Rome*, fig. 15; Pani Ermini, ed., *Christiana Loca*, 62, fig. 1. There is no need, therefore, to think that the apses were made specially to fit such tables (at a gigantic scale)!

154. Ward-Perkins, "Memoria." It appears in St. Ambrose's comparison of the basilica with transept to the cross, Forcella *Iscrizioni*, no. 229, "Forma crucis templum est," and about the same time in Gregory of Nyssa, ca. 380, PG vol. 46, 1093.

155. An idea originally espoused by Krautheimer, "Beginnings."

156. Krautheimer, "Mensa-Coemeterium-Martyrium," 39.

157. Eusebius *Ecclesiastical History* IV, 26.

158. Didache 4, 8. I owe the suggestion of this line of reasoning to the wide perception of pagan and Christian antiquity of my wife.

159. In Ezekiel 12, 40. There are some sixty catacombs. They have not been fully explored even today.

A thorough summary of the state of exploration was made by Weiland, "Katacomben Forschung." See also Pergola, *Catacombe.*

160. For the sorry plight of such people, see Bodel, "Dealing with the Dead."

161. *Apologeticus* 29, 6.

162. *Apostolic Tradition* 34.1–2, trans. G. Dix. What was done for those who could not afford the hire of the workman and the price of the tiles is left to the imagination. However, a series of pits each capable of holding fifty or more corpses has been found in the catacomb of Commodilla, E. Josi in *Enciclopedia Cattolica,* 3:1626.

163. *Divine Institutes* VI, 12.

164. Rebillard, "L'église de Rome."

165. Rutgers, *Jews in Rome.*

166. See chap. 1.

167. Testini, *Archeologia Cristiana,* 151, fig. 30; Fiocchi Nicolai et al., *The Christian Catacombs of Rome,* 117, fig. 134.

168. Guyon, "La vente des tombes"; Conde Guerri, *Los "fossores,"* and Testini, *Archeologia Cristiana,* chaps. 4, 8.

169. Fiocchi Nicolai et al., *The Christian Catacombs,* 16, fig. 6.

170. Fiocchi Nicolai et al., *The Christian Catacombs,* 25, fig. 20.

171. In some cases the development of catacombs from existing quarries with irregular tunnels led to a different layout, as for example in the Coemeterium Maius on the Via Nomentana.

172. On the increase in conversions, Augustine *Letters* XXIX, 11. For the catacombs and Via Appia, see Nuzzo, *Tipologia.*

173. Guyon, *Deux lauriers,* 321.

174. Pani Ermini, "L'ipogeo dei Flavi."

175. Kötzche-Breitenbruch, *Die Neue Katakombe;* Tronzo, *Via Latina,* with other bibliography. Ferrua, *Catacombe sconosciute.*

176. Février, "La date des peintures." Today, just as in 1965, the words of L. De Bruyne, "La peinture," hold true, "Le grand problème qui domine tout . . . est celui de la chronologie des monuments."

177. Guyon, *Deux lauriers,* chap. 4. Following the advent of Constantinian rule, the mausolea, coemeterium teglatum, and surface tombs set the development of the cemetery on another course.

CHAPTER IV.   *The Tomb of St. Peter.*

1. Matthew 16, 18.

2. The cavity, which clearly was venerated from Constantinian times onward as the tomb of the apostle, is situated below the floor of the confessional just in front of the Niche of the Pallia.

3. *The Glory of the Martyrs* XXVIII.

4. Liverani, *Topografia,* 138–40.

5. "Le tombe apostoliche al Vaticano ed alla via Ostiense," in his *Analecta Romana,* 259–306.

6. Mgr. Kaas was no simple Vatican functionary but one of the closest collaborators of the pope. The former leader of the Catholic Center Party in Germany before the creation of the National Socialist state, Mgr. Kaas played an important role in the negotiation of the concordat of 1933 between the Vatican, the policy of which was guided by the future Pius XII as cardinal secretary of state, and the new German government.

7. Apollonj-Ghetti et al., *Esplorazioni.*

8. Prandi, *La zona archeologica.*

9. Ravasi, *Pietro,* 224. On the pagan necropolis, see Mielsch and von Hesberg, *Heidische Nekropole.*

10. Father Kirschbaum left a readable account of the excavations in *Die Gräber der Apostelfürsten* (Frankfurt, 1957), which appeared in English under the title *The Tombs of St. Peter and Paul.* Apart from its

authorship by one of the excavation team, this work is valuable because it provides a narrative account of the progress of the work.

11. Kirschbaum, *The Tombs,* chap. 3, esp. 112. The defective drawings are figs. 79 and 86, the more trustworthy figs. 99, 100, 101. Unfortunately, the trustworthy drawings are admittedly reconstructions, the defective drawings documentation of the actual state of the excavation. For an extended litany of shortcomings of the initial excavations, see Guarducci, "Le reliquie di Pietro," esp. 84–92.

12. Tomb excavated in 1935, Liverani, *Topografia,* no. 19. See also Ministero P I, *Carta Archeologia di Roma* (Florence, 1962), nos. 27–40.

13. In addition to Mielsch and von Hesberg, *Heidische Nekropole,* there is an excellent summary of this aspect of the excavations by J. B. Ward-Perkins and J. Toynbee, *The Shrine of St. Peter.* One of the Roman mausolea under the basilica had already been discovered in early work in front of the papal altar in 1574.

14. Throughout most of the basilica up to and partway along the confessional, the architects of the Renaissance church opened up an underground level between the floor of the new basilica and that of its Constantinian predecessor, the so-called Grotte Vaticane. Except for a corridor around the inner edge of the foundations of the apse, the so-called Grotte Nuove, this lower level does not extend into the area where the pre-Constantinian ground level rises to almost that of the Constantinian pavement.

15. LP XXXIII (Duchesne 1:176).

16. The same waterproofing coat of stucco covers both below-ground and above-ground surfaces.

17. Guarducci, "La capsella eburnea."

18. LP XXXIII (Duchesne 1:176).

19. Kirschbaum, *The Tombs,* 65–66.

20. Ibid., 66.

21. This is wall *s* of figs. 4.15, 4.16.

22. What the excavators took to be part of the same slab was observed close to the Red Wall. They believed that the slab was socketed into the Red Wall. However, the photographic documentation offered in regard to this statement does not permit one to judge, Apollonj-Ghetti et al., *Esplorazioni,* pl. LIVb. That a board shelf formed by this and other missing pieces of travertine once existed and that its central part was socketed into *N2,* as suggested by the restoration offered by the excavators, fig. 4.12, seems a matter only of conjecture as we see from the statement, ibid., 137, "Le due nicchie [i.e., *N2* and *N3*] non si spiegano architettonicamente se non si ammette che proprio fra di esse fu inserita, fin dall'inizio, la grossa lastra di travertine."

23. Ibid., 126; Kirschbaum, *The Tombs,* 67.

24. The excavators paid little attention to this successor to wall *s.* Since it was incorporated in the Constantinian marble and porphyry monument, however, it must be earlier than that structure.

25. Father Kirschbaum describes the situation as follows, Kirschbaum, *The Tombs,* 75, "A heavy travertine slab at the end of which would be detected the base of the pillar discovered at the south\side [of the Memoria]—but only with considerable difficulty because of the extremely confined space." Apollonj-Ghetti et al., *Esplorazioni,* pl. LVIa, shows what little the excavators could see and makes it clear that they never directly observed the contact between the column and travertine piece below.

26. Apollonj-Ghetti et al, *Esplorazioni,* 128, fig. 93, and 129, fig. 94.

27. The excavators reasoned that the travertine slab had been cut back at a later time in the history of the Memoria when wall *g* was constructed north of the niches, necessitating a reposition of the column southward. However, the length of the slab as found (following the supposed reduction in its length to suit the new circumstances) was such that there could be no possibility of its serving as the foundation for a column placed symmetrically with respect to the southern member of the pair in the later arrangement. The fragment of travertine observed by the excavators at the same level as the travertine slab associated with the southern column (Apollonj-Ghetti et al., *Esplorazioni,* 127–28) hardly proves

the existence of a slab resting on the northern column in the manner of the construction hypothesized for its southern counterpart. Father Kirschbaum did not think this element worth mentioning
in his account, *The Tombs*.

28. Compare Apollonj-Ghetti et al., *Esplorazioni*, fig. 100, hypothetical original state of the Memoria,
with fig. 101, hypothetical second state of the Memoria.

29. Ibid., 162; Kirschbaum, *The Tombs*, 71. Further coins were attributed to the cavity by M. Guarducci,
one coin of Constantine II and nine medieval coins; see *Le reliquie*, esp. 14–15.

30. See Prandi, *La zona archeologica*, 373.

31. Kirschbaum, *The Tombs*, 74.

32. Precisely Mausoleum E.

33. The excavators have made much of the fact that the covering slabs of the cavity were set at an oblique
angle to the Red Wall, suggesting, to their minds, that they maintained an orientation over an even
earlier grave, Apollonj-Ghetti et al., *Esplorazioni*, 137; Kirschbaum, *The Tombs*, 75.

34. The evidence for this earlier cover is tenuous. Speaking of the two remnants of walling which give the
basis for the theory, Father Kirschbaum says, *The Tombs*, 75, "The other *(m2)* was partially destroyed at
the top, and its upper corner had a groove that must once have contained a slab for closing the space."
That the groove "must once have contained a slab" is only a hypothesis.

35. Apollonj-Ghetti et al., *Esplorazioni*, 119–31; Prandi, *La zona archeologica*, 391. I incline toward the
opinion of the original excavators and find reassurance in observations of von Gerkan, "Petrusgrabes,"
86, "Die unterste Nische N1 hat nur rohes eingebrochenes Mauerwerk, das garnicht so mauern kann,
und darum is auch die Ansicht von Prandi unhaltbar, MR sei hier gegen ein unbekanntes X gemauert
worden; es ist ein noch späterer Einbruch, also gewollte Nische aber völlig sinn- und zwecklos."
Thus von Gerkan dismisses Prandi's theory that a cippus recording the martyrdom of Peter (now
lost) stood on the spot and that the Red Wall was built over and around it, thus creating *N1*. See
also Thümmel, *Die Memorien*, 37.

36. Kirschbaum, *The Tombs*, 90.

37. C. Serafini, in Apollonj-Ghetti et al., *Esplorazioni*, 229–44, coins denoted as (A), Niche of the Pallia.

38. "Il sistema medioevale-barocco di chiusura del vano sotterraneo e il modo con cui fu sistemata la
nicchia dei Pallii non permettono di controllare il muro e la sua nicchia più in alto," Apollonj-Ghetti
et al., *Esplorazioni*, 127.

39. E.g., the Columbarium of Pomponius Hylas, della Portella, *Subterranean Rome*, figs. on 115, 119.

40. Kirschbaum, *The Tombs*, 150.

41. As already noted, the excavators invoke an apparent groove at one corner of wall *m1* as a sign of the
original closing of the cavity by means of a movable slab.

42. Prandi, *La zona archeologica*, 289–90. The original excavators had argued that the Isidorus slab was a
repair to an earlier system consisting of a hatch supported in part by walls *m1* and *m2*.

43. "Secondo noi, non ci fu mai quella tomba obliqua, sotto il muro rosso," ibid., 410.

44. Relying on the legend preserved under the name of Linus (the second pope) and Marcellus (whose
pontificate in the first decade of the fourth century is dubious) that St. Peter was crucified and buried
beside a turpentine tree (terebinth), F. Tolotti proposed that what was honored in the Vaticano was
not the grave but the spot on which the tree beside the grave grew, Tolotti, "Terebinto." Much of this
paper is given over to an ingenious restoration of the Memoria (as proposed by the excavators) as
a shrine through which the tree grew upward.

45. For this development, see Prandi, *La zona archeologica*, 232.

46. Kirschbaum, *The Tombs*, 104.

47. Such stamps were applied to tiles (which were also used as the facing of Roman brickwork) during
much of the Roman Empire to identify the kiln where the tile was produced with the date of its
production. Prandi also observed that grave gamma was dug into a level above the foundations
of mausoleum *O*, which borders Campo *P* on the south and is dated similarly by its brick stamps,

La zona archeologica, 347–53. The brick with a stamp of 69–79 in grave theta is clearly an old and reused piece. The excavation of Campo *P* makes it clear that the statements of the *Liber Pontificalis* to the effect that the first ten popes (excepting Alexander) were buried with Peter in the Vatican are fiction.

48. Prandi held that *Q* was originally a cistern, and according to his observations the steps in the clivus were built at two separate times. Contra Kirschbaum, *The Tombs,* 113, but the argument is accepted by Thümmel, *Die Memorien.* The same red plaster that gives the Red Wall its name was used on the upper steps of the clivus. This red coating was applied at different times in different places because the below-ground parts of the Red Wall could not have received their coat at the same time as the steps laid up against the same Red Wall above ground level. This reflection negates any argument of common date for the Red Wall and the steps based on their common red plaster.

49. Prandi, *La zona archeologica,* 361.

50. Apollonj-Ghetti et al., *Esplorazioni,* 102, and Prandi, *La zona archeologica,* 361.

51. See the section in Prandi, *La zona archeologica,* fig. 18. Kirschbaum, *The Tombs,* 80, says, "In the earth in front of the entrances to *S* were found fragments of pipes that extended the Clivus canal," but this statement leaves unanswered the question of when the canal was ripped up.

52. Prandi, *La zona archeologica,* 316–17. The same stamp occurs on one of the facing tiles of the tomb enclosure *R1* (ibid., 341), and another stamp of the period of Marcus Aurelius was found by Prandi on one of the risers of the stairs of the clivus, 355.

53. Thümmel, *Die Memorien,* 37–40.

54. Klauser, "Petrustradition." His point is not that the marker at the tomb should have been omitted but that given the situation it should have been made differently.

55. V. Correnti, "Risultati dello studio compiuto su tre gruppi di resti scheletrici umani rinvenuti sotto la Confesssione della Basilica Vaticana," in Guarducci, *Le Reliquie,* 83–160, with L. Cardini, "Risultati dell' esame osteologico dei resti scheletrici di animali," ibid., 161–68.

56. Guarducci, *I Graffiti,* 2:396–407. She extended her search for Peter in the graffiti of wall *g,* finding numerous instances of *P*'s and *E*'s, see her *La Tomba di San Pietro,* 57–69. But these interpretations have not always met with favor, cf. among others, notable for his incisive expression, Pietrí, *Roma Christiana,* 59.

57. OSSA.VRNA.GRAF. Guarducci gave, on several occasions, a full bibliography relating to the discovery and discussion of it, most recently in *Le Reliquie.*

58. See the caustic exchanges between him and Guarducci in her *Le chiavi.*

59. The reassembled skeleton is presented by V. Correnti, "Le Reliquie di Pietro," in Guarducci, *Le Reliquie,* 86–112.

60. In dealing with the excavations below S. Sebastiano carried out largely by Styger, Marucchi, and Prandi, I have relied on R. Krautheimer, *CBCR* 4, Thümmel, *Die Memorien,* Klauser, "Petrustradition," and the articles of von Gerkan, "Petrusgrabes," "Petrus in Vaticano," and "Basso et Tusco," as well as Jastrzebowska, *Untersuchungen zum Totenmahl,* and Tolotti, "S. Sebastiano." It will become clear that I do not agree with the theory put forward by Kjaegaard, "Memoria Apostolorum," that the cult of the Via Appia was merely a "commemorative veneration." This paper is useful, however, for its criticism of several attempts to find Christian funeral monuments below the basilica, Prandi, *La Memoria* and "Mensa martyrum," and Testini, "Memoria Apostolorum." For the history of the excavation, see Schumacher "Die Gräbungen."

61. Another partially excavated house to the north of the cemetery is known as the Villa Piccola.

62. For the debate on this point, see Jastrzebowska, *Untersuchungen zum Totenmahl,* 45, and, arguing for a Christian presence, Carletti, "Pagani e cristiani."

63. Armin von Gerkan maintains that it was actually enclosed; he also restores a portico on the west side of the courtyard, see "Petrus in Vaticano" and "Basso et Tusco." His work on the problem began with his contributions to the volume of Lietzmann, *Petrus und Paulus.*

64. Inscriptiones Christianae Urbis Romae no. 12907–13096, also in Snyder, *Ante Pacem,* 141–43.

65. Marichal, "La date."

66. XXII (Duchesne, 1:151, discussion on 67). On the Templum Apollonis, see Giordani, "In Templum Apollonis."

67. Styger, "Pietro e Paolo," esp. 175–76. He might have added that disturbing graves was not a Roman custom, among either Christians or pagans, as Pope Gregory the Great pointed out to a Byzantine empress seeking relics, Letters I, 30. But relic hunting belongs to a very different order of things from a translation undertaken to consolidate the Roman community in an hour of danger, and a long series of applications to the emperor by citizens of the empire intent on moving the bones of family members shows that moving a body was far from uncommon, cf. Millar, *Emperor,* 359–60.

68. "Mese Iunio III Kal. Iul. Petri in Catacumbas et Pauli Ostiense, Tusco et Basso consulibus." *Monumenta Germaniae Historiae,* auct Ant. IX, 71.

69. Because Peter and Paul suffered under Nero, their *Dies natalis* cannot be the day of their martyrdom but the day of the institution of the cult.

70. Damasi Epigrammata no. 26.

> Hic habitasse prius sanctos cognoscere debes
> Nomina quisque Petri pariter Paulique requiris.
> Discipulos Oriens misit, quod sponte fatemur;
> Sanguinis ob meritum Christumque per astra secuti,
> Aetherios petiere sinus regnaque piorum.
> Roma suos potius meruit defendere cives,
> Haec Damasus vestras referat, nova sidera, laudes.

71. Ecclesiastical History II, 25, 6.

72. Full discussion by O'Connor, *Peter,* chap. 7.

73. This material has been collected by Styger in "Pietro e Paolo," 182–88, and in *Märtyrer-Grüfte,* 18–23.

74. Quoted in *Epistola Hugonis Monachi Cluniacensis* (*Bibliotheca Hagiographica Latina* 4011), ed. Crowley in "Two Studies": "Nosti pater quia papa Cornelius martyr gloriosus Petri e Pauli ossa de catachumbis levata Pauli via Hostiensi, Petri in Vaticano sagaciter posuit." This precious thread of the *vera traditio de sepulcris apostolorum* was unearthed by my indefatigably learned wife.

75. Vegio, "De rebus antiquis," 69–70. For treatments of the problem in the nineteenth and early twentieth centuries, see Styger "Pietro e Paolo," 170, and O'Connor, *Peter.*

76. For other contributions one may consult the recent bibliographies of Thümmel, *Die Memorien,* and Arbeiter, *Alt-St. Peter.*

77. Kirschbaum, *The Tombs,* 91.

78. Von Gerkan, "Petrusgrab," "Petrus in Vaticano," and "Basso et Tusco."

79. Klauser, "Petrustradition."

80. Thümmel, *Die Memorien.*

81. Ruysschaert, "Les premiers siècles," with references to his earlier contributions. Ruysschaert summarizes the evolution of Duchesne's ideas, beginning with the prefaces to his edition of the *Liber Pontificalis* in 1886, pp. civ–cvii.

82. "Corpora animadversorum quislibet petentibus ad sepulturam danda sunt." *Digest,* XLVIII, 24, 3.

83. Letters LVIII (LV), 9. For the full text, see pp. 5–6.

84. Styger, *Märtyrer-Grüfte,* 62.

85. Eusebius, *Ecclesiastical History,* VII, 13, 1 (noting the restoration of the cemeteries by Gallienus).

86. *CBCR* 4:115.

87. A strip of cloth such as that described by Gregory of Tours.

88. Luther, *Reformation Schriften,* 18:1333–37 and 12:1145–62. On the Petrine problem in general, see O'Connor, *Peter in Rome.*

89. So in England in the words of the *Act of Supremacy* of 1559 put into practice by the visitations of the

Commissions for the Establishment of Religion, "No foreign prince, person, prelate, state, or potentate hath or ought to have any jurisdiction, power, superiority, pre-eminence, or authority, ecclesiastical or spiritual, within this realm." It was this spark of independence, carried in the breasts of the English colonists of North America, which in 1775 ignited a beacon of liberty that has burned ever after.

Glossary

Ambulatory: the passageway around the apse of a church.

Arris: the edge formed by the meeting of two planes.

Atrium: a courtyard preceding the entrance to a church.

Baldacchino: a canopy, also a permanent canopy.

Chancel: that part of a church farthest removed from its entrance and generally reserved for the use of the clergy.

Chrism-paten: tray used to support a container for consecrated oil.

Ciborium: a canopy over the high altar of a church.

Clivus: street or alley.

Confessional: the tomb of a martyr and the structures erected in relation to it.

Cryptoporticus: an enclosed, usually semisubterranean passageway.

Domus: town house.

Fenestrella: a small window, especially an opening onto a shaft leading to the resting place of a martyr's relics.

Gehenna: The Valley of Hinnon, near Jerusalem, used as a receptacle for refuse, fires being kept up to prevent pestilence. Hence, in the New Testament, hell. *(Webster's New Collegiate Dictionary)*.

Haruspex: a diviner skilled in the examination of the entrails of sacrificial victims to ascertain the disposition of the pagan gods toward the undertakings of the sacrificer.

Loculus: burial cavity cut into the wall of a catacomb.

Martyrium: shrine of a Christian martyr.

Narthex: the vestibule of a church.

Nave: the central aisle of a Christian basilical church.

Paten: a plate employed in the eucharistic service.

Refrigerium: a commemoration before a tomb, including the taking of a meal by the participants.

Rostra: the speakers' platform in the Roman Forum.

Scyphus: a cup.

Spandrel: The space left between the curve of an arch and the rectangular frame enclosing it.

Transept: that element in the plan of a church set at right angle to its principal axis, between the nave and the chancel and extending beyond the nave at either side.

Bibliography

Act of Supremacy 1559, *http://history.hanover.edu/texts/engref/lxxix.html*

Alexander, S. S. "Studies in Constantinian Church Architecture." *RAC* 49 (1973): 33–44.

Alföldi, A. "Die Ausgestaltung des monarchischen Zeremonials." *RM* 49 (1934): 1–118.

———. *The Conversion of Constantine and Pagan Rome.* Oxford, 1948.

———. *Constantinisches Goldprägung.* Mainz, 1963.

———. "Die Sol Comes Münze vom Jahre 325." In *Mollus, Festschrift Theodor Klauser* (*JAC, Ergängzungsband* 1, 1964), 10–16.

Amadio, A. A. *I mosaici di S. Costanza* (*Xenia Quaderni* 7). Rome, 1985.

Amelung, W. *Die Skulpturen des Vaticanischen Museum.* Volume 1. Berlin, 1903.

Apollonj-Ghetti, B. M., A. Ferrua, E. Josi, E. Kirschbaum. *Esplorazioni sotto la confessione di San Pietro in Vaticano, eseguite negli anni 1940–1949.* Città del Vaticano, 1951.

Arbeiter, A. *Alt-St. Peter.* Berlin, 1988.

Barnes, T. D. *The New Empire of Diocletian and Constantine.* Cambridge, 1982.

———. *Constantine and Eusebius.* London, 1981.

Bauer, F., A. M. Heinzelmann, A. Martin, and A. Schaub. "Untersuchungen im Bereich des Konstantinischen Bischofskirche Ostias." *RM* 106 (1999): 289–341.

Bauer, F. A., and Heinzelmann, M. "The Constantinian Bishop's Church at Ostia." *JRA* 12 (1999): 342–53.

Beard, M., and R. North, eds. *Pagan Priests.* London, 1990.

Berenson, B. *The Arch of Constantine or the Decline of Form.* New York, 1954.

Bianchi Bandinelli, R. *La fine dell' arte antica.* Milan, 1970.

Bodel, J. "Dealing with the Dead: Undertakers, Executioners and Potters' Fields in Ancient Rome." In *Death and Disease in the Ancient City,* edited by V. M. Hope and E. Marshall, 126–15. London and New York, 2000.

Bonamente, G., and F. Fusco, eds. *Costantino Il Grande.* Macerata, 1992.

Bosio, A. *Roma Sotterranea.* Rome, 1632.

Bowersock, G. W. "Peter and Constantine." In *Humana Sapit: Études d'antiquité tardive offertes à Lellia Ruggini,* ed. J.-M. Carrié and R. Lizzi Testa, 209–17. Paris, 2002.

Brandt, O. "Il battistero lateranense da Costantino a Ilario." *Opuscula Romana* 22–23 (1997–98): 7–65.

———. "Il battistero lateranese dell' Imperatore Costantino?" *Acta Hyperborea* 8 (2001): 117–44.

Brenk, B. "Microstoria sotto la Chiesa di SS. Giovanni e Paolo: La cristianizzazione di una casa privata." *RINA,* Series 3, 18 (1995): 169–206.

Bruun, P. "The Christian Signs on the Coins of Constantine." *Arctos* 3 (1962): 25–35. Reprinted in P. Bruun, *Studies in Constantinian Numismatics,* 53–57. Rome, 1991.

———. *Studies in Constantinian Chronology.* Numismatic Notes and Monographs 146. New York, 1961.

———. *The Roman Imperial Coinage.* Volume 7, *Constantine and Licinius.* London, 1966.

———. "Victorious Signs of Constantine: A Reappraisal," *Numismatic Chronicle* 157 (1997): 41–59.

Burckhardt, J. *The Age of Constantine the Great.* Translated by M. Hadas. New York, 1956.

Calza, R. "Un problema di iconografia imperiale sull' arco di Costantino." *RendPont* 32 (1959–60): 133–66.

Cameron, A. "Orfitus and Constantius: A Note on Roman Gold-Glasses." *JRA* 19 (1996): 295–301.

Camp, J. *The Archaeology of Ancient Athens.* New Haven, 2001.

Caporicci, G. *Torpignattara.* Rome, 1976.

Cardini, L. "Risultati dell' esame osteologico dei resti scheletrici di animali." In M. Guarducci, *Le Reliquie di Pietro sotto la Confessione della Basilica Vaticana,* 161–68. Rome, 1965.

Carletti, C. "Pagani e cristiani nel sepolcreto della 'pizzola' sotto la Basilica Apostolorum a Roma." *Vetera Christianorum* 18 (1981): 287–307.

Carpiceci, A. C., and R. Krautheimer. "Nuovi Dati sull' Antica Basilica di San Pietro in Vaticano." *BdA* 93–94 (1995): 1–70 and 95 (1996): 9–84.

Caspar, E. L. E. *Geschichte des Papsttums.* Volume 1. Tübingen, 1930.

Castiglione, Baldassare. *Le Lettere.* Edited by Guido La Roccca. Verona, 1978.

Catalano, P., S. Minozzi, and W. Pantano. "Le necropoli romane di età imperiale: Un contributo all' interpretazione del popolamento e della qualità della vita nell' antica Roma." In *Urbanizzazione delle Campagne nell' Italia Antica* (*Atlante Tematico di Topografia Antica* 10), 127–37. Rome, 2001.

Cecchelli, C. *Sant' Agnese fuori le Mura e S. Costanza* (*Le Chiese di Roma illustrate* 10). Rome, n.d.

Cirone, D. "I risultati delle indagini stratigrafiche all' arco di Costantino." *RendPont* 66 (1993–94): 60–76.

Colli, D. "Il palazzo sessoriano." *MEFRA* 108 (1996): 771–815.

Conde Guerri, E. *Los "fossores' de Roma paleocristiana.* Città del Vaticano, 1979.

Conforto, M. L. A., Melucco Vaccaro, et al. *Adriano e Costantino.* Milan, 2001.

Corcoran, S. S. *The Empire of the Tetrarchs.* Oxford, 1996.

Corpus Inscriptionum Latinarum. Berlin, 1862ff.

Correnti, V. "Risultati dello studio compiuto su tre gruppi di resti scheletrici umani rinvenuti sotto la Confessione della Basilica Vaticana." In M. Guarducci, *Le Reliquie di Pietro sotto la Confessione della Basilica Vaticana,* 83–160. Rome, 1965.

Crema, L. *Architettura romana.* Turin, 1959.

Crowley, H. E. "Two Studies in Cluniac History." *Studi Gregoriani* 11 (1978): 111–17.

Calcani, G. "I tondi adrianei el 'Arco di Costantino." *RIN* ser. 3, 19–20 (1996–97): 175–201.

Cullhed, M. *Conservator Urbis Suae* (*Skrifter Utgivna av Svenska Institutet I Rom, octavo* 20). Rome, 1994.

Curran, R. *Pagan City and Christian Capital.* Oxford, 2000.

Dalton, M. *Catalogue of the Early Christian Antiquities of the British Museum.* London, 1901.

Dark, K., and F. Özgümïs. "New Evidence for the Byzantine Church of the Holy Apostles from Istanbul." *Oxford Journal of Archaeology* 21 (2002): 393–413.

de Blaauw, S. *Cultus et Décor* (*Studi e Testi* 35). Città del Vaticano, 1994.

De Bruyne, L. "La peinture cemeteriale constantinienne." In *Akten des VII Internationalen Kongresses für Christliche Archäologie,* 159–214. Città del Vaticano, 1995.

de Maria, S. *Gli archi onorari di Roma e dell' Italia romana.* Rome, 1988.

Deichmann, F. W. "Märtyrerbasilika, Martyrion, Memoria und Altergrab." *RM* 77 (1970): 144–69.

Deichmann, F. W., and A. Tschira. "Das Mausoleum der Kaiserin Helena und die Basilika der Heiligen Marcellinus und Petrus an der Via Labicana vor Rom." *JdI* 72 (1957): 44–110.

Delehaye, H. *Les Origines du Cult des Martyrs.* Brussels, 1912.

della Portella, I. *Subterranean Rome.* Cologne, 2000.

Dölger, F. J. *Ichthys, Das Fischsymbol in frühchristlicher Zeit.* Rome, 1910.

Drake, H. A. *Constantine and the Bishops.* Baltimore, 2000.

Duchesne, L., ed. *Le Liber pontificalis: Texte, introduccion et commentaire,* 2d ed. Paris, 1955–57.

Dunbabin, K. *Mosaics in the Greek and Roman World.* Cambridge, 1999.

Elliott, T. C. *The Christianity of Constantine the Great.* Scranton, 1996.

Elsner, J. *Art and the Roman Viewer.* Cambridge, 1995.

———. "From the Culture of Spolia to the Cult of Relics: The Arch of Constantine and the Genesis of Late Antique Form." *Papers of the British School at Rome* 68 (2000): 149–84.

Elworthy, F. T. *The Evil Eye.* London, 1895.

Enciclopedia Cattolica. Vatican City, 1949–54.

Enciclopedia di Arte Antica. Rome, 1958–66.

Encyclopedia of the Early Church. New York, 1992.

Ensoli, S., and E. La Rocca, eds. *Aurea Roma.* Rome, 2000.

———. "I colossi di bronzo a Roma in età tardoantica: Dal colosso di Nerone al Colosso di Costantino: A proposito dei tre frammenti bronzei dei Musei Capitolini." In *Aurea Roma,* edited by S. Ensoli and E. La Rocca, 66–90. Rome, 2000.

Favez, L. "L'épisode de l'invention de la Croix dans l'oration funèbre de Théodose." *Revue des Études Latines* 10 (1932): 423–29.

Ferrua, A. *Catacombe sconosciute.* Florence, 1990.

Février, A. "A propos de la date des peintures des catacombes romaines." *RAC* 65 (1989): 105–33.

Fiocchi Nicolai, V. "La nuova basilica circiforme della Via Ardeatina." *RendPont* 68 (1999): 69–233.

Fiocchi Nicolai, V., F. Bisconti, and D. Mazzoleni. *The Christian Catacombs of Rome.* Regensburg, 1999.

Forcella. V. *Iscrizioni Cristiane di Milano.* Milan, 1897.

Frazer, A. "The Iconography of the Emperor Maxentius' Building in the Via Appia." *Art Bulletin* 48 (1966): 385–92.

Frutaz, A. *Il complesso monumentale di Sant' Agnese.* Vatican City, 1969.

Gatti, G. "Una basilica di età costantiniana recentemente riconosciuta presso la via Prenestina." *Capitolium* 34 (1960): 3–8.

Gauer, W. "Ein Dakerdenkmal Domitiens." *JdI* 88 (1973): 318–50.

Geertmann, H. "The Builders of the Basilica Maior in Rome." In *Festoen opgedragen aan A. N. Zadoks-Josephus Jitta bij haar zeventigste verjaardag,* 277–95. Groningen, 1974.

Giardina, A., ed. *Società romana e impero tardo antico.* Volume 2. Rome, 1986.

Gibbon, E. *The History of the Decline and Fall of the Roman Empire.* Volume 1. London, 1776.

Giordani, R. "In Templum Apollonis." *RAC* 64 (1988): 61–188.

Giuliani, A. *L'arco di Costantino.* Milan, 1955.

———. "L'arco di Costantino come documento storico." *Rivista Storica Italiana* 112 (2000): 441–47.

Gordon, R. "The Veil of Power, Emperor, Sacrifice and Benefaction." In *Pagan Priests,* edited by M. Beard and R. North, 201–34. London, 1990.

Grenier, J.-C., and F. Coarelli. "La tombe d'Antinoüs à Rome." *MEFRA* 98 (1986): 217–53.

Grisar, H. *Analecta Romana.* Volume 1. Rome, 1899.

Guarducci, M. *I Graffiti sotto la Confessione di San Pietro in Vaticano.* Città del Vaticano, 1958.

———. *Le Reliquie di Pietro sotto la Confessione della Basilica Vaticana.* Rome, 1965.

———. "Le reliquie di Pietro sotto la confessione della Basilica vaticana, una messa a punto," *AC* 19 (1967): 1–96.

————. "La capsella eburnea di Samagher." *Atti e Memorie della Società Istriana di Archeologia e Storia Patria* 26 (1978): 5–139.

————. *La Tomba di San Pietro.* Milan, 1989.

————. *Le chiavi sulla pietra: Studi, ricordi e documenti inediti intorno alla tomba di Pietro in Vaticano.* Casal Monferrato, 1995.

————. *Le reliquie di Pietro in Vaticano.* 1995.

Guyon, J. "La vente des tombes à travers l'épigraphie de la Rome chrétienne (IIIe–VIIe siècles): Le role des Fossores, Mansionarii, Praepositi et Pretres." *MEFRA* 86 (1974): 549–96.

————. *Le Cimetière aux deux lauriers* (*BEFAR* 264). Rome, 1987.

Harl, W. *Coinage in the Roman Economy, 300 B.C. to A.D. 700.* Baltimore, 1996.

Hoffmann, V. "Die Fassade von San Giovanni in Laterano." *Römisches Jahrbuch für Kunstgeschichte* 17 (1978): 1–46.

Holland, L. A. *Janus and the Arch* (*Papers and Monographs of the American Academy in Rome* 21). 1961.

Holloway, R. R. "The Spolia of the Arch of Constantine." *NAC* 14 (1985): 261–73.

————. "Remarks on the Arch of Titus." *Antiquité Classique* 56 (1987): 183–91.

Hope, V. M., and E. Marshall, eds. *Death and Disease in the Ancient City.* London, 2000.

Hülsen, C. *Il libro di Giuliano da Sangallo.* Leipzig, 1910.

Jastrzebowska, E. *Untersuchungen zum christlichen Totenmahl auf Grund der Monumente der 3 und 4 Jhrs. Unter der Basilika des Hl. Sebastian im Rome.* Frankfurt, 1981.

Jobst, W. "Die Büsten im Weingartenmosaik von Santa Costanza," *RM* 83 (1976): 431–37.

Jones, H. M. *Constantine and the Conversion of Europe,* 2d ed. London, 1962.

Jones, M. W. "Genesis and Mimesis. The Design of the Arch of Constantine in Rome." *Journal of the Society of Architectural Historians* 59 (2000): 50–77.

Kinney, D. "Spolia, Damnatio and Renovatio Memoriae." *MAAR* 43 (1997): 117–48.

Kirschbaum, E. *The Tombs of St. Peter and Paul.* London, 1959.

Kjaegaard, J. "From Memoria Apostolorum to Basilica Apostolorum." *Analecta Romana Instituti Danici* 13 (1984): 59–76.

Klauser, T. "Die römische Petrustradition" (*Arbeitsgemeinschaft für Forschung des Landes Nordrhein-Westfalen, Geisteswissenschaften* 24). Cologne, 1956.

Knudsen, S. E. "Summary of Papers on the Arch of Constantine Presented at Annual Meetings of the Archaeological Institute of America." *AJA* 93 (1989): 262, 94 (1990): 313, and 97 (1993): 317.

Koeppel, G. "Die historischen Reliefs der römischen Kaiserzeit." *Bonner Jahrbucher* 190 (1990): 1–64.

Kötzche-Breitenbruch, L. *Die Neue Katakombe an der Via Latina in Rome* (*Jahrbuch für Antike und Christentum, Ergänzungsband* 4). 1976.

Kraeling, C. H. *The Excavations at Dura Europos, Final Report II. The Christian Building.* New Haven, 1967.

Kraft, K. "Das Silbermedaillon Constantins des Grosses mit dem Christusmonogram auf dem Helm." *Jahrbuch für Numismatik und Geldgeschichte* 5–6 (1954–55): 151–78.

Krautheimer, R. *Corpus basilicarum christianarum Romae.* Vatican City, 1937–77.

————. "The Beginnings of Early Christian Architecture." *Review of Religions* 3 (1938–39): 127–48.

————. "Mensa-Coemeterium-Martyrium." *Cahiers Archéologiques* 11 (1960): 15–40.

————. *Three Christian Capitals.* Berkeley, 1983.

————. "The Ecclesiastical Building Program of Constantine." In *Costantino Il Grande,* vol. 1, edited by G. Bonamente and F. Fusco, 509–52. Macerata, 1992.

Kultermann, U. *Die Maxentius-Basilika: Ein Schlüsselwerk spätantiker Architektur.* Weimar, 1996.

L'Orange, H. *Art Forms and Civic Life in the Late Roman Empire.* Princeton, 1965.

L'Orange, H., and A. von Gerkan. *Der Spätantike Bildschmuck des Konstantinsbogens.* Berlin, 1939.

La Rocca, E., ed. *Rilievi storici capitolini.* Rome, 1987.

————. "Le basiliche cristiane 'a deambulatori' e la sopravivenza del culto eroico." In *Aurea Roma,* edited by S. Ensoli and E. La Rocca, 204–20. Rome, 2000.

Leeb, R. *Konstantin und Christus.* Berlin, 1992.

Lehmann, K. "St. Costanza." *Art Bulletin* 37 (1955): 193–96.

Lietzmann, H. "Das Problem der Spätantike." *Sitzungsberichte der Preussischen Akademie der Wissenschaften* (1927): 342–58.

———. *Petrus und Paulus in Rom.* Berlin and Leipzig, 1927.

Liverani, P. "Il monumento antonino di Efeso." *RIN*, Series 3, 19–20 (1996–97): 153–74.

———. "Dalle Aedes Laterani al Patriarchio Lateranense." *RAC* 75 (1999): 521–33.

———. *La topografia antica del Vaticano.* Città del Vaticano, 1999.

Lorenz, T. "Überlegungen zur Vorgeschichte der frühchristlichen Basilika." *Boreas* 23–24 (2000–01): 113–31.

Lugli, G. *Itinerario di Roma Antica.* Milan, 1970.

Luther, M. *Reformation Schriften.* St. Louis, Mo., 1880–1910.

Mackie, G. "A New Look at the Patronage of Santa Costanza, Rome." *Byzantion* 67 (1997): 381–406.

MacMullen, R. *Constantine.* New York, 1969.

Magi, F. *I rilievi flavi del Palazzo della Cancelleria (Monumenti Vaticani di archeologia e d'arte 6).* Florence, 1945.

"Il coronamento dell' arco di Costantino." *RendPont* 29 (1956–57): 83–110.

Maischberger, M. *Marmor in Rome* (Palilia 1). Wiesbaden, 1997.

Marcone, A. *Pagano e cristiano, vita e mito di Costantino.* Rome, 2002.

Marichal, R. "La date des graffiti de Saint Sébastien à Rome." *Comptes Rendus de l'Academie des Inscriptions et Belles-Lettres* (1953): 2–26.

Matthiae, G. *Mosaici medioevali delle chiese di Roma.* Rome, 1967.

Mattingly, H. *Roman Coins.* London, 1928.

Maurice, H. *Numismatique Constantinienne.* Paris, 1911.

Mazzarino, S. *L'impero romano.* Volume 2. Rome and Bari, 1973.

McCormick, S. G. *Art and Ceremony in Late Antiquity.* Berkeley, 1981.

Melucco Vaccaro, A. "L'arco dedicato a Costantino: Analisi e datazione della decorazione architettonica con un contributo di Dora Cirone." *RM* 108 (2001): 17–82.

Melucco Vaccaro, A., and A. M. Ferroni. "Chi costruì l'arco di Costantino?" *RendPont* 66 (1993–94): 1–76.

Messineo, G. *Malborghetto (Lavori e Studi di Archeologia* 15). Rome, 1989.

Meyer, H. *Antinoos.* Munich, 1991.

Mielsch, H., and H. von Hesberg. *Die Heidische Nekropole unter S. Peter in Rom,* 2 vols. (*Atti della Pontificia Accademia Romana di Archeologia* 16). Rome, 1986–95.

Millar, F. *The Emperor in the Roman World.* London, 1977.

Mingazzini, P. "É mai esistito l'arco di trionfo di Marcaurelio sul Clivo Argentario?" *RM* 70 (1963): 147–55.

Morey, C. R. *Early Christian Art.* Princeton, 1942.

Morin, L. "La basilique circiforme et ses antécédents." *Echos du Monde Classique, Classical Views* 34 (1990): 263–77.

Münz, E. "Notes sur les mosaiques Chrétiennes de l'Italie, V, Sainte Costance de Rome." *Revue archéologique,* New Series 35 (1878): 353–67.

Muller-Wiener, W. *Bildlexicon zur Topographie Istanbul.* Tübingen, 1977.

Nestori, A. *La Basilica Anonima della Via Ardeatina.* Città del Vaticano, 1990.

Nilgen, U. "Das Fastigium in der Basilica Constantiniana und vier bronze Säulen des Lateran." *RQ* 72 (1977): 1–31.

Nock, A. D. *Conversion.* Oxford, 1933.

Nuzzo, D. *Tipologia sepolcrale delle catacombe romane: I cimiteri ipogei delle vie Ostiense, Ardeatina e Appia. British Archaeological Reports* 905. Oxford, 2000.

O'Connor, D. W. *Peter in Rome.* New York, 1969.

Osborn, E. "The Apologists." In *The Early Christian World,* edited by E. Esler, 1:525–51. London, 2000.

Packer, J. E. *The Forum of Trajan in Rome: A Study of the Monuments.* Berkeley, 1997.

Patrologia Graeca. Paris, 1857–1904.

Pallottino, M. "Il grande fregio di Traiano." *BC* 66 (1938): 17–56.

Pani Ermini, L. "L'ipogeo dei Flavi in Domitilla." *RAC* 45 (1969): 119–74 and 48 (1972): 235–69.

————, ed. *Christiana Loca.* Roma, 2000.

Parrot, A. *Le Refrigerium dans l'audelà.* Paris, 1937.

Pensabene, P. "Riempiego e nuove mode architettoniche nelle basiliche cristiane di Roma fra IV e VI secolo." *Akten des XII Internationalen Kongresses für Christlichen Archäologie* (*JAC Ergänzungsheft* 20 [1995]): 1076–96.

Pensabene, P., and C. Panella. "Riempiego e progettazione architettonica nei monumenti tardo-antichi di Roma." *RendPont* 66 (1993–94): 110–283.

————. "Riempiego e progettazione architettonica nei monumenti tardo-antichi di Roma II." *RendPont* 67 (1994–95): 25–67.

————, eds. *Arco di Costantino* (*Studi di Archeologia* 100). Rome, 1999.

————. *Arco di Costantino.* Rome, 1999.

Pergola, P. *Le catacombe romane.* Rome, 1997.

Perrotti, R. "Recenti ritrovamenti presso S. Costanza." *Palladio* 6 (1956): 80–83.

Pietrí, C. *Roma Christiana.* Volume 1 (*CEFR* 224). Rome, 1976.

Pohlsander, A. *The Emperor Constantine.* London, 1995.

Prandi, A. *La zona archeologica della Confessio Vaticana: I monumenti del II secolo.* Città del Vaticano, 1957 (limited edition). Also printed under the title "La tomba di S. Pietro nei pellegrinaggi dell'età medievale in Pellegrinaggi e culto dei santi in Europa fino alla Ia crociata." In *Convegno del Centro sulla spiritualità medievale* 4, 283–447. Todi, 1963. Page references in this work are to this latter edition.

Prandi, A. *La Memoria Apostolorum in Catacumbas* (*Roma sotteranea cristiana* 2). Rome, 1936.

————. "Sulla dicostruzione della 'mensa martyrum' nella Memoria Apostolorum in Catacumbas." *RendPont* 19 (1942–43): 344–53.

Rash, J. J. *Das Mausoleum bei Tor de' Schiavi in Rom* (*Spätantike Zentralbauten in Rom and Latium* 2). Mainz, 1993.

Rasmussen, K. B. "Traditio Legis." *Cahiers archéologiques* 47 (1999): 5–37.

Ravasi, G., et al. *Pietro, la storia, l'immagine, la memoria.* Milan, 2000.

Rebillard, E. "L'église de Rome et le développement des catacombes." *MEFRA* 109 (1997): 741–63.

Richardson, L., Jr. *A New Topographical Dictionary of Ancient Rome.* Baltimore and London, 1992.

Ridley, R. T. *Zosimus, New History.* Sidney, 1982.

Riegl, A. *Spätrömische Kunstindustrie.* Wien, 1927.

Ristow, S. *Frühchristliche Baptisterien* (*Jahrbuch für Antike und Christentum* 27). 1998.

Rodenwaldt, G. "Eine spätantike Kunstströmung." *RM* 36/37 (1921–22): 8–110.

————. "Römische Reliefs als Vorstufen zur Spätantike." *JdI* 55 (1940): 12–43.

Rohmann, J. "Die Konstantinsbogen in Rom." *RM* 105 (1998): 259–82.

Rostovtseff, M. I. *Social and Economic History of the Roman Empire,* 2d ed. Oxford, 1957.

Rutgers, L. V. *The Jews in Late Ancient Rome.* Leiden, 1995.

Ruysschaert, J. "Le tableau Mariotti de la mosaique absidal de l'ancien S.-Pierre." *RendPont* 40 (1967–68): 295–317.

————. "Les premiers siècles de la tombe de Pierre: Une discussion dégagée d'une hypothèse." *Revue des archéologues et historiens d'art de Louvain* 8 (1975): 7–47.

Ryberg, I. S. *Panel Reliefs of Marcus Aurelius* (*Monographs on Archaeology and the Fine Arts* 14). 1967.

Salzman, M. R. "The Evidence for the Conversion of the Roman Empire to Christianity in Book 16 of the Theodosian Code." *Historia* 42 (1993): 362–78.

Sapelli, M. "La Basilica di Giunio Basso." In *Aurea Roma,* edited by S. Ensoli and E. La Rocca, 137–39. Rome, 2000.

Saxer, V. "Charles Pietrí et la topographie paléochrétienne de Rome." *MEFRA* 111 (1999): 597–608.

Schneider, A. M. *Refrigerium*. Freiburg, 1928.

Schumacher, W. N. "Die Gräbungen unter S. Sebastiano." *RQ* 82 (1987): 134–66.

Selinger, R. *The Mid–Third Century Persecutions of Decius and Valerian*. Frankfurt am Main, 2002.

Sena Chiesa, G., and A. Arslan, eds. *Felix Temporis Reparatio*. Milan, 1992.

Smith, R. R. R. "The Public Images of Licinius I." *Journal of Roman Studies* 87 (1997): 170–202.

Snyder, G. F. *Ante Pacem*. Macon, Ga., 1985.

Sordi, M. *The Christians and the Roman Empire*. Norman, 1986.

Southern, P. *The Roman Empire from Severus to Constantine*. London, 2001.

Speidel, M. *Die Denkmäler der Kaiserreiter: Equites Singulares Augusti (Beihefte der Bonner Jahrbücher 50 [1964])*.

Stanley, D. J. "New Discoveries at Santa Costanza." *Dumbarton Oaks Papers* 48 (1994): 57–261.

Steinby, M. "L'industria laterizia di Roma nel tardo impero." In *Società romana e impero tardo antico*, volume 2, edited by A. Giardina, 99–159. Rome, 1986.

Steinby, M., ed. *Lexicon topographicum urbis Romae*. Rome, 1993–2000.

Stern, H. "Les mosaiques de l'église de Sainte-Constance à Rome." *Dumbarton Oaks Papers* 12 (1958): 157–218.

Stucchi, S. "Tantis virtutibus, l'area della colonna nella concezione generale del Foro di Traiano." *AC* 41 (1989): 237–92.

Styger, P. "Gli apostoli Pietro e Paolo ad Catacumbas sulla via Appia." *RQ* 29 (1915): 149–205.

———. *Römische Märtyrer-Grüfte*. Berlin, 1935.

Süssenback, U. *Christuskult und kaiserliche Baupolitik bei Konstantin*. Bonn, 1977.

Syme, R. *Historia Augusta Papers*. New York and Oxford, 1983.

Tedone, G. "Roma, Velabro, la fabbrica superiore dell' Arco di Giano." *Bollettino di Archeologia* 23–24 (1993): 195–202.

Testini, P. "Noterelle sulla Memoria Apostolorum in Catacumbas." *RAC* 30 (1954): 209–31.

———. *Archeologia Christiana*. Bari, 1980.

Thümmel, H. G. *Die Memorien für Petrus und Paulus in Rom*. Berlin, 1999.

Töbelmann, F. *Der Bogen von Malborghetto (Abhandlungen der Heidelberger Akademie der Wissenschaften 2)*. 1915.

———. *Römische Gebälke*. Heidelberg, 1923.

Tolotti, F. "Dov'era il terebinto del Vaticano?" *MEFRA* 91 (1979): 491–524.

———. "Le basiliche cimiteriali con deambulatorio del Suburbio romano: Questione ancora aperta." *RM* 89 (1982): 153–211.

———. "Sguardo d'insieme al monumento sotto S. Sebastiano." *RAC* 60 (1984): 123–61.

Torelli, M. "Le basiliche circiformi di Roma, iconografia, funzione, simbolo." In *Felix Temporis Reparatio*, edited by G. Sena Chiesa and A. Arslan, 202–17. Milan, 1992.

———. "Topografia e iconografia dell' Arco di Portogallo." *Ostraka* 1 (1992): 105–31.

Tronzo, W. *The Via Latina Catacomb*. University Park and London, 1986.

Turner, E. S. *Gallant Gentlemen*. London, 1956.

Vasari, G. *Le vite d' più eccellenti pittori, scultori ed architettori*. Sansoni edition, 1906.

Vegio, M. "De rebus antiquis memorabilibus Basilicae S. Petri Romae." In *Acta Sanctorum* Junii t. 7, 69–70. Antwerp, 1717.

Vermeule, C. C. *Roman Imperial Art in Greece and Asia Minor*. Cambridge, Mass., 1978.

von Gerkan, A. "Zu den Problemen des Petrusgrabes." *JAC* 1 (1958): 79–93.

———. "Basso et Tusco consulibus." *Bonner Jahrbucher* 158 (1958): 88–105.

———. "Petrus in Vaticano et in Catacumbas." *JAC* 5 (1962): 22–32.

Ward-Perkins, J. B. "Memoria, Martyr's Tomb and Martyr's Church." *Journal of Theological Studies*, New Series 16 (1966): 20–37.

Ward-Perkins, J. B., and J. Toynbee. *The Shrine of St. Peter and the Vatican Excavations*. London, 1956.

Weiland, A. "Zum Stand der städtromischen Katacomben Forschung." *RQ* 89 (1994): 173–98.

Williams, S. *Diocletian and the Roman Recovery.* London, 1985.

Wissowa, G. *Religion und Kultus der Römer* (*Handbuch der Klassischen Altertumswissenschaft.* Volume 4). Munich, 1902.

Wohl, B. L. "Constantine's Use of Spolia." *Acta Hyperborea* 8 (2001): 85–115.

Zeggio, S. "La realizzazione delle fondazioni." In P. Pensabene and E. C. Panella, *L'arco di Costantino,* 117–37. Rome, 1999.

Index